Library of Congress Cataloging-in-Publication Data

Cleve, Jay.
    Out of the blues: strategies that work to get through the down times / by Jay Cleve.
        p. cm.
    Bibliography: p.
    ISBN 0-89638-154-4
    1. Depression, Mental — Popular works. 2. Depression, Mental — Prevention —
Popular works. 3. Conduct of life. I. Title.
RC537.C54 1989
616.85'27 — dc 19
                                                                                88-38627
                                                                                CIP

Cover design by Susan Rinek

Interior design by Pam Arnold

Inquiries, orders, and catalog requests should be addressed to
CompCare Publishers
2415 Annapolis Lane
Minneapolis, MN 55441
Call toll free 800/328-3330
(Minnesota residents 612/559-4800)

To the children:

Aimee
John
Patrick
Seann

Contents

Long-Range Techniques to Help Reduce Depression-Proneness

Improving Your Interactions with Others

When the Going Gets Tough

Foreword

If ever the world needed a book about the oxymoron-like phenomenon of depression and wellness, it's now—and Dr. Cleve has filled the need. It's all here—the fundamentals and most fine points about personal responsibility, personal wellness planning, stress management and boredom-avoidance, time management, communications, self-nurturing, humor and play, positive thinking and action, self-esteem, commitment to personal excellence, imagery and visualization, the relativity of past versus present/future.

If you ever wondered about the connection between wellness and spirituality, your curiosities will be satisfied reading *Out of the Blues*. Dr. Cleve shows that the connection is similar to that between your heart and the rest of your body, namely, intimate and interconnected.

An important part of what I mean by spiritual wellness is feeling confident and positive about your life! I think a person is spiritually well if he/she likes himself/herself, is excited about life, has satisfying relationships and is enthused about the way he/she spends time, with the direction of his/her interests, and the way the future seems to be shaping up. That's the ethic I read in *Out of the Blues*. While spirituality can be complex and controversial, Dr. Cleve believes it need not be either; it can instead be fun, challenging and invaluable . . . and it belongs in therapeutic settings, especially when depression is suspected or confirmed.

You are in for a treat instead of a treatment. Enjoy *Out of the Blues*. I know I did.

Donald B. Ardell, Ph.D.
Director, Campus Wellness Center
University of Central Florida
Author of *High Level Wellness: An Alternative to Doctors, Drugs and Disease*
Publisher of *Ardell Wellness Report*

My Thanks:

To all of my clients over the years who have taught me so much about depression—and life.

To Dr. Bert Kamstra, who reviewed and made suggestions on the manuscript.

To the staff and interns at the Portage County Mental Health Clinic, who responded to the material and furthered my knowledge of depression.

To Ronelle Ewing, my editor at CompCare Publishers.

Introduction

If you're feeling "blue" right now, you're not alone. It has been estimated that at any given time in this country, up to 30-45 percent of the population struggle with feelings of depression. Everyone feels "down," "blue," or "bummed out" at one time or another. And accompanying these moods are feelings that can affect the quality of life for an hour, a day, or longer: fatigue, anxiety, guilt, dependency, sadness, inertia, self-hate, and despair.

It could be said that *occasional* and *brief* bouts with depressed moods are relatively normal. Unfortunately, though, many people struggle for years with a low level of chronic depression that permits functioning but severely restricts personal growth and fulfillment. How much better it would be if people would allow themselves to experience an hour or even a *whole day* of the blues occasionally, then productively work through those feelings before they gain a foothold in the psyche and become deep and incapacitating.

The National Institute of Mental Health defines depression as *"An emotional state of dejection and sadness, ranging from mild discomfort and down-heartedness to feelings of hopelessness and despair."* Types of depression can extend from simply feeling "blue," through normal grief, to psychotic depression. The various warning signals or symptoms of depression (see pages 3-12) must be taken very seriously, particularly if these symptoms are severe, if they linger, or if they recur frequently. Even with self-motivation and careful application of their best efforts and skills, people sometimes are unable to pull themselves out of the blues. At times like this, professional help is not only appropriate, it is *essential*. Remember, a person need not be suicidal, irrational, or immobile to seek professional help. *Anyone who is severely depressed, or depressed for long periods of time, or frequently depressed is advised to seek professional help without delay.* It is a fact that more is being learned about depression every day and help *is* available. Fortunately, through health insurance plans and public clinics, good psychological and psychiatric care is more accessible than it has been in the past (see Chapter 29).

Despite the fact that depression feels like an ominous black cloud that suddenly descends, bringing emptiness, listlessness and doom, it is not a mysterious, unexplained phenomenon. In fact, depression is most often a relatively predictable, comprehensive, and learned way of reacting to situations that involve stress, threat, or conflict. And *unless depression is biochemical in nature or accompanies a period of grief and readjustment, it can be mitigated, interrupted, counteracted, or sometimes even prevented with some practical coping strategies.*

It is perhaps useful to know that health care professionals do not determine the severity of a depression from the subjective feeling state. Rather, the severity of a depression is determined by its intensity, its duration, and the effects it has on eating and sleeping habits and a person's overall adjustment to and conduct of his or her daily life. It is therefore possible for a person to feel *profoundly* depressed, yet continue to function quite normally. When this is the case, the condition is more likely to be a *depressive phase*, rather than a full-blown depression. But when otherwise normal and well-adjusted people are in this kind of depressive phase, they feel anything *but* normal and well-adjusted. *You may be a depression-prone person if you are frequently stuck in a depressive phase or you struggle with more severe depressive moods for no readily apparent reason and you have ruled out physiological reasons as well as a stressful situation, event or growth stage as a primary source of your feelings.*

Though I wrote this book primarily for depression-prone people (described in Chapter 3), the concepts and suggestions included have also proven helpful to people who suffer from severe depression, as well as those who are depressed due to a stressful life event, situation, or growth stage.

The fact is, many people fail to take advantage of the opportunity for personal growth that a bout with depression provides. In a society that regularly confronts the threat of nuclear war, along with the realities of environmental destruction, crime, and economic uncertainties, many people choose to avoid "more bad news" concerning *themselves.* And when people consciously or subconsciously avoid confronting their pain, they become externally focused and other-directed. They may become codependent in their relationships and focus almost exclusively on the wants, feelings, needs, and ideas of others. Or, they may become dependent upon others and compulsively seek approval, acceptance, or caretaking from them.

But depression, like the grieving process, can be an opportunity for growth. At the deepest level, depression may involve *grieving the loss of self*. When we can no longer avoid the pain within ourselves, we *must* focus inward to resolve that pain. The pain forces us to turn inward and look squarely at ourselves. A bout with depression can be an internal challenge to face our pain and actively participate in our own healing. This book provides techniques to help people return "home" to themselves through an honest but gentle self-examination—not for the purpose of furthering guilt and self-punishment but to activate the healing powers *within* through self-acceptance, self-compassion, and new self-assurance, and to catalyze the love and vitality which at the deepest level is the self.

The information in this book is distilled from my own professional experience and observations. I came to write it when I looked back over more than twenty years of counseling depression-prone people and realized that time and again, I've suggested many of the same strategies to people who are struggling with depression. I guess you could say that I operate almost like a "depression coach"—suggesting strategies to a client in one session, finding out how these strategies worked at the next session, and subsequently suggesting new strategies. As a professional counselor, I have seen that people who are motivated to deal with their depressed feelings are, quite often, able to pull themselves out of a depressive phase or actually *prevent* a full-blown depression from occurring. And if they're motivated, they can accomplish this relatively quickly.

This book features the short-term tactics and long-range techniques my clients have found most helpful. Many of these strategies are so simple and straightforward that once you understand how and why they work, you can try them out immediately and on your own. This is a *self-help* book based on the following premise: the more aware you are of how you get depressed and perhaps unknowingly *maintain* that depression, the more adept you will become at recognizing depression, dealing with it, and moving through it with your hope and health intact. With awareness, practice of new skills, and work, you might even get to the point where you can counteract a depression entirely; in other words, when you feel a depressed mood coming on, you recognize it, counteract it, or work through it, and find effective ways to pull yourself away from its downward spin.

What I intend to do in this book is show you how to recognize, work through, and combat specific episodes of depression and/or your overall depression-proneness. To that end, I've included practical information about the notable symptoms, recognized causes and effects of depression, along with the strategies that have been effective for so many people. Please read the descriptions of the symptoms of depression as well as the possible causes of depression before going on to these self-help strategies.

Many of the depression-prone people I've worked with through the years are among the most perceptive, aware, sensitive and compassionate people I've ever known. The sensitivity they have toward others and themselves—which, incidentally, is likely to have *contributed* to their depression in the first place—eventually proved to be an important asset in lifting them out of the blues. As you learn new ways to recognize and deal with depression and depression-proneness, you will also learn to get on with your life and focus on the fulfillment that you deserve to experience. I believe you'll find that when you have the ability to lift yourself out of the blues, you've taken another important step toward being in close touch with your feelings and actively involved in determining the direction and quality of your life.

Jay Cleve
March, 1989

A Note from the Author

Confidentiality is an essential element in my work as a counseling psychologist. In order to protect the privacy of my past and present clients, I have designed case histories in this book that are composites and adaptations of cases that I have worked with during my career. Many details in these case histories have been altered or fictionalized in order to obscure the identity of any one individual or situation. Quotes within case histories are paraphrases or remarks that I consider relatively typical of a person in a similar situation to that which is being described.

Any similarities between these case histories and any real person or situation — past or present — is purely coincidental.

A Look at Depression

1.

Warning Signals

Occasional depressed moods seem to "go with the territory" of being human and relating to others in this complex world. It just isn't realistic to expect to be forever free of the blues; in fact, I don't think most of us would even choose to be totally immune from depressed moods. The introspection and self-awareness that sometimes result from "down" periods can provide a person with valuable information and insights.

If recognized and dealt with constructively, a period of depression can actually help motivate a person to take positive action and change destructive, self-defeating behaviors. Because it may ultimately lead to much-needed rest and revitalization, a mild depression might even be a way for the mind and/or body to call a halt to a detrimental situation. A depression may require a person to re-examine and even reorder priorities. Or, if a person's energy is being undermined by some ambivalent situation in his or her personal or professional life, a depression might force that person to scrutinize the situation, weigh the assets and liabilities involved, and move toward a satisfactory resolution.

If the blues seem to come out of nowhere and for no apparent reason, you might *initially* accept the feelings as an inner request or demand for brief withdrawal from an overbooked schedule or from some disturbing, unresolved issue or troublesome relationship. If a specific event or situation triggered the depression, the correlation will probably become evident relatively quickly. In the end, you may well be thankful for a bleak but merciful period of time that, in the end, forced you to do some difficult but absolutely necessary thinking, feeling, and decision-making.

But take note if you get depressed often and/or if your depression is severe. For example, if you're struggling with depressed moods every few weeks and those moods last for more than a few days at a time, or you're sometimes so severely depressed that you have difficulty carrying out the tasks and activities of your daily life, the underlying problem may be severe depression or depression-proneness. *In either case, help is available.* Remember, something can be done about *every* depressed state. Severe depression can and should be treated without delay. There is no reason to suffer the pain and torment of depression when it can be alleviated—whether banished almost completely or somehow lessened.

The warning signs of depression—physical, emotional, and psychological symptoms—are interconnected, though some seem to be contradictory. The following informal survey, loosely adapted from three well-known depression tests[1] may help you identify the areas of your life that seem to produce the greatest number, frequency, and intensity of problems. From your answers, you can at least roughly estimate the nature and intensity of your depression, as well as the aspects of your life that are creating the most problems. With this knowledge, then, you can pursue recommended courses of action and specific strategies described in later chapters of this book.

Check each symptom that has affected you in the past or is affecting you at the present time. Then, make some notes about the frequency and/or intensity of each particular symptom you experience:

I. Physical Symptoms:

Sleep problems:

☐ Difficulty getting to sleep at night _____

_____

_____

☐ Waking up too early in the morning _____

_____

_____

☐ Difficulty getting out of bed in the morning _____

_____

_____

☐ Restlessness or light sleep; easily awakened _____

_____

_____

Physical vitality problems:

☐ Feelings of physical weakness _____

_____

_____

☐ Tiredness; fatigue; exhaustion _____

_____

_____

Health problems:

☐ Inconsistent body weight (gaining or losing) _____

_____

_____

☐ Bowel irregularity _____

_____

_____

☐ Susceptibility to colds, flu, minor infections _____

_____

_____

☐ Frequent stomachaches, headaches, backaches _____

_____

_____

☐ Reduced interest in sex _____

_____

_____

☐ Lack of interest in food _____

_____

_____

☐ Anxious about general health _____

_____

_____

II. Behavioral Symptoms:

☐ Difficulty getting started on projects and activities _____
_____
_____

☐ Less active than in the past _____
_____
_____

☐ Move more slowly than usual _____
_____
_____

☐ Cry frequently _____
_____
_____

☐ Moodiness _____
_____
_____

☐ Restlessness and agitation _____
_____
_____

☐ Tend to overreact to people and situations _____
_____
_____

☐ Argue with others frequently and/or blow up easily _____
_____
_____

☐ Withdraw from others _____
_____
_____

III. Mental Symptoms:

Difficulties in:

☐ Concentration _____
_____
_____

☐   Remembering _____

_____

_____

☐   Understanding _____

_____

_____

☐   Thinking clearly _____

_____

_____

☐   Exercising judgment _____

_____

_____

Troubled by:

☐   Indecisiveness _____

_____

_____

☐   Brooding, obsessing, ruminating _____

_____

_____

☐   Thoughts of suicide _____

_____

_____

IV. Feelings within Self:

☐   Self-criticalness _____

_____

_____

☐   Pessimism and negativism _____

_____

_____

☐   Helplessness _____

_____

_____

☐ Guilt _____

_____

_____

☐ Shame _____

_____

_____

☐ Regret _____

_____

_____

☐ Dependency _____

_____

_____

☐ Hopelessness regarding the future _____

_____

_____

V. Self-Concept:

☐ Disappointment in self _____

_____

_____

☐ Lack of confidence _____

_____

_____

☐ Self-doubting _____

_____

_____

☐ Feelings of being incapable of doing things _____

_____

_____

☐ Feelings of uselessness _____

_____

_____

☐ Feeling like a failure _____

_____

_____

☐   Uncertainty _____

_____

_____

☐   Feelings of emotional weakness _____

_____

_____

VI. Feelings with Regard to Others:

☐   Lonely, even when in the presence of others _____

_____

_____

☐   Needy; vulnerable; easily hurt _____

_____

_____

☐   Misunderstood _____

_____

_____

☐   Unappreciated _____

_____

_____

☐   Exploited, manipulated, taken advantage of _____

_____

_____

☐   Disappointed in others _____

_____

_____

☐   Fearful of rejection _____

_____

_____

☐   Intensely concerned about opinions and judgments of others _____

_____

_____

VII. Social Behavior:

☐   Self-sacrificing _____

_____

_____

☐   Compliant; non-assertive _____

_____

_____

☐   Choose highly critical friends _____

_____

_____

☐   Unfavorably compare self with others _____

_____

_____

☐   Depend upon others for approval, acceptance, support _____

_____

_____

☐   Feel responsible for the well-being of others _____

_____

_____

☐   Reject compliments _____

_____

_____

☐   People-pleasing tendencies _____

_____

_____

VIII. Perceptions of Other People:

☐   People are too critical _____

_____

_____

☐   People are not sympathetic toward me _____

_____

_____

☐　　People are unfriendly toward me _____

_____

_____

☐　　People are pushy and quarrelsome toward me _____

_____

_____

☐　　People take advantage of me _____

_____

_____

☐　　People are disappointed in me _____

_____

_____

☐　　People are unappreciative toward what I do _____

_____

_____

☐　　People are manipulative and exploitative _____

_____

_____

After completing this brief survey, review the specific symptoms you've checked, as well as your notes pertaining to the frequency and intensity of these symptoms. It should be said here that everyone experiences at least some of these symptoms from time to time; many people regard occasional bouts with some of these symptoms as well within the range of normal. But depression is an individual matter. As with tolerance to physical pain, individuals differ greatly in their abilities to recognize, accept, cope with, and work through depressed feelings. And, some people have been depressed for so long that they're quite accustomed to those depressed feelings and may no longer even realize that it *is* possible to feel much better than they do.

Note that the symptoms listed here vary in their significance. For example, one wouldn't weigh frequent colds as heavily as suicidal thinking. For this reason, look carefully at the symptoms that trouble you most. *Intense and/or frequent experiences with disruptive, life-affecting items should alert you to the need for professional help.*

Occasional and/or less intense experiences with several of the items listed, especially if they are long-standing, may point to a chronic, low-grade depression which has never seemed severe enough to warrant action. Moderately intense and relatively frequent experience with items in several symptom areas may alert you to consider professional help as well as the way you are organizing and conducting your life.

This informal survey does serve to illustrate the way in which depression spills over into many areas of life—beginning with a poor self-concept and ultimately undermining interpersonal relationships and the quality of life itself.

References

1.   Depression tests by William Zung, Aaron Beck and the *Minnesota Multiphasic Personality Inventory.*

2.

What Kind of Depression Is It?

In all instances of prolonged, severe, and/or recurring depression, it is important to differentiate between the physiological and psychological aspects of causes. These aspects are always intertwined, making the task of differentiation quite difficult and most appropriately carried out by a professional.

Physiological Depression

Physical illnesses, even relatively minor ones like head colds and flu, can temporarily deplete a person's energy level so that the mind tends toward depressed thinking and feeling. Serious illnesses and major surgery affect a person's energy level contributing to feelings of vulnerability and low spirit. Hormonal factors may also precipitate mild to severe depression. For example, puberty, a time of over-production of a variety of hormones, may result in generalized physical excitation and disruption. Puberty is often characterized by intense confusion and moodiness; in this case, it is sometimes difficult to separate the physical from the mental or emotional components of that time of life. In a similar way, depression among post-partum mothers, particularly first-time mothers, is probably as much hormonally induced as it is an emotional reaction to new responsibilities and pressures. PMS (premenstrual syndrome) is another condition related to hormone production that may be responsible for recurrent monthly depressions in women. Some women also have depressive reactions to the hormones contained in birth control pills.

Hyperthyroidism and other glandular malfunctions can cause physical and mental depression. And some cases of chronic depression have been traced to hypoglycemia, a disorder characterized by low blood-sugar. Alcohol is known to act as a chemical depressant on body and brain. Consider, then, the irony that people frequently use alcohol to mask or otherwise seek relief from feelings of depression. Overuse and misuse of tranquilizers and barbiturates also can create depressive thinking and behavior.

Physiological and biochemical sources of depression represent controversial areas of research. It is known that biochemical imbalances affect the central nervous system and can produce the widely fluctuating mood swings that characterize the manic-depressive syndrome. Also, the mental health disorder of schizophrenia, which frequently manifests itself in extreme depressive symptoms, evidences definite abnormal biochemical components that disturb brain function.

Psychological Depression

The majority of people who seek professional treatment for depression are suffering from psychological depression. Psychological depressions usually have three main sources: 1. an upsetting or stressful event or situation; 2. a developmental vulnerability; 3. a depression-prone personality. One of these sources alone could be enough to trigger and/or aggravate a depression. All three sources sometimes interact to catalyze, then perpetuate and reinforce a severe depression. I'll describe each in a bit more detail here:

Situational Depression
Psychological depression is often triggered initially by a personal loss, such as the death of a loved one, the ending of a marriage, or the termination of a job. This loss, then, leads to a grieving process that commonly involves intense self-examination. In this case, grieving is a completely natural and necessary part of the healing process. And unless this period of grieving is complicated with self-blame, guilt, severe hurt or anger, it usually proceeds with few complications.

Some psychological depressions are generated by major role transitions: from spouse to widow or divorced person; from front-line worker to laid-off worker; from employer to retired person. Any role change requires an adjustment and may involve giving up something or losing something, including a portion of one's identity.

During the time a person is actively functioning as a parent, he or she needs regular, dependable relief from ongoing parenting responsibilities. Single parents who have sole custody of their children face a particularly onerous child-rearing task and related potential for depression.

With the departure of grown children from their everyday lives comes a notoriously difficult period of time for some parents. If these parents have nothing as yet to "replace" their children in their attention-giving priorities, they may feel that their fundamental function in life is severely threatened.

Loss of a job seems to make most people vulnerable to depression. No two ways about it, being laid off or fired can be extremely damaging to the ego. In fact, losing a job can create a depression that is really an internalization of the external economic depression over which an individual has no control. Unless another equally good or better job can be secured in a timely manner, the unemployed person is likely to feel rejected, unwanted, devalued, and perhaps even incompetent and worthless. Unrewarded or otherwise unproductive efforts to find new employment, along with additional rejections or lack of response, may further damage the ego and make a person vulnerable to depression.

Other situational stresses may include interpersonal conflicts with relatives, friends, lovers, or work associates that continue on— for months or even years—without effective resolution. These situational stresses come from anything that requires emotional, social, and economic readjustment to unforeseen or radically altered circumstances. These alterations might include a job change involving a geographic move, or accidents and illnesses—one's own or someone else's—that involve major life changes and possibly create financial uncertainties and strain.

Developmental Vulnerability to Depression

Just as situational variables make a person more vulnerable to depression, a person's susceptibility to depression would appear to be greater during certain life stages.

For example, adolescents seem to be more depression-prone than their grade-school counterparts. Also, parents of colicky babies or active young children can become physically and emotionally depleted by the constant demands on their attention, time, and energy. Depressive periods and severe "cabin fever" are likely to occur in parents with young children when all are confined (such as in small apartments and during weather when mobility is limited).

The unique stresses and disillusionments sometimes associated with adults in their twenties and thirties are many: attempts to consolidate careers, raise families, and deal with conflicting demands of job ambitions, personal desires, and family needs can make individuals highly vulnerable to depression.

When children become teenagers and demonstrate less and less interest in family socializing, along with the tendency to criticize or reject parents, those parents may look to each other for solace and support—and all too often discover in the process that without the parenting role to share, they are drifting apart. Sometimes, when the difficulties of parenting adolescents coincides with a shrinkage in job options, as well as a feeling of restlessness in a marital relationship, and/or the onset of menopause or the male climacteric, a mid-life crisis and depression may well result. The outcome of depression at this stage of life may be a radical change in career, domestic arrangements, and lifestyle.

Dealing with middle-age does seem to increase the likelihood of a major depression. Lofty career ambitions of early life often must be modified, compromised, or even completely abandoned at this time. At the same time, one must somehow reconcile gray and thinning hair, wrinkles, and a less-than-perfect body with the youthful and perfect body images so prevalent in advertising. Also at this time of life, there is heightened awareness of the increased susceptibility to degenerative diseases such as cancer, arthritis, and cardiovascular illnesses.

The aging person may have special vulnerabilities to depression aggravated by forced retirement, boredom, and shrinking financial resources. Along with and related to the deaths of friends and relatives, the aging person confronts the inevitability of his or her own mortality. This realization often leads to a sort of rumination over the meaning and value of life as it has been lived.

During these particularly vulnerable life stages, people should not be too hard on themselves, or too proud or stubborn to ask for and accept help and support from relatives, close friends, and professionals. Unfortunately, however, many people who have always prided themselves on their self-sufficiency and inner strength choose to "keep their own counsel" and find themselves becoming more and more disturbed, isolated, and depressed.

The Depression-Prone Personality

Both situational and developmental vulnerability can and often are complicated by a third ingredient: a depression-prone personality style. People who adhere to perfectionistic standards, experience strong feelings of guilt, are self-critical and self-punishing, and think in negativistic or pessimistic ways will suffer more frequent and serious bouts of depression than those people who are easier on themselves, have reasonable expectations, and maintain an optimistic outlook about themselves and life in general.

Consider the possibility that you may be depression-prone if you experience frequent "down" moods or occasionally more severe depressive periods for no readily apparent reason and you have ruled out some aspect of physiology as a primary source of your "down" feelings. If you're like most depression-prone people, you're probably lugging around a variety of detrimental thought processes, self-defeating emotional underpinnings, and negative behavior responses that date back to your early, formative years. Perhaps you've been traveling with this extra emotional baggage for so long that you feel it will be an integral part of you forever. *It doesn't have to be that way at all.* You need to know that you can do a lot to rid yourself of this unwanted emotional baggage. This emotional baggage only serves to weigh you down and prevent you from ever feeling fulfilled in your life and at peace with yourself. You can begin the unloading process *right now*, just by recognizing the causes and effects of these negative emotions, thinking styles, and social habits.

3.

Characteristics of the Depression-Prone Person

In order to take a closer look at the characteristics of the depression-prone person, we need to examine the components of psychological depression as well as the personality styles and response patterns that contribute to depression-proneness.

Basic Components of Psychological Depression

In my twenty-plus years of experience counseling depressed and depression-prone people, I have come to recognize the following components of psychological depression: Perfectionism - Self-Criticalness - Guilt - Self-Hate.

Perfectionism
When excellence isn't enough

Perfectionism is a person's expectation—insistence even—that he or she will do some things, many things, or *everything* perfectly. By its very nature, perfectionism pervades all other characteristics and it is therefore an important contributing factor in depression. But perfectionism may be subtle and hidden away to the extent that people don't even recognize it in themselves. Most people who have a tendency to get depressed will find perfectionism lurking somewhere in their psyches, pushing them on every moment. Unfortunately, perfectionism ultimately can hold people back to the extent that they never feel satisfied that they've met the rigorous demands they place upon themselves.

In order to identify perfectionism and the impact it has on their lives, people may have to work backward by examining their behaviors and thought processes. For example, upon the successful completion of a task or project, they need to examine the depth of their disappointment, the intensity of their guilt, and the extent of their overall dissatisfaction with the results. You see, even excellent isn't *enough* for the perfectionist. Perfectionists are likely to think that *anyone* can do adequate, many can do very good, and some can do excellent; they strive, instead, for *absolute perfection*. And no matter how enthusiastically and genuinely other people around the perfectionist acknowledge, appreciate, and compliment the achievements of perfectionists, no one ever seems able to convince them that what they have accomplished is worthwhile, much less wonderful. Perfectionists truly feel that their accomplishments are never adequate; always, it seems, they want to do more, they want to do it better, and they probably want to do it in record time as well.

Many perfectionists are driven by unrealistically high standards that they may have set for themselves relatively early in their lives. In many cases, a parent or parents initially set extremely high standards for them, standards that were subsequently reinforced and perhaps even rewarded by society. Furthermore, many perfectionists almost always feel that they are in competition with *someone*, even if it's only their past and/or future selves. Perfectionists have an erroneous belief that in order to get genuine love and approval from others, they must make some extraordinary mark on the world. This competitive drive probably begins very early in a person's life, then the ambitions grow right along with him or her. That magical mark they strive for starts small and just continues to become more and more impressive (and unrealistic).

But in reality, of course, the reach of perfectionists far exceeds their grasp. Whatever they accomplish is, to their way of thinking, merely a stepping stone to something more significant. And rarely, if ever, is any accomplishment *good enough* for the perfectionist. As they work through their thoughts and behaviors, many perfectionists come to realize one reason why they're almost always disappointed in the results of personal efforts: they are more focused on the drive for perfection than on the tasks themselves.

Over-responsibility — Inherent in perfectionism is a person's belief that he or she is somehow accountable for *everything* in and around his or her life. For example, a perfectly capable preteen accidentally leaves her warm hat on the school bus and eventually develops pneumonia. This young woman's mother, as an overly responsible person, subsequently feels guilty about the turn of events and finds ways to prove her own accountability: *"I should have bought her a hat she liked, so she'd keep it on her head." "I should have picked her up at school that day, so I could have seen for myself that she had her hat."* If it rains on the day of the company picnic, the overly responsible person feels accountable for that predicament: *"I should have planned the picnic for later in the season, after the chance of rain had passed." "I should have made arrangements for an alternative site in case of rain." "If only I had listened to my boss; she suggested a different day for the event, and that day turned out to be perfect."*

It seems that other people are able to shrug or laugh off blunders, large and small. *Not so the perfectionist.* In fact, the casual attitudes exhibited by others in the face of their own mistakes might *amaze* the perfectionist; he or she may even feel somewhat envious of the low-key, devil-may-care attitudes they see in others. It's true that most people don't tend to brood over their responsibilities and accountabilities the way perfectionists do. In fact, some people seem to avoid getting involved in situations where they might be unduly criticized or blamed for doing something wrong or producing less-than-perfect results. But perfectionists are likely to seek out just such situations and take on impossible tasks out of guilt, fear, obligation, or perhaps to demonstrate to others a highly developed sense of responsibility.

Feelings of Inadequacy — When perfectionists are told that they're being awfully tough on themselves, they might agree at first. But in the next breath, they'll probably say "... But I deserve it." Perfectionists are usually their own harshest critics. And when it's suggested to them that they're too tough on themselves and have perfectionistic standards, chances are very good they'll deny it and say something like this: *"How can you say that?" "I'm a hopeless case." "I can hardly get myself to work in the morning."*

Many perfectionists publicly declare that the standards they set for themselves are, indeed, quite minimal. One might wonder, then, why they're never satisfied with their performance if their standards are so "low." A persistent questioner might be able to coax a revealing admission out of the perfectionist: that he or she consistently evaluates himself or herself negatively because the idealized image carried deep within is *flawless*. Because perfectionists know that the inner model is *perfect*, they still have a degree of security, even if they never measure up to this image. But carrying an unrealistically idealized image within while striving for absolute perfection contributes to ongoing feelings of inadequacy. Obviously, even exceptional achievements fall short; human beings simply cannot measure up to a model of absolute perfection.

Because perfectionists focus on their observable behaviors, they may not even realize that their standards are excessive. But ongoing impatience with oneself, frequent dismissal or trivialization of real accomplishments, and deep self-dissatisfaction clearly reflect an idealized image of super-worker, super-spouse, super-friend, super-parent, and on and on. The situation gets more complicated when perfectionism is non-selective. Using perfection as a model, some people choose a few high-priority skills and abilities to develop and refine. But many perfectionists erroneously believe that they must be perfect at *everything*. And since perfection is an ideal that can only be approached—never attained—people who strive for perfection in all things are setting themselves up for frequent and devastating disappointments.

Self-Criticalness

"They seem to feel that they don't deserve to be happy."

Although perfectionism is sometimes difficult to identify, the pointed and sometimes harsh self-criticism that results from failure to meet perfectionistic standards is relatively easy to identify. No doubt about it, depression-prone people are very tough on themselves. And because perfectionists expect and perhaps even demand so much from themselves in terms of ideal accomplishment, they never "measure up"—even in the best of times. For example, people who are highly self-critical probably have vague feelings of guilt if they go through a period of feeling good about themselves and their lives. They seem to feel they don't *deserve* to be happy. Then, when these same people feel "down," they tend to regard those feelings as punishment for having had things a bit too easy for a time.

Depression-prone people tend to critique everything they do, and they perceive that nothing they do is good enough. When feeling depressed, a self-critical person might add to the feeling with non-affirming statements like, *"I know I'm worthless and a failure; I deserve to feel bad."* Unfortunately, they may believe that the only way to get themselves out of a slump is to beat themselves into proper shape with even *more* name-calling and self-reproachment.

When people feel good about themselves, they tend to be quite realistic about their capabilities and their performance. But when people feel bad about themselves, they feel they must somehow accomplish great things in order to feel better about themselves. It follows, then, that the more depressed people are, the higher they tend to set their standards and expectations for themselves. Consequently, when they're least capable of doing well, they impose the most exacting and unrealistic standards on themselves. They're likely to feel that only the most magnificent achievement could pull them out of their depression. But since such magnificence seems completely beyond their weakened grasp, they spiral deeper into despair instead. And they begin to believe that nothing they can do will ever help them feel better about themselves.

When people are being extremely tough on themselves and becoming increasingly depressed as well, they may sense that they need other opinions to counteract their own self-criticism. At times like this, they tend to seek out people who they hope will correct their misperceptions about themselves and convince them of their worth. Sometimes, though, these people aren't chosen with a great deal of care. But even when highly self-critical people seek out and receive positive opinions from the right people, they aren't likely to accept or even *believe* the feedback they receive. In fact, they may dismiss perfectly appropriate and genuine compliments with self-critical remarks like these: *"Well, those people really don't know me. If they did, they wouldn't be so positive in their opinions." "Anyone could have done that job as well as I did, or better, if he or she had worked as hard." "I was just lucky." "He/she just said that to make me feel better."* To the supportive friend or associate, it sometimes seems that one just

cannot "win" with a depressed person who is self-critical—
particularly since the very thing the depressed person needs and
wants — positive input from others — is the same thing that
ultimately is rejected and used to fuel further self-criticism.

Guilt
". . . a person actually may begin to crave punishment."

The criticism people level at themselves for not living up to their own
unrealistically high expectations ultimately produces guilt for
perceived failures and regret for perceived "sins" and "errors" of the
past. If, deep down, people feel responsible for everything and
everybody, and they really believe they must do all things perfectly,
they can't help but feel disappointed in themselves most of the time.
But why do they feel guilty? In my opinion, some of the techniques used
to socialize children and shape them into good, law-abiding citizens
utilize guilt to instill a work ethic and a social conscience. Many
people—even those who appear to blame others for whatever is amiss
in their lives—feel burdened, guilty, overly responsible. From parents,
these people may have heard, *"You should be ashamed of yourself!"*
From teachers, they may have heard, *"You didn't work hard enough!"*
From the pulpit, they may have heard, *"You are a sinner!"*

Feelings of guilt in the adult perfectionist are sometimes
accompanied by a sense of panic particularly if, as children, misdeeds
or imperfections resulted in disapproval or even *withdrawal* of love by
parents or significant others. Because some of the internalized,
subconscious tenets of conscience remain unchanged when people
reach adulthood, some perfectionistic adults tend to feel anxious and
guilty merely *in anticipation* of some transgression. When guilt
feelings become overwhelming, a person actually may begin to *crave*
punishment. Whether carried out directly or indirectly by others or
by oneself, punishment may have the effect of purging these people of
their guilt temporarily and *very briefly* restoring the feelings of being
loveable and deserving of acceptance by others.

Self-Hate
*Once it develops, the mechanisms for magnifying and escalating it are
always present.*

Self-criticism for failing to meet perfectionistic standards and the guilt
and regret that result eventually lead to self-hate. A person may not
be fully aware of the progression of feelings at first, but it continues

on just the same. Consumed by guilt, people may become angry with themselves. Then, when they turn the anger inward, the self-hate emerges full-blown. It could be that just moments before this, the person didn't feel self-hate at all. A person might then believe that this particular incident simply triggered existing feelings of self-hate and brought them to the surface where they could be seen and felt. It can be frightening to see the rapidity with which any one set of good feelings can come crashing down; *how fast everything can fall apart.*

But self-hate isn't an ongoing condition; it is, in fact, *created* by overwhelming feelings of guilt and failure. Certainly, though, once self-hate develops, the mechanisms for magnifying and escalating it are always present. And, after years of practice and conditioning, these mechanisms become knee-jerk reactions. Is it any wonder, then, that a small error can summon forth strong self-insult? "*You stupid idiot!*" someone mutters to himself or herself after trying the wrong key in the car door. Indeed, self-criticism bred of self-hatred can be so automatic (and subconscious) that a person doesn't even *hear* it.

As I see it, there are two primary routes from self-demanding perfectionism to self-hate: 1. *Imposing excessive demands on oneself and not being mobilized for action*; and 2. *Imposing excessive demands on oneself and being mobilized for action.*

People who impose excessive demands on themselves but are not mobilized don't even *try* to do things. They are likely to spend their time and energy criticizing themselves for not initiating certain behaviors, for not possessing certain traits, or for not feeling certain ways. They feel guilty over failure and slowly settle into self-hate. As I see it, this is the progression of feelings they experience:

Perfectionism $\longrightarrow$ Self-Criticalness $\longrightarrow$ Guilt $\longrightarrow$ Self-Hate

On the other hand, *people who impose excessive demands on themselves and are mobilized might actively (and perhaps compulsively) struggle to meet their perfectionistic self-expectations.* Gradually, they begin to feel anxious and fearful that they might not meet these lofty expectations after all. (And, realistically, how could they?) Since the attainment of absolute perfection is, by definition, impossible, they quickly see their efforts as insufficient, then they begin to perceive themselves as failures and finally collapse into self-hate. Because it involves mobilization for activity, this route of progression from perfectionism to self-hate incorporates a few additional variables: self-demand, fear of failure, and perceived failure. This is the progression of feelings they are likely to experience:

Perfectionism ⟶ Self-Demand ⟶ Fear of Failure ⟶ Perceived Failure ⟶ Self-Criticalness ⟶ Guilt ⟶ Self-Hate.

A patient of mine named Lisa brings to mind the first route from perfectionistic self-demand to self-hate:

> Lisa was so demanding of herself and so self-critical that she was immobilized. Seeing her dishes pile up and her house get more disordered with each passing day, she said that she felt completely overwhelmed and didn't even know where to begin to get her surroundings in manageable condition again. Still, Lisa's internal dialogue reflected her perfectionism. She'd say things to herself like this: "I'll never get this oven clean enough." "I'll never get all the sand out of this rug." "These walls will never look completely clean." She thought that every room of her house should look like the "after" picture of a Mr. Clean advertisement— realized she couldn't possibly get her house to sparkle like that— felt enormous guilt— criticized herself for not being good enough— and began to hate herself.

Rich, a fourth-year college student, brings to mind the second route from perfectionistic self-demand to self-hate:

> Though depression-prone, Rich maintained a high level of nervous energy. He was always a bit "hyped up" and never seemed to sit still. But he was also very demanding of himself and tended to be depression-prone. One time, Rich received an assignment in his sociology class to write a term paper on world hunger. That happened to be a topic he was very interested in; in fact, he already knew a great deal about the topic. Rich felt that because of his interest and background, he should be able to do an extraordinary job on the paper; he placed himself under a great deal of pressure to write a paper of perfect quality. But when Rich was in the early stages of developing the paper, he began to sense that he could never really do the extraordinary job on the project that he

expected himself to do. He looked at his outline and notes, judged them to be mediocre, concluded he'd ultimately do a poor job, and began to detest himself for his "failure."

Even though the circumstances and reactions of Lisa and Rich differ, both ultimately experienced depression, in the form of anger turned inward, at the end of their respective journeys from per-fectionistic self-demand to self-hate.

Personality Styles and Response Patterns Contributing to Depression-Proneness

The components of psychological depression are exacerbated by the following personality styles or response patterns: Self-Alienation, Learned Helplessness, Deprivation Script, Anger-Proneness, and Negative Thinking and Despair.

Self-Alienation
"... a detachment from self that is disorienting."

Some people repress or otherwise "neutralize" the impact of their most painful feelings by placing a black shroud — a blanket of depression — over the feelings, making them feel vague and diffuse. This repression ultimately leads to feelings of numbness and extreme emotional distance. But repression of feelings isn't the only characteristic that contributes to self-alienation. People may also be particularly susceptible to these painful feelings of self-alienation when they develop people-pleaser interpersonal styles. Their hyper-alertness to the expectations, demands, and needs of others may have produced a pronounced "other-directedness" which ultimately results in people feeling that they aren't really themselves. Always feeling that they must respond to people with what is thought to be the *proper* thing to do, say, feel, and believe leads to a detachment from self that is disorienting. In time, such behavior may even lead to difficulty in differentiating between what they actually feel and what they think they "should" feel, and where their needs and issues end and the needs and issues of other people begin.

Many people who are alienated in this way use *projection*—the process, in this case, of attributing to others one's own negative feelings. Projection enables people to give up unacknowledged or rejected feelings in themselves by attributing those feelings to others. This technique "seems" to work at first because the negative focus shifts away from oneself and onto others. In a sense, they "empty" themselves onto others. But the more people disown their feelings through repression or projection, the more self-alienated and empty they feel. What begins as an internal dynamic involving perfectionism, self-criticalness, guilt, and self-hate begins to affect interpersonal dynamics.

Learned Helplessness

"... it's as if some people are programmed to collapse under the weight of their own overwhelming 'shoulds' and 'ought to's ..."

The roots of learned helplessness are often found in the dynamics of a person's early family situation. Perhaps a parent, guardian, or other significant adult encouraged or demanded the subservience or dependency of a child in order to feel authoritative or needed. The tendency to feel helpless may have come from modeling a parent or guardian who demonstrated a "we are all victims of fate" attitude, or from an individual who may have had so many setbacks that he or she came to view life as basically a "no-win" situation.

People who grow up with a belief that they are basically helpless will almost certainly find it difficult to meet adversity with decisiveness, firmness, and confidence. Some individuals reinforce this helplessness by forming relationships—marriages, in particular— that are highly protective, relationships that in some way insulate them from the need to be self-sufficient and autonomous. Then, when circumstances change through separation, divorce, or death, these people succumb to feelings of utter helplessness and confusion.

Sometimes feelings of helplessness result from the immobility that occurs when a person finally shuts down, so to speak, from the strain of dealing for a long period of time with exceedingly high self-expectations. Indeed, it's as if some people are programmed to collapse under the weight of their own overwhelming "shoulds" and "ought tos," then give up. They feel terribly indecisive and exhausted. In these cases, helpless feelings may create panic so that these people just want someone else to take care of them.

When people feel good about themselves, they don't rely on others to assure them that they're okay; they reassure themselves. But when people feel bad about themselves, it just follows that they're not likely to look to themselves for approval or kindness. So they look to others for the vital affirmation or reaffirmation they're unable to give to themselves. Having undermined their own self-esteem with self-criticism, they need *others* to provide them with constant acceptance, reassurance, and support.

Deprivation Script

". . . some people . . . become 'comfortable' with the idea of receiving very little from others."

Many depression-prone people grew up receiving very little warmth or support from parents, guardians, siblings, teachers, or peers. In fact, many times it appears that depression-prone adults were somehow emotionally deprived as children. Emotional deprivation in childhood often results in weak ego development. Also, people who are somehow deprived of experiencing—or even seeing—true intimacy as children may, as adults, be unusually distant, aloof or reserved with others because of feelings of awkwardness or fear. Unfortunately, some people who experienced emotionally deprived childhoods eventually become "comfortable" with the idea of receiving very little from others. The state of deprivation has, for them, familiar and expected qualities and is therefore perceived as relatively "safe" as well; they come to believe that they don't deserve love *anyway*. And what they *are* used to, they perpetuate in the present—they become resigned to a particular, solitary fate and consciously or subconsciously structure their lives to ensure the deprivation they somehow feel they "deserve." They feel somewhat comfortable in their negative predictions—not realizing that their negative expectations and thought patterns actually may have contributed to negative outcomes in the first place.

When deprivation is a person's script, he or she may feel so unworthy and despicable that withdrawal from others seems to be the only option. In this case, the avoidance of contact with others is simply a form of extreme self-protection. It all becomes a vicious cycle: Depressed and lonely people are more vulnerable to hurt from others. Even when they most need interaction with other people, they are not willing to risk rejection. For this reason, they stay away from people, causing even more isolation and depression for themselves. And they continue to focus on their separation from others.

People who experienced emotionally deprived childhoods may also go to the opposite extreme: out of a desperate need for the approval and support of others, they may actually drive others *away* with their unrealistic demands for love, reassurance, and attention. Again, a vicious cycle develops: others flee or remain distant; ultimately the person who has become "safe" with deprivation doesn't even have to deal with the desperately hoped-for but basically feared intimacy.

It is true that depressed people are likely to bring about their own social abandonment and isolation. When people remain in depressed states for long periods of time, they may severely test the patience of friends, relatives, and colleagues. Think about it: when every compliment is met with rejection or disavowal and every constructive suggestion is countered with an argument or rejection, the time will come when other people won't even *try* to converse with, much less comfort, the depressed person who is dependent. Also, many people would shy away from anyone's desperate or extreme dependency upon them, especially if they feared they might somehow get dragged down into the pit as well.

People maintain deprivation in a number of ways: with self-denial and self-sacrifice; by constantly neglecting their own personal needs for the "good" of others; by befriending or marrying a person who is selfish and ungiving; by sabotaging themselves; and by demanding things in ways that ensure that they won't be successful in getting them. And if these people do happen to get close to someone who *is* giving, they may feel confused, uncomfortable, and *guilty*. Such people believe that they don't deserve to be happy until they've "earned" that happiness through guilt, self-punishment, self-sacrifice, or by achieving perfection at last.

Anger-Proneness
". . . they may feel they can only reduce the control others have over them with an act of rage."

A tendency to overreact and "fly off the handle," so to speak, is another characteristic that both exacerbates and perpetuates depression. What makes a person so susceptible to angry outbursts when he or she is depressed? Dependency and helplessness make a person *feel* "thin skinned"; in this state, he or she feels terribly vulnerable—and is easily hurt by others. Deprivation and neediness make people supersensitive to thoughtless remarks and slights. And extreme forms of self-criticism make a person hypersensitive and prone to overreact to the slightest criticism from others—the very people who might be most needed for non-critical, totally accepting support. These people "ask" others for the honest truth, but they really don't want or need it, since they're already functioning as their own harshest critics and worst enemies. Even fairly minor negative remarks or innocuous responses may trigger enormous hurts in anger-prone people, hurts that can easily turn to rage. The "touchiness" of these people may make others somewhat wary of dealing with them; the wariness they sense in others, in turn, makes them feel even more rejected and isolated.

People who are already highly critical of themselves may just expect that other people have high expectations and harsh criticisms of them, too. And if they are also lacking a strong inner sense of self-identity and direction, they may be extremely reliant on the expectations of others and susceptible to both guilt and manipulation. The tension builds: at the same time they feel vulnerable toward others, they feel anger toward them as well. And they tend to feel that people are trying to manipulate them, even when facts and reality do not bear this out.

"Helpless" people are likely to respond in anger when they imagine that others are trying to make them feel guilty, take advantage of them, use them, or in some way dominate or control them. When people give their power to others and consider themselves worthless while elevating others to lofty heights, they may feel they can only reduce the control others have over them with an act of rage. Sometimes this rage is suppressed externally and experienced internally as profound sadness. At other times, this rage becomes misplaced, surfaces in response to an inconsequential matter, then causes remorse, guilt, suppression, depression and, of course, more anger.

Negative Thinking and Despair

". . . both cause and effect of depression."

Two other components complete the dynamics of depression: negative thinking and despair. In my work with depression-prone people, I have discovered that many of them were exposed, early in their lives, to pessimistic, cynical, and/or negative thinking, possibly "modeled" for them by a relative, a sibling, or a close friend.

When people are disturbed, exhausted, and emotionally depleted, their thinking tends to become muddled. As the world closes down around them, it becomes more and more negative as well.

They feel stupid and worthless and that they'll never feel better again; they begin to believe that nothing will ever turn out as it should. Life, then, seems profoundly disappointing and meaningless. In fact, negative thinking and despair function as both cause and effect of depression. There is no doubt that negative, distorted thinking and despair intensify feelings of depression. When people are cynical, pessimistic, and selectively focused on what they feel is wrong with them and the world around them, their distorted thinking creates and/or perpetuates a negative sense of themselves and their world. Negative and distorted thinking is the kind of thinking that tends to make people perceive and react to minor mishaps as major catastrophes, small problems as absolutely unsolvable and situations not completely positive as proof that a pessimistic view of reality is appropriate and justified. But these people may go for long periods of time without feeling depressed, and during those times their thinking may be quite positive. Then, situational crises may provoke negative thinking, which then perpetuates depression through the conviction that things are terrible and unsalvageable.

Perhaps the most painful feeling that causes and perpetuates depression is the pervasiveness of despair and hopelessness—the wearing of the darkest of dark glasses. When they look at the past, negative thinkers see the dark side of things in the form of regret, guilt, resentment, and unfulfilled longing. When they look ahead, negative thinkers see the dark side of things with thoughts of futility and impending doom. The present, too, is fraught with dismal thoughts and ruminations for the negative thinker.

The experience of depression can be oddly and powerfully seductive. Even when depressed people have been truly happy for six months prior to onset of the depression, in the midst of that depression, they believe that they only "imagined" past happiness; they assume that they were fooling themselves, avoiding or merely postponing the unavoidable, underlying reality of despair. The current depression permits this gloomy "reality" to creep in and prove that things are, "in fact," *terrible*.

The psychodynamics of depression in the diagram that follows clearly illustrate the factors that can be targeted with depression-combating strategies.

Diagram of Psychological Depression Process

Internal Dynamics of Depression

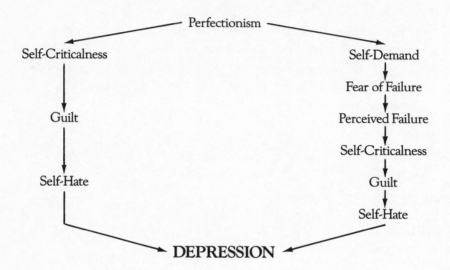

Interpersonal Dynamics of Depression

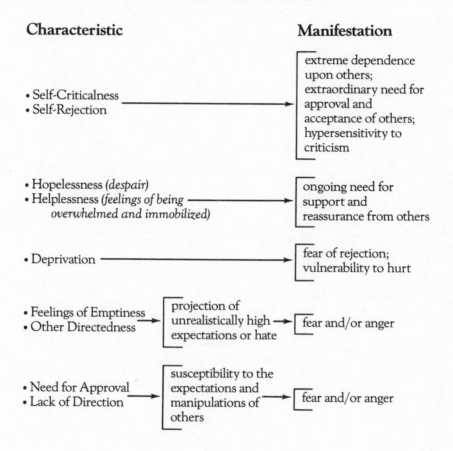

Characteristic	Manifestation
• Self-Criticalness • Self-Rejection	extreme dependence upon others; extraordinary need for approval and acceptance of others; hypersensitivity to criticism
• Hopelessness (*despair*) • Helplessness (*feelings of being overwhelmed and immobilized*)	ongoing need for support and reassurance from others
• Deprivation	fear of rejection; vulnerability to hurt
• Feelings of Emptiness • Other Directedness → projection of unrealistically high expectations or hate →	fear and/or anger
• Need for Approval • Lack of Direction → susceptibility to the expectations and manipulations of others →	fear and/or anger

Short-Term Tactics to Help
You Through the Blues

The short-term tactics presented here are designed to remove a person from the grip of depression as quickly as possible. If you feel blue now and then, these short-term tactics may be all that you need to help you rid yourself of an *occasional* and *brief* bout with depression. And then, once you're feeling good again, you may decide to look at your life . . . and wonder why you were "down" in the first place. Perhaps it will be a long time before you feel blue again. But if you're a depression-prone person, the mechanisms that initially caused and subsequently perpetuated the depression will continue to be operative, even after the immediate signs of depression lift and dissipate. In other words, your thinking and behavior will probably remain unchanged. If you fail to face or you otherwise avoid issues that need to be resolved after depression lifts, you'll probably find yourself back in the blues again in the not-too-distant future.

The short-term tactics detailed here won't help you repeatedly and successfully avoid the depression-inducing aspects of your personality style or response patterns. Some of these tactics appear to "let you off the hook" by instructing you to refrain from being hard on yourself. There's a reason for this: when we're depressed, we're simply not capable of the hard work and sustained effort necessary to change ourselves and our circumstances. I'm not advocating an evasion of problems that need to be faced; what I *am* advocating is that you not try to tackle everything head-on and all at once. At first, your efforts must be channeled into relieving your depression. Later on, you can begin to use the long-term techniques I suggest for confronting and dealing with the primary sources of your depression-proneness and for enhancing your interactions with people.

Of course, none of these self-help strategies constitute effective substitutes for psychotherapy, if your depression is negatively affecting your life for significant periods of time. *Remember that if you are seriously or repeatedly depressed, these short-term techniques can serve only as ways to assist you in gaining some perspective on your situation so that you can seek appropriate professional help.* Use these strategies with the knowledge that they can help you find a more comfortable place where you will be a little stronger and more clear-headed than before, and therefore better able to make some significant changes in your life.

4.

Acknowledge and Accept
Your Feelings

"The problem isn't the brief period of feeling blue,
but what you do about it."

Feeling blue needn't be cause for panic. In fact, acknowledging and
accepting your feelings of depression can be beneficial. Remember
the wisdom conveyed by a Chinese proverb: *"When the typhoon*
blows, it is wise to bend with the gale."

Many people *deny* having the blues because they're reluctant to
think of themselves—or to have others think of them—as
emotionally flawed. Some people take *pride* in their strength,
stoicism, and ability to function—regardless of the external and
internal forces they're dealing with. Some people are so unaccepting
of themselves that they make strong, negative judgments about their
feelings of depression; to their way of thinking, it's wrong to have
feelings about feelings! When people reject their feelings in this way,
they become depressed about their depression and anxious about
their anxiety.

But, of course, being depressed and admitting it has nothing to
do with being "bad," lazy, sinful, deprived, depraved, or emotionally
unstable. Feelings of depression might simply indicate some or all of
the following: that you are "blessed" with both sensitivity and a well-
developed conscience, that you have established unrealistically high
standards for yourself, and that you tend to put yourself down.
People who are feeling blue often ask me this question: *"But how can*
I possibly be okay when I feel so bad about myself?" My answer is that
feeling blue is just a *feeling*, not proof that something is wrong.

Oftentimes, the blues can be dealt with quite simply once they're
acknowledged—just so long as you don't use your feelings of
depression as an opportunity to characterize yourself as "screwed up,"
"disturbed," or "mentally ill." There's a big difference between a

person who says, "*Hmm, I feel a little depressed today . . . what can I do to get through this and maybe even cheer myself up?* and the person who says, "*Oh no; here I go again! What's wrong with me? I'm always getting depressed. I must be neurotic.*" It is realistic and healthy to accept some moodiness, some ebb and flow, some positive and negative emotions and energies in your life. But even though occasional down times are perfectly normal, there seems to be a subtle yet pervasive pressure to always be "up" in this culture.

> A woman I know moved to the United States after spending her childhood in Norway. This woman grew up in a country where days are short, winters are long, and people accept occasional periods of depression as normal. After living in the United States for a few years, this woman decided to move back to Norway. When I asked her why she was leaving the United States, she said: "In Norway, it's all right to feel depressed. Here, though, I always feel that I have to act pleasant and be happy. People around me seem to be disturbed when I'm sad or depressed. It is just more comfortable and reassuring for me to have people accept me *as I am* at any time and not to feel under pressure always to be 'up.'"

I believe that this woman's words contain a very useful message. Even though I present tactics here for dealing with and/or combating depression, there are times in all our lives when no short-term tactics are effective and we just don't have the wherewithal to struggle against the blues. At times like this, you might just say to yourself: "What the heck, I *feel* like being depressed. And I don't feel like wasting my energy trying to deny it, avoid it, or fight it."

Generally, it's no big deal to submit to a brief session with the blues. If you feel blue or down, fine—as long as you don't scold or in other ways punish yourself for feeling the way you do. In a simple, philosophical way, it can be helpful to learn to accept the fact that some days are good and some days are not. *The problem isn't the brief period of feeling blue, but what you do about it.* If you use your blue feelings to judge, criticize, or berate yourself, you can be sure that those feelings will last and probably intensify as well. But if you can let go of the sense that you "should" or "must" be happy all the time, and if you can learn to take the bad with the good, the natural rhythms of life probably will help dissipate your blues in a day or two—as long as you don't hang on to them. (And if you *do* have a tendency to hang on to the blues in this way, Chapters 15-23 will help you explore some solutions to that problem.)

5.

Resist Analyzing Your Feelings

*" . . . unless you're able to identify rather quickly what triggered
your feelings of depression, abandon your search."*

When you're feeling down, try to resist analyzing yourself and your
situation. Actually, depression analysis is quite tempting because it
requires relatively little activity; you can think for *hours* about what
may have caused your depression—while you toss and turn in bed or
sit in a chair and stare at the wall. Depression analysis is also likely to
give you a false sense that you're doing something active and
substantive to deal with down feelings and overcome them. But, in
fact, this self-analysis is likely to make you feel even *more* depressed.
When people are depressed, they're *already* focused on real and
perceived negatives in their lives, so a litany of bad feelings and
distorted beliefs just naturally becomes the "reason" for the depressed
state of mind.

    If, like some people, you feel that you require "brutal honesty"
from yourself in your efforts to snap out of a depression, I'm
predicting you'll be far more brutal with yourself than honest.
Usually in this so-called "honest" self-analysis, people spend time and
energy reviewing their emotional baggage in an effort to ascertain
what's wrong with them. In the process of this self-analysis, they
manage to root out and dig up every imaginable failure, flaw, and
shortcoming—and they do this at a moment in time when they most
need to know what's *right* with them. You're far more likely to snap
out of your depressed state of mind if you postpone that supposedly
honest self-examination, try not to take yourself too seriously, avoid
ruminating . . . and avoid melancholy music.

    During the period of time you're feeling blue, beware of people
who—however well-meaning they seem to be—attempt to draw you
into intense sessions of analysis to "help" you discover the true cause
of your depression. These self-appointed analysts, who might be

friends, family members, or work associates, may encourage you to scrutinize yourself closely and perhaps even "get tough" with yourself. Don't buy into that game; when you're down, encourage (and ask for) simple, unquestioning, non-judgmental and positive support from the people in your life.

Now that I've recommended that you not analyze your depression—at least not until after you feel better and have mobilized yourself again—I'll qualify that statement somewhat: when the blues *first* hit it might be helpful, for a moment, to ask yourself what, specifically, may have triggered the depression (*identify, don't analyze*). If the answer doesn't come immediately, drop the question at once. But if at the "gut" level, you're aware of some specific event that preceded the depressed feelings, it will probably come to you almost immediately. Being able to identify the precise source of the blues—inconsequential as it may seem to someone else—might possibly help you feel less helpless and less overwhelmed by your feelings. If you can identify a specific factor that led to your feelings, your depression may begin to lose its black-cloud quality. But instead of asking yourself "Why am I depressed?" ask this: "What happened to *trigger* my depressed feelings?" You might briefly review what happened in your life shortly before you began feeling down. (Perhaps you received a disturbing piece of news by letter or phone, or you experienced confrontation or conflict with someone, or you felt betrayed or manipulated.)

Remember, I'm only suggesting here that you try to identify *a specific incident that may have triggered the feelings*, not that you engage in a comprehensive inventory of your life and everything that you perceive is wrong with it. In attempting to answer this one quick allowable *why*, don't overlook minor incidents, small acts of thoughtlessness, or slight criticisms from others. You may discover that something relatively trivial or seemingly unimportant launched the tailspin you're experiencing. And if you do identify this incident or act, don't ridicule yourself for getting depressed over "nothing." Instead, congratulate yourself for being perceptive enough that in the midst of the blues, you were able to identify the source of your feelings and then move on. With that kind of natural inner awareness at work, you can learn to combat depression-proneness by identifying and "catching" a reaction or response before it takes hold and precipitates a downward spiral of feelings.

But, it's worth remembering this: unless you're able to identify rather quickly what triggered your feelings of depression, abandon your search. Additional efforts may only intensify your depressed state of mind. Visualize a car stuck in the mud with its wheels spinning—the more the driver tries to blast out of the quagmire, the deeper the car sinks into the mud.

Often, it's only *after* you've pulled yourself out of the worst of the depression that the event or events that triggered it can be accurately identified. Fortunately, knowing exactly how you got depressed is in no way a prerequisite for mobilizing yourself and using depression-combating techniques. When you've come through a bout with the blues and are feeling better again, that's a good time to take a look at your life and engage in a self-inventory of your work, relationships, avocations, and finances. You'll be in a better position, at that time, to consider the gaps in your life, to modify or clarify relationships, to explore job options, to reappraise values, and to review financial goals. This activity will help you determine if you're wanting in some area, if you have some unresolved problems or issues, or if you need to clarify and/or modify your lifestyle, plans, and priorities. Rethinking and resolving these issues when you're feeling better may help to reduce the number of problem areas in your life that could trigger or intensify psychological depression.

6.

Challenge Your Passivity and "Act As If"

"Slow motion is better than no motion."

When people are *anxious*, they're likely to be restless and fidgety; anxious people usually want to take action and do something—anything—to lessen the effects of their anxiety. But when people are *depressed*, they're likely to find that mobilizing themselves for action is no easy task. In fact, depressed people may be so overwhelmed that they essentially lose hope and collapse into a state of inactivity. Given the guilt feelings so common in depression-prone people, they may even subconsciously *choose* to continue suffering by *maintaining* their depression.

Hopelessness, helplessness, and passivity are significant barriers to change and these feelings seem to intensify during a depression. For example, the person who tends to look on the dark side of things anyway will find *more* to be negative about during a depression; the person whose behavior is already inconsistent will be inconsistent in his or her efforts to work through a depression; the person who is passive is likely to make only half-hearted attempts to implement depression-combating tactics. It is useful to note that the helplessness so common in depression is thought to be learned behavior.

Though I'm an animal lover and uncomfortable about reporting the details of the laboratory research I'm about to summarize, this research does serve to explain and illustrate an important concept. Research psychologist Dr. Martin Seligman tested the hypothesis of learned helplessness in the following laboratory experiment with an animal: A dog was placed in a cage with an electrified floor. Initially, electricity was turned on for only one side of the cage floor. As soon as the dog felt the electrical shock, he jumped around in the cage; the dog quickly learned to escape the discomfort of the electric current by moving to the other side of the cage. Then, when electricity was turned on for the entire cage floor, the dog continued moving about, trying to avoid the discomfort. Learning that his efforts were futile, he appeared to give up even *trying* to avoid the electric current. As the shock was repeatedly administered, the dog simply lay on the floor, doing nothing. Next, the electricity was turned off on one side of the cage floor. But because the dog was no longer responsive at that point, he did not discover that he now could escape the electric current. This experiment illustrates that the dog *learned* to be helpless and had, therefore, given up. Similarly, some depression-prone people come to believe that *no* action is worthwhile because their efforts are already doomed to failure. You've heard the telltale remarks of this helplessness and hopelessness; perhaps you've even uttered them yourself: *"Why even bother?" "What good will it do?" "I might try, but I know it won't work!" "I give up!"*

Continuing on with his laboratory experiment, Seligman then attempted to reverse the helpless behavior the dog had learned. He did this by placing a harness on the dog and pulling him to the side of the cage where the electricity had been turned off. Once the dog passively experienced the "success" represented by the absence of electric current, he began to actively avoid it once again. Through this experiment, Seligman thus "taught" the dog to overcome his learned helplessness.[1], [2] Extrapolating to the human condition, it *is* possible in the midst of a depression to do things that will pull you out of that depression, contrary to how you might feel at the time. In order to pull yourself out of a depression, you don't necessarily have to feel or believe that you can get out of it—you only need to "act as if" you can.

> I once treated a college student named Jeff. Now, Jeff was abso-lutely *certain* that he wouldn't be able to mobilize himself unless he understood *all* of the factors that contributed to his feelings of helplessness and his tendency to procrastinate. I agreed to ex-plore Jeff's feelings in depth with him. But because an explora-tion of that kind can be very time-consuming, I wanted him to work, in the meantime, on changing a few of his deeply-en-trenched habits—habits that were contributing to his problems.
> Since Jeff evidenced very little *internal* motivation, I asked him to cooperate with me in setting up a series of simple external

"motivators" to use in working through and overcoming his problem. One of the problems he frequently mentioned was his difficulty in getting out of bed in the morning, so we began there: I suggested to Jeff that he place his alarm clock across the room from his bed. (Jeff hated the sound of the alarm and usually kept it close at hand so that he could turn it off as soon as it rang.) By placing the clock across the room, of course, Jeff would have to get out of bed and somehow get to the other side of the room in order to turn off the alarm. Together, we devised the following plan: if Jeff returned to bed after turning off the alarm, a student football player in the dorm (who, incidentally, was nicknamed "The Beast") was to come to his room and throw him out into the hallway. The first few mornings, Jeff returned to bed even after being tossed into the hallway (who said this guy isn't motivated?). When I suggested that he pay "The Beast" to throw him in the shower if and when he went back to bed, he decided to simply "act as if" he *wanted* to get out of bed in the morning. And he did.

Next, I suggested to Jeff that he start jogging again. To help motivate him to get back in the jogging routine, I suggested that he give a jogging buddy fifty dollars to hold for him. Jeff would then receive five dollars from his friend each day that he jogged. But if he didn't jog on a particular day, his friend would keep the five dollars allotted for that day. Jeff, who was on a tight budget already, gave up *fifteen dollars* (three days of jogging activity) before he got back into the habit of jogging on a daily basis.

Once Jeff began his new routine in earnest—getting up early in the morning, arriving at his classes on time, and experiencing the kind of energy that comes from regular exercise—he found that other changes in his life were easier to make. And he subsequently abandoned his exhaustive search for all the "reasons" for his feelings of helplessness. Once Jeff began to focus on *doing something* rather than just thinking about why he *wasn't* doing something, he stopped procrastinating. For example, he looked for part-time work when he needed money, rather than spending time and energy worrying and complaining about his financial difficulties; he applied for grant money on time; he began searching for a summer job during the month of April, rather than waiting until after final exams in June.

If, like Jeff, you try a few specific tactics to combat depression and you subsequently begin to feel somewhat less depressed, you will know firsthand that *any* effort is likely to bring at least some reward. At a deeper level, then, the elements of helplessness and passivity so prominent in depression can be undermined by realizing that you do, after all, have some control over your life and that any/every effort can make a difference in how you feel. Think of it like this: it takes more energy to get an idling car up to a speed of fifty miles an hour than it does to maintain a fifty-mile-per-hour cruising speed; in a similar way, it is easier to *stay* mobilized once you *are* mobilized. *Slow motion is better than no motion.*

Don't give up the struggle. Ignore the voices of doom and discouragement inside your head that nag at you and say "This isn't going to work." Being passive will only reinforce your helpless feelings and serve as "evidence" (to you) that you're trapped and incapable of changing your situation. Lack of effort translates into lack of reward and thereby serves only to *maintain* depression. If you force yourself to do a few things each day, you'll get a pleasant feeling of accomplishment, however slight it may be. Maybe you'll find some activity that actually makes you feel *better* for a while. It's not true that you have to "hit rock bottom" before you can begin to come out of a depression.

A period of depression often dramatically curtails your activities, slows down your life, and narrows your interests and options. As a result, you are likely to be less stimulated and subsequently you'll become bored. A vicious cycle, for sure. If you're *waiting* to become motivated and mobilized before undertaking change or other activities, consider this: productive, healthy people usually don't put off tasks until the mood hits them or until they otherwise *feel like* doing them.

Productive, healthy people don't believe they have to *feel* like doing work and they don't think they necessarily must be *motivated* to do it. In fact, true motivation is more likely to *follow* activity. Activity stimulates further interest and involvement, thus setting in motion a positive cycle. We really don't get involved in an activity until we move from talking about it to *actually doing it*. Think about your own experience. Doesn't a project often look more appealing and manageable from the inside—as it's being tackled and accomplished—than it does from the outside—as we ponder whether or not we're in the mood and/or have the necessary energy to begin the project at all? Remember that small efforts to mobilize yourself with specific tasks on a daily basis could end up working wonders in lifting your spirits. The sense of ongoing progression will contrast dramatically and constructively with the nothing's-done-and everything's-falling-apart feelings that are so pervasive in a depression.

References

1. Abramson, L.Y., M. Seligman, and J.D. Teasdale. 1978. Learned helplessness in humans: Critique and reformation. *Journal of Abnormal Psychology.* 87 (1): 49-74.

2. Seligman, M. and S.F. Maier. 1967. Failure to escape traumatic shock. *Journal of Experimental Psychology.* 74: 1-9.

7.

Mind Your Body

" . . . improper nourishment and lack of exercise increase anyone's vulnerability to depression."

New research findings on the mind-body connection are published frequently. But since I'm neither a nutritionist nor an exercise physiologist, and because it would require another full-length book to adequately explore these topics, I'm opting to provide only a few summary statements and suggestions here. An overriding note of caution: for guidance regarding the relationship between diet, exercise, and depression, consult sources of information that you know to be reputable and that you trust. Anyone who is interested in specific nutritional and/or physical exercise strategies for combating depression would do well to consult with an appropriate health care specialist. Depending upon your own experience, what I'm offering here are either reminders or considerations regarding the vital connection between mind and body.

• Many people drink large quantities of coffee when they feel listless and depressed. But caffeine really produces only temporary, artificial "highs." These false, short-lived feelings of false energy tend to make people feel "wired" and "edgy," and send them crashing downward when the effects wear off. Caffeine increases the metabolic rate, body temperature, blood pressure, and peripheral blood flow, so it's not surprising that this drug promotes an overall "stressed out" feeling that disturbs rest and sleep.

• Glucose is the preferred "fuel" that supplies energy to the body's cells for growth and repair. Every tissue in the body needs glucose to function properly. But the process of converting carbohydrates—sugars and starches—into blood glucose utilizes needed B-complex or "nerve" vitamins, upsets the blood-sugar level, and tends to make both body and mind more prone to nervous unrest. Of course, most of us consume excessive amounts of "hidden" sugar simply by eating processed foods. In fact, studies show that people in this country consume an average of 110 pounds of sugar each year—much of it contained in processed foods that are also very high in starch content. White flour, white rice, and other refined starches so prevalent in the American diet also contribute to physical difficulties because of their empty calories. In other words, the body converts these refined starches to pure sugar; therefore, they add calories and tend to make a person feel satisfied or full, but they offer very little in terms of nutrients. Salt, too, is implicated in a number of health problems. Like sugar, it is quite prevalent in the American diet, particularly in packaged foods. Salt also contributes to the loss of potassium from the body, thus changing the delicate acid/alkaline or electrolyte balance in the cells of the tissues.

• Some studies have shown that foods rich in the B vitamins and vitamin C may help people deal more effectively with the stress in their lives. Vitamin C is essential to the body's immune system and helps body tissues repair themselves following injury or severe physical exhaustion. But regarding any kind of vitamin supplementation program, be wary of suggested optimal dosages. Because of the vast individual differences among people—their activity and stress levels, nutrient absorption, size, and unique body chemistry—there is no one optimal dose or vitamin regime appropriate for everyone. Note, especially, that mega-doses of some vitamins can be toxic; sudden and/or significant increases in the intake of some vitamins and minerals may produce imbalances that can be quite harmful. As with other considerations involving mind and body, your best source of information is a medical professional with special training in nutrition.

• In his book, *Feeling Good*, Dr. David Burns contends that in his extensive review of research literature, he found documentation of only *one* dietary substance which in some cases helped to alleviate depression: *L-Trytophan*. [1] L-Trytophan is one of the dietary building blocks the body uses to manufacture proteins. L-Trytophan, an essential amino acid, is used by the brain to manufacture serotonin, one of the neurotransmitters in the brain's emotional centers. The level of serotonin in the brain is directly influenced by the amount of L-Trytophan in one's diet. Since the body is unable to manufacture its own L-Trytophan, it must obtain this substance from food items such as milk, eggs, bananas, and turkey. Dietary supplements of L-Trytophan are now available, but again—by way of caution—therapeutic doses of this substance and/or other dietary supplements should be supervised by an appropriate health care specialist.

• Both body and mind benefit greatly from regular physical exercise. When you're feeling depressed, it's important to get out and *do* something. It it widely accepted that maintenance of a regular exercise program and a variety of enjoyable, physically engaging activities can serve as solid defenses against depression. Think about it: it's more difficult to feel depressed when one is running, biking, dancing, walking. People who are unable to do much of anything other than walk can benefit greatly—physically and psychologically—from a half-hour brisk walk each day. Certainly it's difficult for us to motivate ourselves when we feel exhausted and lacking in energy. But in a psychological depression, the fatigue and inertia experienced are *subjective feelings*, as opposed to *physical states*. You may be physically depleted because you've not been taking proper care of your body. Inadequate rest, improper nourishment, and lack of exercise increase *anyone's* vulnerability to depression.

• The most direct way for depression-prone people to become mobilized and stay mobilized is to keep up their energy levels through daily—or at least regular—physical exercise. One-half hour per day of strenuous aerobic (oxygen-demanding) exercise (swimming, biking, jogging, jumping rope, or brisk walking) has the effect of increasing the oxygen intake of the body's cells and the rate of the blood circulation supplying oxygen and carrying away cellular waste products. Aerobic exercises are physical activities that stimulate heart and lung activity for a time period sufficiently to produce beneficial changes in the body. Aerobics have one thing in common: by making you work hard, they demand plenty of oxygen. The primary objective of an aerobic exercise is to increase the maximum amount of oxygen that the body can process in a given time (aerobic capacity). This aerobic capacity is dependent upon efficient lungs, a powerful heart, and a good vascular system. And these physiological positives are particularly beneficial to the brain.

• Physical exercise also serves to "burn off" the inevitable buildup of nervous agitation and accompanying tensions that seem to be rather common byproducts of contemporary life. Though not as beneficial to the cardiovascular system, vigorous but nonaerobic sports like racquetball, handball, or tennis can also help decrease the kind of ongoing stress that can lead to depression.

• Exercise provides several other mental-health benefits: It stimulates our bodies to produce *natural* antidepressants (endorphins), morphine-like substances thought to play a role in producing what is sometimes referred to as a "runner's high." These natural antidepressants produced by the body also appear to facilitate restful, sound sleep and, in fact, help the body renew itself with less sleep.

• When people begin to pay attention to their bodies in performing various movements and exercises, they are more likely to notice physical habits that both *reflect* and *perpetuate* feelings of depression. For example, dejected posture—head down and shoulders slumped— creates a feeling of depression through the body sensations associated with the posture. Because this "depressed" posture prevents a person from breathing deeply enough, it can also rob the body of adequate oxygen. Poor posture may, indeed, prevent a person from breathing deeply enough. A slow, faltering gait—with head down—also perpetuates *feelings* of dejection. One particularly good way to "act as if" you're not depressed is to consciously concentrate on holding your head high, squaring your shoulders, breathing more freely and deeply, and walking more briskly. An alert, erect stance may, in fact, signal the mind that the body is not depressed.

• Many posture, movement, and body therapy techniques have proven to be useful in creating and maintaining energy, alertness, and feelings of physical well-being. The gentler techniques of Hatha Yoga,

Feldenkrais, and the Alexander Technique work more directly on posture, gait, and breathing. Other body therapies work exclusively on breathing, dissolution of body blocks, and freeing of respiratory apparatus. Some of the more dramatic forms of body work— Bioenergetics and Rolfing—work to free or realign the body.

• Dr. John Greist, Professor of Psychiatry at the University of Wisconsin Medical School in Madison, Wisconsin, has studied the exercise of running as a treatment for depression. In one of his early studies, Greist compared running, meditation, and group therapy as treatment modalities and found running to be most effective in alleviating depression.[2]

In most of Greist's subsequent studies on running and depression, the individuals studied were not being treated with antidepressant medication; these individuals were considered to be non-psychotic and at low risk of suicide. Instead, they were diagnosed as having neurotic or reactive depression. In one of Greist's studies (published in *Comprehensive Psychiatry*), he and his colleagues studied thirteen men and fifteen women between the ages of 18 and 30.[3] For the first four weeks of the program, subjects ran three to four times per week with a running leader; during the fifth and sixth weeks, only two sessions were scheduled with the leader; during the seventh and eighth weeks, only one session was scheduled. The basic idea in this scheduling was to gradually have the patients run on their own. In this particular study, running proved to be more effective than either short- or long-term psychotherapy.

Positive treatment effects were attributed to the following: 1. *Mastery*: individuals who became independent runners developed a sense of success and mastery of what they correctly perceived as a difficult skill; 2. *Patience*: to become an independent runner takes time, and one learns again the necessities of patience and making regular efforts until the activity becomes a habit; 3. *Capacity for change*: subjects learned they can change themselves for the better; 4. *Generalization*: changes through running helped subjects feel capable of becoming competent in other areas; 5. *Distraction*: subjects noticed new and very real bodily sensations that distracted them from preoccupations with minor, but annoying, physical symptoms of depression; 6. *Positive habit or "addiction"*; 7. *Symptom relief*: reduction in depression, anger, and anxiety — subjects began to feel better physically and mentally; 8. *Consciousness alteration*: subjects reported positive, creative, less conscious, and more insightful interludes; 9. *Biochemical changes*: improvement in blood pressure, resting heart rate, kicks in neurotransmitters like the endorphins.

References

1.   Burns, David P. *Feeling Good*. New York: William Morrow, 1980.

2.   Greist, John. *Anti-Depressant Treatment. The Essentials.* Baltimore: William and Wilkins. 1979.

3.   Greist, John, et al. Running as a treatment for depression. *Comprehensive Psychiatry.* 20 (1): 41-54 (January/February, 1979).

8.

Structure Your Time

"It's like having a good road map on a foggy night . . ."

Depression-prone people seem to be even more susceptible to depression when they're unemployed or retired, especially if they fail to build some kind of structure into their daily lives. Regardless of the nature of the job itself, employment usually brings at least some degree of structure to daily living because it requires that a person do some or all of the following: • be somewhere on time • respond to external expectations and demands • carry out the tasks of the job itself.

Unless his or her depression is severe, a depressed person will benefit much more from just coasting along within a structured situation than he or she will from giving up, staying in bed, and staring at the walls. When depressed people schedule activities on a daily basis, they'll probably find that there's less time available for brooding. All of this is another way of saying that in order to reduce the potential for depression at any given time, depression-prone people probably need to create structured situations and time-oriented frameworks for themselves. *How to add structure to one's life?* With short-range activities (tasks) and long-range objectives (goals).

Here's a plan of action I frequently recommend to depressed clients: when you awaken in the morning feeling exhausted, overwhelmed and blue, make a list of the bare essentials in terms of activity necessary—only things you absolutely *must do that day.* You may decide, for example, to limit yourself to a few life-maintenance functions: getting out of bed, fixing breakfast, walking the dog, and phoning a few friends or family members. Accomplishing a few simple tasks serves to "prime the pump," so to speak, and make you feel less "zombie-like." (You may even experience some feelings of surprise or satisfaction when you actually manage to outdo your pet rock that day.) On days like this, you're likely to engage in negative self-talk, self-talk that says you don't stand a chance of accomplishing *anything*. All the more reason, then, to focus on the accomplishment of relatively minor tasks that might help to dispel self-doubts. Slowly and methodically, with one small step of activity at a time, you can begin to move out of your depression.

You can begin to put some positive structure into your life by making a list each morning—or each night—of several things you hope to accomplish during the coming day. You might prioritize these items either by their functional importance or their pleasurableness. Write the date or the day of the week at the top of the list. Then, identify a few tasks that you're reasonably sure you can accomplish that day. Your list will serve as a reminder of the things you *could* do that day—not of the things you feel you *should* do. Recheck your list from time to time during the day; as you complete each activity, place a check mark alongside that item or cross it off your list completely.

In your daily list of activities, you might insert just one task that involves doing something to make your immediate surroundings more pleasant—even if the task simply requires that you shove some clutter into a box or closet or under a bed to await a time when you feel like sorting through it. Or you could improve your surroundings simply by picking a single flower or a leafy branch, putting it in a small vase, and placing it where you can look at it often during the day. Taking better care of your surroundings is an important part of taking better care of *yourself*. And, in spite of the guilt feelings and self-punishment that come so quickly to the depression-prone person, remind yourself that you *deserve* to dwell in attractive and orderly surroundings.

At first, make a list of daily activities as simple as the following: • prepare scrambled eggs for breakfast • take a shower • wash hair • call a friend or family member on the telephone • go for a brisk walk around the block. Resist any temptation you might feel to judge these activities; that's simply an empty exercise that will lead to another round of self-criticism. *Also, don't assign yourself too many tasks. And make sure that at least half of the tasks are activities you don't mind doing or, better yet, even enjoy doing.*

As you become more comfortable with these structured activities, you could perhaps add another one to your list each day. But avoid overwhelming yourself with too many activities by setting an upward limit. If you start out with three structured activities per day, you might get to the point where you can handle a dozen or more. As you begin to feel more capable and energetic, you could gradually increase the complexity and difficulty of the tasks. Of course, if you're working outside the home while coping with a bout of depression, you could make similar lists related to your job tasks. Setting up even a rather loosely structured program on a daily basis will give you some immediate objectives. *It's like having a good road map on a foggy night*: you may feel lost; you're unable to see ahead; the fog appears to be never-ending. But the structure you've set up serves as a "map" to confirm that, despite your doubts, the road ahead *will* take you where you want to go.

Checking off items on your list will give you a simple, visible sense of accomplishment each day. Save the lists. Then, periodically—especially if you start to berate yourself for being down and not accomplishing anything—you can review just how much you really *have* accomplished.

If you set goals for yourself that are too low, accomplishing them may not bring you much sense of achievement. On the other hand, if you set goals for yourself that are too high, you risk sabotaging yourself. Unfortunately, depression clouds judgment about what is necessary or reasonable in attaining the kind of fulfillment that is life-enriching. When people are depressed, they may feel that regardless of what they accomplish—short-term or long-term—it won't help them feel better about themselves. Regardless of how strong this feeling is at the time you're depressed, don't give in to it. Most people are surprised and pleased to realize that the accomplishment of even small daily tasks begins to perk them up.

I once worked with a college student named Ted whose depression seemed to be related to his goals. Ted's primary problem wasn't a lack of goals or a lack of clarity in expressing those goals. In fact, he was very clear on what his goals were; it seemed to me that he had hundreds of them! And he held fast to each and every one. In fact, I don't think that at first I could have wrenched a single goal away from Ted with a crowbar! He wanted to do everything; beyond that, he seemed to feel that everything he wanted to do was of equal importance and therefore carried the same priority. To complicate matters, Ted also held a belief that prior to tackling any goal, there were several related goals he'd have to accomplish.

Here's an example of the self-defeating situation Ted was placing himself in every day as he worked toward his goals with a series of self-imposed rules: • he set up a rigid study schedule for himself that required he get started extremely early in the morning, even though he knew that he wasn't a "morning person" • he scheduled himself so tightly, he really had no time left for recreation or even relaxation • he set a B + average as his goal for that semester, even when he knew that he was already falling behind and lacked the background to pull his grades that high • he would not begin studying until his room was completely uncluttered and neat—even though he was basically what he called a "slob" • even when he was running only twenty minutes late in the morning, he insisted on completely revising his daily schedule before studying • he'd tear up a paper and start over *completely* unless everything was, to his way of thinking, perfect • though studying was a priority for him, he felt that he must jog four miles each day in order to "keep fit" • he'd be unmercifully hard on himself whenever he strayed off a rigidly nutritional diet • he never allowed himself to watch television because he felt that was a non-intellectual activity.

But Ted was never sure which goal to tackle first. So, rather than make a mistake in prioritizing and putting energy into a goal that wasn't the "perfect" one to start with, Ted remained immobilized. And he was aghast when I suggested to him that since all of his goals apparently held the same value for him, he should just arbitrarily pick one goal to focus on for starters. Could he possibly be effective in achieving his goal, he wondered, if he was not completely sure which goal to start with? Ted found the following exercise quite difficult: (I suggested to him that he select and focus on three long-term goals, three intermediate goals, and three short-term goals.) He did successfully complete the exercise, but was still concerned that there were many goals he'd overlooked for the purposes of this exercise.

Another source of Ted's depression was a lack of productivity related to procrastination. Once Ted began working on *some* of his goals, even though in his perception they may not have been exactly the "right" goals to start with, he began to feel some sense of accomplishment. He also learned that despite his hopes and best efforts, he simply could not do *everything*. Furthermore, once Ted's depression began to lift—at least in part because he was beginning to accomplish so many things—he learned that he didn't have to accomplish everything he hoped to in order to feel okay about himself. Once he began to actively pursue specific goals, genuine and clear-cut priorities began to emerge.

Indeed, what Ted learned is that effective goal-setting cannot occur in a vacuum. Instead, goal-setting is really a developmental process in which prioritizing and decision-making grow out of trying one activity for a while, then trying another. When you feel up to it again, begin jotting down a few longer-range objectives to think about and to act on only when you have put more time and space between you and your depression. Then, if you start to slip back into the blues, consult your list-in-the-making. You could say to yourself: "Three days ago when I wasn't feeling quite so low, I believed that X, Y, and Z were important to me and that accomplishing these things would give me a sense of genuine satisfaction. Even though I don't believe that *anything* would make me feel better right now, the goals I have set give me something positive to consider. And they remind me that I *can* (and will) feel better again."

9.

Try Some Tenderness

" . . . treat yourself as considerately and sympathetically
as you'd treat a good friend."

Many people find that when they develop an awareness of the energy
they expend in *maintaining* depression, they can learn to short-circuit
it. But how and why do people maintain their depression in the first
place?

People maintain depression when they continue to tell
themselves how worthless they are. Right now, in fact, you may be
berating yourself and telling yourself what you should or should not
do—or should or should not have done. In addition to telling
yourself that you're a failure and will never change, you probably
continue to place many unrealistic expectations and demands on
yourself. Also, you may be depleting your energy by feeling sorry for
yourself, or by fighting the past, or by gathering ample proof that
you've been unjustly dealt with by others.

Many people succeed in turning the blues or a relatively mild
depression into absolute despair and severe depression by reaching
into a "black box" of negative feelings. This is most likely to happen
in the process of analyzing a depression—trying to figure out its cause
or source. You can reach into your own personal "black box" and
begin pulling out past unpleasant incidents, childhood traumas,
examples of deprivation, "proof" of failures, feelings of shame, guilt,
resentment, longing, and unfulfilled needs. Once you really get
going, there's no end to the nasty treasures you'll find! In other
words, a blue mood might serve as an occasion for you to produce
enough emotional garbage from your past and present to nurture a
full-blown depression. In cases like this, the issue that initially
triggered your depression is not the same issue that *maintains* your
depression. Some people find it helpful to actually visualize this so-
called "black box" and figuratively pull their hands away from its dark

collection of negative thoughts and feelings. In the midst of a depression, you might visualize yourself taking hold of the lid of this "black box," purposefully lowering it, shutting it, then locking it. You simply don't need to go back into that box to seek out more things to disturb and depress you.

Instead of digging around in the "black box," here's one of the first things you can do when you're feeling depressed: *stop being so critical of yourself and stop punishing yourself further for being depressed. I think most of us would agree that depression itself is punishment enough!* Whenever you find yourself engaged in self-criticism, ask yourself these questions: "*Could I ever be this vindictive and punitive toward a friend?*" "*Would I ever knowingly make a friend feel guilty, depressed, worthless, or sick?*" "*If I did hurt a friend and make him or her feel badly, would I proclaim that he or she has no right to wallow in self-pity?*" At this point, I think you'll see quite clearly how utterly merciless you've been with yourself. Indeed, if you caught yourself being *one-tenth* as demanding toward someone else as you are toward yourself, I think you'd be horrified! And isn't it awful how you can be so tough on yourself and then, instead of letting up and giving yourself some compassion or sympathy, you attack yourself further for being weak, dependent, and self-pitying? Depressed people need their own patience and kindness as much as they need the patience and kindness of others; nevertheless, they tend to kick themselves mightily when they're feeling down.

You know yourself better than anyone does, right? By being fully open and honest with yourself, by exposing all your vulnerabilities and failings, you are creating an inner dynamic that parallels a deep, intimate relationship. Would you knowingly violate this trust by rejecting yourself? Many depression-prone people are inclined to do just that. But there is every good reason to treat yourself as considerately and sympathetically as you'd treat a good friend. Consider it a variation of the Golden Rule: *Do unto yourself as you would do unto others.* Or, in a negative form: *Don't do to yourself what you wouldn't do to others.*

Try some tenderness. It may be difficult at first, but you need to treat yourself to some self-administered compassion. Compassion is a form of loving sympathy that develops quite naturally when you make an effort to understand the challenges and hurts of others and how they truly deserve some measure of happiness. This time, give *yourself* the gift of compassion. *And don't mistake compassion for self-pity*—the psychic whip that depression-prone people tend to use to undermine their self-respect. Masochistic, self-indulgent, self-pitying people are clearly misguided. They slash away at themselves, then pour salt on the wounds to sustain the hurt they feel. So, how does one distinguish between compassion for oneself and self-pity? Don't attempt to make this distinction by examining your feelings, because depressed people tend to judge themselves harshly. Instead, *look directly at your behavior*. It's likely that you've slipped into self-pity if you do the following: • reject the efforts of others to help you or cheer you up • decline opportunities to make yourself feel better • respond to reasonable advice from others with "Yes, but . . ." • make excuses for why nothing works • do nothing to work your way out of a depression.

Compassion for oneself can go a long way in alleviating depression. By contrast, self-pity leads to further negative "self-indulgence" and perpetuation of the depression. You'll find, also, that having compassion for yourself is likely to bring support from others. Feelings of self-pity will tend to discourage people from maintaining their show of concern and offers of assistance. Besides, self-pity ultimately makes a person feel even more isolated, gloomy, and abandoned. Of course you can make a conscious choice about which route to take, but I strongly recommend the route of compassion.

Without compassion for themselves, people are more likely to engage in self-punishment. And then, because they already feel so guilty, some people find it almost *impossible* to stop their self-punishing behaviors. They seem to feel that this ongoing punishment confers genuine benefits—believing, for example, that suffering makes them more deserving or strengthens them for the adversities of life. Some people even believe that suffering puts them in touch with deeper levels of being, making them more interesting, more sensitive to others, more alive. But because self-punishment is, by its nature, unproductive and often brutally excessive as well, it isn't likely to effect any positive changes in people at all. Instead, self-punishment tends to aggravate feelings of anxiety, exhaustion, and despondency, thereby increasing susceptibility to more guilt and depression in the future.

Sometimes people begin punishing themselves even *before* they fail. On close examination, what's operative in situations like this is much more than a simple attitude of "starting early to avoid the rush"; instead, it's a kind of "black magic" routine, a self-fulfilling prophecy. This routine is often used to appease self-hate mechanisms and it deflects even harsher punishment that might come later, when the "returns are in," so to speak, and failure conquers. Maybe dedicated self-punishers believe that if they punish themselves harshly enough, other people—or God—will be forgiving. These self-punishers also maintain control over their punishment by allowing themselves to be vulnerable to the criticisms of others or by beating themselves verbally before anyone else has an opportunity to do so.

After years of practice in skillful self-punishment, you may find it almost impossible to stop the practice. At first, you may need to compromise with yourself. If you realize you can't stop yourself until you've engaged in at least *some* self-punishment, ask yourself the following: "Exactly how long must I punish myself until I've received my 'just due'?" Then determine precisely how long you "deserve" to suffer as payment for some fault or transgression that's troubling you. And hold to the exact period of time you specify. For example, if you decide that your "sin" warrants two entire days of unremitting self-criticism, *go to it for two days . . . then stop completely*! Now I realize that this may seem like a rather grotesque exercise, but it *is* worth trying if you find it difficult to break the habit of self-punishment. This exercise can result in three positive outcomes: 1. You give yourself permission to do something you would have done anyway. 2. You rigidly impose a time limit on your self-punishment sentence. 3. As a result of the first two outcomes, you will know (and feel) that you're assuming some degree of control over your self-punishment; becoming aware of this underlines the absurdity of the "need" to inflict self-punishment and also helps people realize that they *can* stop this unproductive and harmful habit.

People often *do* grow and become stronger by adjusting to hardships and crises. But self-punishment simply ensures the perpetuation of a guilt/depression lifestyle. We simply cannot become better people through exaggerated, self-initiated punishment and suffering; these activities only serve to reinforce self-defeating habits. Self-imposed suffering over issues or situations beyond your control will drain your internal resources and undermine your self-esteem. Then, when a *real* crisis occurs, you might be too exhausted to respond to it appropriately, much less handle it effectively.

Perhaps surprisingly, though, depression-prone people often do handle sudden, major crises quite well, provided they're not already exhausted from bouts of self-punishment. In fact, some depression-prone people even seem to have a sense of *relief* when they encounter a genuine external problem they must solve. The relief comes partially from the temporary respite from painful self-punishment, as well as from the necessary distraction from inner self-absorption. But the crisis confrontation and related problem-solving also helps depression-prone people realize—if only briefly—that they, in fact, have competence in coping with the real world outside of themselves and their internal spheres. In other words, when chronically depressed people face actual emergencies, they simply don't have time or energy to devote to problems that are distorted or invented in their minds.

10.

Examine Your Feelings of Guilt

" . . . guilt is almost always at the very center of depression."

Why do people punish themselves? Oftentimes, it's because they feel guilty about something—or they feel guilty about *many things*; some people actually feel guilty for being alive! Guilt is a factor not only in relation to issues of the past, but also in relation to present and future issues. And guilt is almost always at the very center of depression.

Some people actually fear that unless they use feelings of guilt to restrain themselves, they might "run amok" and become compulsive pleasure-seekers or slaves to wild impulses. Other people seem to fear that if they accept themselves just as they are (with no guilt and regret), they'll become complacent and never acquire the ability or desire to change. To some extent, I think many of us believe that guilt has some essential function for individuals and society as a whole. This belief, I suspect, comes from the long-held tradition of utilizing guilt as a tool for instilling conscience and socially acceptable behavior. Some people have come to believe that only guilt can restrain unethical or antisocial behavior—and that guilt can be effective in facilitating character change. The following examples illustrate the erroneous belief that guilt is an effective way to bring about desirable character changes in others:

> Because Betty was very intelligent and attractive, her mother didn't realize how unsure of herself she really was. When Betty left home to take a job in another town after high school gradua- tion, her mother worried that Betty might become neglectful in her efforts to improve herself. Since Betty had a tendency to gain weight when she wasn't diligent about diet and exercise, her mother began quizzing her by telephone about her progress in these areas. As it turned out, Betty missed the security of having family around and she felt anxious about her new job. She had developed a habit of "nervous nibbling" and because of her de-

manding schedule had difficulty finding adequate time to exercise regularly. Her mother expressed grave concern about Betty's laxity and strongly hinted that she was fearful that Betty would just let herself go and become lazy and slovenly. Her mother's criticisms increased Betty's disappointment in herself and triggered more anxiety and guilt. She had bad feelings about herself much of the time and was therefore often fatigued and agitated. Her fatigue made it "impossible" for her to exercise and she began to binge on sweets whenever she felt agitated and restless.

Les, a 22-year-old recent college graduate, began working for his father in the family's clothing store. His father, a workaholic, felt that after "playing" for four years of college, it was "high time" Les get down to business and "do some honest work for a change." Actually, Les—whose studies didn't come easily—had worked very hard in college and found little time for recreation. He had hoped that a nine-to-five job would give him an opportunity at last to enjoy free time in the evening. When Les failed to put in long hours at the store, his father expressed disappointment in him and periodically reminded him that he'd helped him financially through school. At first, Les felt guilty and tried very hard—but never hard enough for his father. Eventually, Les's guilt turned to resentment—which he quickly buried. The buried resentment eventually took its toll in the form of an increased susceptibility to colds and flu. Thus, Les often was unable to work at all because of illness.

In both of these cases, manipulation through guilt backfired and the desired behavior change was sabotaged by fatigue, guilt, anxiety, buried resentment, and illness.

Most people have had the experience of feeling guilty when they perceive that they haven't measured up to their own expectations or the expectations of others. Feelings of guilt become a *major* factor at this point if, somehow, early in our lives, we learned to associate that feeling with competition and the drive for success. But let's take a look at guilt feelings for what they really are: Feelings of guilt are most likely to develop when we feel we've done something "wrong" or feel we've failed to do something "right"—as defined by significant others or society as a whole. This internalized system of "do's" and "don'ts" imbedded in one's conscience is created by early influences: family, school, church, and peers. The "rules" we learned were actually an amalgam of personal preferences, religious and moral beliefs, and concerns about what others may think, along with a few practical and logical behavioral guidelines.

Since we were exposed to many of these rules of conduct as very young children, some of the "shoulds" we learned may have been pre-verbal—that is, imposed upon us prior to our understanding of language. At this stage, thought processes are simple, concrete, literal, and subjective. If our parents or other significant people in our lives were rigid yet non-specific in conveying their expectations to us, the expectations we subsequently operate with as adults may be unclear, all-pervasive and therefore unmanageable. Consider, also, the fact that very young children tend to think in absolutes and are unable to differentiate between major and minor issues. Therefore, even if our parents didn't *intend* to be so exacting and demanding with us, we may have carried their rigidity to an extreme and become forceful, demanding, and uncompromising with *ourselves*. As a result, it may be difficult for us to prioritize our inner commands and we give relatively unimportant issues as much emotional attention as vital, life-affecting issues.

Most of the things we feel guilty about don't involve moral transgressions. Instead, most of us feel guilty about real or perceived outcomes of the following process: *ignoring or rejecting behavioral preferences and attitudinal beliefs of authority figures, preferences and beliefs that are augmented by the prejudices of peer groups and even casual acquaintances.* Intellectually, we may feel that we have evolved far beyond such influences when we mature. Emotionally, though, these internalized elements are still very much with us, creating guilt with their very presence. But, as most of us have come to understand, intellect is often in conflict with feelings. Upon close examination, we may find that the early lessons we absorbed and internalized are actually contradictory in nature. The work ethic predominant in western culture seems to further complicate matters: How can we be obedient and well-behaved in the parental home, yet learn to assert ourselves effectively on the school yard and, later, in the marketplace? And can a person be enormously successful in business while conforming to the pure, self-effacing altruism of certain religious teachings? There is confusion in *our own minds* as to what we were taught to feel guilty about. So, it seems, many people decide it's easier to just cover all the bases and feel guilty about *everything*.

The feelings of guilt that seem to contribute most to depression are the feelings of guilt that accompany self-criticalness, over-responsibility, and hypersensitivity to the disapproval of others. And this guilt is usually followed by self-blame. Next time you're depressed, try this: promise yourself that for a period of time, you simply won't allow yourself to feel guilty about *anything*. You may have to start slowly, initially giving this "guilt-free existence" an hour or two at a time. Then you can add on to that block of time each day in order to build a resistance to guilt. At first, you'll probably feel uneasy and disoriented with this restrictive contract. Because you've permitted guilt to control you for so long, you may have come to regard it as part and parcel of your identity. *But it's not.*

When these automatic guilt feelings begin, you've probably learned to shift *immediately* into the self-blame routine. Now, if you're a dyed-in-the-wool, government-certified self-blamer, you have perfected this art to the point that you won't allow *anything* to be the result of circumstances beyond your control. Nothing is due to genes, chemicals, unexpected events, quirks, or luck. Therefore, because you feel that you're responsible for the world around you, you almost automatically feel as if you're to blame if anything *anywhere* goes wrong.

When you're depressed, your mind will tend to ruminate over past and present guilts for which you accept blame and feel you must punish yourself, thereby becoming even more distressed and depressed. But self-punishment only intensifies the guilt and contributes to the vicious cycle. This cycle can be practiced to the point where it goes on "automatic pilot" without any need for your control or awareness. Held together by a consistent emotional "logic," it becomes a self-contained, self-reinforcing system like the following:

" *I feel bad.*"

"If I feel bad, *I must be bad.*"

"If I'm punishing myself this much, *I really must be guilty.*"

"If I'm bad, *I must feel guilty.*"

"If I'm guilty, *I must punish myself.*"

"If I feel guilty, *I must be guilty.*"

Russian Roulette, anyone? Ironically, the worse people feel about themselves, the more inclined they are to hike their standards. And then, the more they fall short of those standards, the more intense their personal sense of failure is likely to be. They subsequently pile on more guilt and self-blame, considering themselves all the more "deserving" of self-punishment. There's an elusive but very potent element at work, though, that you might ponder: When you drag around feelings of guilt all the time, you cloud issues of self-responsibility by constantly blaming yourself for everything. If you can be honest with yourself, you'll discover at least two disagreeable aspects of self-blaming:

1. When people believe that they truly are responsible for *everything,* they are unrealistically inflating themselves and their importance. This belief seems both arrogant and inconsistent, doesn't it—coming from people who spend so much time berating themselves and their worth?

2. When people blame themselves for *everything,* their real responsibilities and accountabilities become obscured and sometimes completely lost. In other words, burying ourselves with overwhelming guilt has the effect of masking genuine errors, thereby blocking opportunities for learning and growth. Having ongoing feelings of guilt about everything also interferes with a person's ability to distinguish between innocent, unfortunate, or inappropriate behaviors and genuine transgressions. Of course, sometimes we *are* guilty of deeds that clearly call for both remorse and a serious commitment to change. But if we're already burdened by illogical self-blame, we may be so inclusive in our guilt-arousing behaviors that we avoid or repress our awareness of behaviors that really *do* need our attention.

It is helpful to recognize that self-blame is usually one-sided and selective. You're probably quick to blame yourself for something that goes wrong. *But do you ever take "blame"*—credit, that is—*for something that goes right?* When people are in a self-blaming frame of mind, they're very receptive to blame from others. They just add it to their pack of woes. Self-blamers leave themselves wide open to those exploiters who are only too willing to shift any blame they might feel—or be asked to shoulder—onto someone else who seems willing to absorb it.

But, of course, feeling guilty all the time drags you down, depletes your energy, lowers self-esteem, and immobilizes you. *People use so much energy trying to deal with guilt, they don't have sufficient energy left to make positive changes!* Also, guilt tends to make a person feel as if he or she doesn't even *deserve* to change in order to become a better person. And people who feel they don't deserve positive change and positive outcomes often wind up being their own worst enemies, sabotaging themselves every step of the way. Following are two examples of how people continue to maintain the same self-defeating behaviors for years because of guilt and the low self-esteem that results:

> Mary had always been a rather passive person who never seemed to feel good about herself. Possibly to make up for her feelings of low self-esteem, she was very accommodating to anyone who needed help. Mary ran errands for people, babysat at a moment's notice, and routinely offered rides to people whose cars were being repaired. Frequently, these favors were requested at times that were very inconvenient for her, but Mary always followed through on them. Since Mary asked others for nothing in return, she frequently got just that. Of course, the people who used her most tended to be "takers" anyway, people who don't see or feel the need to reciprocate. Mary made excuses for these people when her other friends pointed out that she was being used. Occasionally, Mary felt a vague sense of disappointment for not being appreciated or acknowledged, then immediately felt guilty for harboring negative feelings. Because Mary felt that she deserved no better treatment, she continued to give in to others in order to bolster her feelings of self-worth. Yet she didn't feel good enough about herself to take genuine credit for being "goodhearted."

Nick, a 46-year-old office worker, needed a great deal of acknowledgment and support from coworkers because of his low self-esteem. One of the ways Nick was able to create in himself a sense
that others cared for him was to set himself up in ways so that
other coworkers would have to "bail" him out. He'd postpone
working on projects until just before the deadline, then he'd be
forced to solicit the help of coworkers. Unfortunately, this became such a pattern that coworkers helped grudgingly and were
clearly resentful of the position Nick placed them in time and
time again. Nevertheless, their help "proved" to Nick that these
other people cared—even though he knew they helped him
grudgingly. Because their "giving" was contaminated by bad feelings, Nick was, in a sense, punished in the very act of gaining
their assistance.

The bottom line here is that guilt is really a rather useless emotion!
Even if you *are* guilty of something, putting yourself down constantly
about it isn't likely to help you at all. People who feel good about
themselves are far more apt to be spontaneously kind, sensitive, and
accepting of others than those who are self-critical and guilt-ridden.
Oftentimes, objectionable, selfish, inconsiderate, and self-defeating
behaviors occur *because* the perpetrators of this behavior already feel
so bad about themselves.

Sometimes people conveniently use guilt as a substitute for not
changing. They salve the guilty conscience with thought strategies
like this: *I probably won't change, but at least I'll make myself feel
terribly guilty about it!* It's as if it would be unthinkable to continue to
do something wrong and have the audacity not to feel guilty about it!
But, paradoxically, when we don't allow ourselves to wallow in guilt
over objectionable behaviors that we regret, we make it more difficult
for ourselves to repeat or continue the guilt-arousing behavior in the
future.

Vulnerability to guilt also has powerful interpersonal
implications. People who are guilt-prone tend to be overly concerned
about the opinions other people have of them; for this reason, guilt-
prone people are easy prey for people who may wish to manipulate
them. Some of us, indeed, have enormous "guilt buttons" that can
be pressed by anyone, anytime. With this guilt button, we leave
ourselves open for feeling guilty at all times. Then, when guilt builds,

it may become so intolerable that we deal with it by blaming others or by resenting them for "making" us feel so guilty. Actually, no one has the power to *make* another person feel guilty. Guilt feelings involve two basic ingredients: someone with a willingness to accept a guilt trip and the person who "makes" him or her feel guilty.

Since guilt and resentment are two sides of the same coin, there is potential for feeling resentment in direct proportion to the amount of guilt felt. Once guilt builds to an unmanageable peak, it always has potential to flip over into angry resentment. As a matter of fact, if you want to stop feeling so much resentment, don't work directly on the resentment itself. Instead, work to examine, deal with, and reduce your feelings of guilt. Then, when guilt subsides, your potential for resentment will diminish as well. When you identify, deal with, and overcome free-floating guilt feelings, you can truly detach yourself from most manipulative attempts by others. It is most gratifying to watch the wife who, after years of feeling guilty and being subtly controlled by her husband, gives up both the feelings and the actions of guilt. For example, now she doesn't even *respond* when her husband mechanically exhibits the behavior once guaranteed to short-circuit her and dissolve her into a puddle of guilt-stricken tears or launch her into an infantile tantrum. He may try again with some very "innocent" insinuation and again meet with no reaction. Finally, in frustration, he may even say (or think): *"Hey, that's not fair. You aren't doing it right. You're supposed to feel ashamed and guilty like you always have!"*

Though the internal mechanisms of guilt and self-punishment may have proven useful to us in peculiar psychological ways, they certainly are not useful to others. For example, if someone wrongs another person, the perpetrator's resulting guilt or self-punishment doesn't really benefit the wronged person at all. In fact, guilt and self-punishment actually interfere with genuine *remorse* over the act committed. Thus, if you genuinely hurt someone—deliberately or inadvertently—your feelings of remorse are appropriate and healthy because they stem from the fact and awareness that you have hurt another person. Remorse is *other-centered*; it focuses on the two most important factors in the interchange—the other person and your hurtful behavior. After directly conveying apologies to the other person, the hurtful behavior can then be examined for the purpose of changing it in the future.

On the other hand, guilt is *self-centered*. The guilt-prone person turns inward and becomes self-absorbed, consumed by his or her distorted feelings of guilt and self-hate. Because a dynamic like this focuses on self-blame, negative self-labeling and self-punishment, the wronged person is neglected and the hurtful behavior itself becomes obscured. Imagine a cartoon-type drawing in which the victim is standing up, bleeding and saying *"What about me?"* while the perpetrator writhes on the floor, whipping himself and yelling, *"I'm terrible, awful, rotten!"* Automatic self-punishment mechanisms serve only to *distract* people from the specific behaviors to be changed as well as the hurt feelings of the wronged person. *Really, the potential for changing damaging behavior in the future most accurately rests in genuine remorse and an empathic awareness of the impact of one's behavior on another person.* The more clearly you can recognize the impact of your own actions and take responsibility for them, the better focused your efforts at self-change will be.

Whenever you feel consumed by guilt, ask yourself these questions: *"Am I really focusing on and examining my behavior for the purpose of future change? Or am I just moping around and obsessing over how terrible I am?"* When things go wrong, ask yourself these questions: *"Am I in any way responsible for this? Could I have anticipated the problem, planned better, been more realistically foresightful? Could I have been more sensitive, thoughtful, honest, or considerate? If so, what was happening that I wasn't? Was I just having a bad day, or is this behavior a pattern of interaction I have with some people—or all people? Could I have been engaged in some exploitation? Exactly what was I doing—what am I doing—and how can I change it?"* If you answer such questions honestly and specifically, you'll be in a better position to identify the areas of your personal responsibility and then deal with them appropriately, *without* paralyzing feelings of guilt. The first step toward overcoming pervasive feelings of guilt is to become fully aware of the frequency with which you feel guilty. But sometimes people block their awareness of guilt feelings or rationalize them away.

Years ago, I counseled a 35-year-old college philosophy teacher named Jill. Jill had been raised by very rigid, dogmatic parents who subtly manipulated her through guilt and provided her with a kind of instantaneous, guilt-inducing mind-set. When, as an adult, Jill studied college-level philosophy and theology, she felt that she had "freed" feelings of "guilt," which she equated with "sin." According to Jill's new (and much more liberal) philosophy, she was not a "terrible sinner" and, therefore, should not feel guilty. But as I worked with Jill, I found her to be *excessively* guilt-ridden, regardless of what she called the feelings. I suggested that even though her current mind-set didn't allow for guilt, this intellectual acknowledgment was purely intellectual and may not have affected her subconscious emotional habits at all. I advised her to forget about the notion of guilt and instead, as an experiment, note the number of times each day she felt "disappointed" in herself, "annoyed" with and/or disgusted with herself. At first, Jill carried a small piece of paper in her pocket and marked it whenever she experienced one of these feelings. When, at the end of the week, she counted an average of twenty-five negative feelings about herself per day, she began recording those feelings. To her surprise, in just a few weeks, she discovered that many of these negative feelings were actually feelings of guilt.

Since once of Jill's definite strengths was her logical, incisive mind, I spent some time urging her to clearly define her personal theology in detail. What were her views about love, giving, sex, and self-care? What were her values and priorities? Once Jill felt that she was on solid ground theologically, we considered her feelings of "annoyance," "disappointment," and "irritation" with herself (guilt) in light of her theology. Jill eventually succeeded in interrupting the automatic guilt feelings that came to her by saying to herself—even shouting when she was alone—"*Not Guilty!*" Each time she experienced vague, gnawing feelings of guilt, she used her firm intellectual beliefs about guilt to challenge those feelings. Jill's new beliefs and her thought-stopping process worked together effectively and she finally was able to conquer her elusive but powerful feelings of guilt.

11.

De-emphasize Your Faults

" . . . self-acceptance will free and enhance your energy."

"What I'm going to say in this chapter probably will strike you as obvious, a collection of common sense statements. But experience tells me that *everyone* needs to be reminded of the fundamental importance of self-acceptance. Regardless of what it is you don't like about you, the most productive, loving things you can do for yourself are really very simple and straightforward: *accept yourself, try to understand yourself, and don't subject yourself to perpetual blasts (or even whispers) of self-criticism.*

When I consider the importance of de-emphasizing faults and moving toward self-acceptance, I'm reminded of my one and only "single-session cure" a number of years ago:

> Meg, a young woman who worked as a secretary in our office, asked me if I could see her for some personal counseling. Meg was then very dissatisfied with herself and was planning to leave her job soon. She asked me to tell her what was wrong with her, and then proceeded to enumerate what she identified as her "faults." As Meg shared her concerns about herself with me, I got the impression that she expected me to chastise her for her perceived faults, add my own negative observations, then give her a Vince Lombardi pep talk concluding with an admonition to "go and sin no more."
>
> Here's what Meg considered her "faults": "I get flustered when I'm rushed"; "I feel very shy and awkward around strangers"; "I say things that sound strained or inappropriate when I try to make conversation"; "I fail to do thoughtful or gracious things in social situations because I'm so self-conscious." Because of her anxieties about doing things wrong or looking ridiculous, Meg rarely sought out new activities and experiences and she almost never took risks; overall, she told me she felt like a "chicken" and believed that she was stifling her own self-improvement efforts. Because Meg's perceived faults consisted pri-

marily of personal quirks or relatively minor problems, they actually seemed a bit humorous to me; in fact, when she began listing them, I chuckled. Annoyed, she demanded to know what I thought was so funny. I told Meg that I enjoyed many of these so-called "faults" of hers and that her faults were actually personality quirks that made her a unique human being. I told her that some of these personality quirks actually endeared her to people. "If they were my faults," I told her, "I wouldn't give them up for the world!"

Together, Meg and I examined each of the faults she had listed. I suggested that she consider a few things before she invested any more energy in worrying about these faults or trying to change them: that if she changed many of these faults, she might actually change her personality; that these faults, though perhaps a bit self-defeating at times, weren't hurting anyone, and that even if she didn't get rid of *one single fault*, she was still a very interesting and enjoyable person. Meg was surprised: "You mean, if I don't change myself *at all* and I stay exactly as I am, that's okay?" "It certainly is," I replied. Meg thanked me and didn't request another session at that time. Two years later, I got a letter from her that I think beautifully articulates one of the most important ingredients in self-acceptance.

" . . . When I left your office two years ago, I was really on a high! I felt as if you had given me permission to simply be myself. I believed that I could abandon all the self-punishing behavior and simply accept myself for what I was: human, a little weird and flaky at times, but really okay. Relieved of the exhausting responsibility of changing myself through self-criticism and tyrannical 'self-improvement' programs, I felt that I had just cut myself loose from an anchor or had just climbed out from under a boulder. I felt light, enthusiastic, and bursting with excitement and energy! I suddenly wanted all kinds of good things for myself because I felt I deserved them. I got into an exercise class, lost weight, took up painting again, and started getting out more because I no longer felt so ashamed of my appearance. After taking some courses at the vocational school, I have a new job I enjoy and a steady boyfriend. And guess what? I still have all of my old 'faults'!"

Self-acceptance—the first and all-important step toward self-love. But self-acceptance isn't a matter of sitting back, being passive, and dismissing personal improvements or change with summary statements like, "Well, that's just the way I am; I can't do anything about it." That certainly sounds more like resignation to me, like giving up on efforts to improve your self-esteem (and giving up on efforts to combat your depression-proneness). On the contrary, people who are able to accept and love themselves *as they are* seem to have natural desires to grow and change as they progress through their lives. People who accept and love themselves tend not to be locked into rigid patterns of thinking and behavior. They freely interact with other people and the world around them in order to receive stimulation for growth and adaptation. As a result, they're able to evolve more spontaneously and fully as people. Actually, a person has to apply psychic brakes in order to avoid moving, changing, and growing in this world. Life is, after all, in constant flux and motion; standing still wastes valuable energy. We cannot *help but change* when we're non-defensive and truly open to life experiences. You'll find that self-acceptance will free and enhance your energy. No longer will you have to spend time and effort thinking about defending and protecting yourself from self-criticism, guilt, and the self-absorbing psychological pain that results. You can harness for life-enhancement the energy that was used in the internal struggle of "I'm bad." No longer preoccupied or wounded by self-abuse, self-punishment, or self-rejection, you can *learn* to feel free, loving, expressive, responsive, and interested in people, situations, and issues beyond your own sphere. Feeling unworthy and guilty is immobilizing; feeling good and deserving of success is energizing. *Break out of the depressing past now!*

12.

Be Good to Yourself

" . . . reinforce the feeling—and the belief—
that you are well worth caring for."

An all-important "exercise" in self-acceptance: *stop* pushing yourself
mercilessly and finding fault with everything about yourself and *start*
making a conscious effort to treat yourself well. Begin this exercise
immediately by practicing simple self-care—you know, the things
we're all aware of but forget, particularly when we're down: • eat
foods you enjoy that are also good for you • get sufficient rest and
exercise • avoid doing things that you know from experience are self-
destructive or self-defeating • make time and space for peaceful
relaxation in your daily life.

     Then, too, consider little things you can do to make yourself feel
special and appreciated throughout the day: compliment yourself—
for the way you look, for something you've accomplished, or for
something you've thought or felt. Give yourself small but pleasant
treats throughout the day. You don't have to spend a *dime* treating
yourself in this way. Though, if you can afford a few longed-for items
that you've not bought because you believe you don't deserve them,
go ahead and spend a few dollars. You're worth it. (After a while, you'll
really begin to believe me.) Basically, though, when I talk about giving
yourself simple treats throughout the day, these are the kinds of
things I'm talking about: • brewing yourself a pot of tea and sitting in
the spring sunshine to watch the buds unfurl • reading a book you
may have denied yourself because you felt it was frivolous or time-
consuming • eating dinner by candlelight • taking a long, hot bath
• picking a bouquet of wildflowers and placing them so that you'll see
them when you first open your eyes in the morning. You probably get
the gist of these suggestions now: each is a simple, external thing, but
each will ultimately help to reinforce the feeling—and the belief—
that you are well worth caring for. And don't allow yourself, even for
a moment, to feel guilty about doing these things for yourself.

As you learn to treat yourself well, beware of self-sacrifice. Depression-prone people tend to be guilt-prone. To assuage their feelings of guilt, they often do things to avoid being (or even appearing) what they consider "selfish" by giving to others compulsively and neglecting their own physical and emotional needs. But this self-denial brings them more pain and, untimately, more intense self-absorption. People who *give up* rather than *give of* themselves to other people or to causes risk serious psychological and physical deprivation. Self-sacrifice of this magnitude is misguided self-indulgence that feeds neuroses, diminishes self-respect, stimulates guilt, and facilitates self-destruction. Take note: when you're down and not functioning well, you may feel guilty about your state of mind, about burdening others, and about being demanding. You might then have a natural tendency to want to "get back to normal" and try to make up for your "selfishness" by sacrificing even *more* of yourself. But when you neglect your own needs, you'll end up feeling more depleted and deprived than before. As a result, your depression will not only continue, it may *intensify* as well.

Oftentimes, I've seen this tendency to overcompensate for feelings of guilt in women who are mothers of young children, and who tend to be perfectionistic and culturally "programmed" for a degree of self-denial in the nurturing of their families. This kind of giving to others requires a great deal of energy—energy that a person simply doesn't have if he or she is depressed. Remember, also, that often the recipients of extraordinary "sacrifices" feel uneasy and guilty, or they fail to demonstrate the measure of gratitude the "giver" might consciously or subconsciously expect. The result for the person who has sacrificed? Resentment . . . and sheer exhaustion, as well.

If you do take good care of yourself and feel that at least some of your own needs are being met on a consistent basis, you'll feel better and your desire to give to others will be *genuine*, not a compulsive need to prove to others that you're not selfish and self-absorbed.

A fundamental step in self-care is to get in touch with exactly what it is you need and want—and to believe that your wants and needs are justified. You have a perfect right to need and want companionship, love, laughter, and beauty in your life, as well as food, shelter, and clothing. When people have too many unmet needs, they feel deprived, embittered, and chronically dissatisfied. But getting in touch with what you need and want is not necessarily an easy thing to do. Your *real* needs and wants may be blurred or completely lost because of "shoulds" or "ought tos." You may feel that you have no "right" to want and need certain things, or you may not wish to admit that you really *want* something, out of a strong fear that you won't get it. People sometimes protect themselves from disappointment by not identifying what their needs and wants are. But when people repress too many needs, they constrict both their inner and outer lives. Consequently, they numb their feelings and live in a state of dull resignation that blocks the development of fulfilling experiences and relationships.

Following is an example of a person who learned to get back in touch with her wants and needs by making a few relatively simple changes in her daily life:

> Karen, a former client of mine, is a homemaker with two school-aged children. Karen grew up on a farm and had learned from her family that a person should not do anything enjoyable until "all the work is done." One could say, of course, that on a farm, the work is *never* done. Consequently, Karen had grown up without models to show her how to effectively balance work with pleasure. And since a homemaker's work is never quite "done" either, Karen had no real idea how to give herself pleasure if and when she *did* catch up with her work. Understandably, Karen became depressed.
>
> When I encouraged her to start doing things she really enjoyed, she seemed to be only vaguely aware of what those things might be. After some experimentation, she learned that despite having disliked piano lessons as a child, she enjoyed "fooling around" on the piano as an adult—without the pressure to practice she'd always felt as a child. Karen also came to realize that as an adult, she enjoyed reading. By developing a few new hobbies, she began to structure her day in blocks of two hours on, one hour off. Karen discovered that she could work efficiently for two hours when she knew that she had several pleasurable activities to look forward to during her "breaks."

Karen's case illustrates another important point about depression:

when people are depressed, frequently they're just not able to determine what they might enjoy doing. In her depressed state, Karen was convinced that no activity or interest would stimulate her or give her any particular pleasure. The interests and hobbies that ultimately gave her pleasure and joy came only *after* a period of experimentation; her enjoyment of these new pursuits evolved more fully as she become more active and less depressed. Like Karen, you probably won't know what you find pleasurable until you *try* various activities and explore old and new interests over a period of time. Some of these activities and interests will provide more pleasure as time goes on, some won't. Just let go of the activities and interests that don't give you pleasure and concentrate on the ones that do.

You can turn your depression around by responding directly to the feelings of deprivation that are behind it. For example, instead of engaging in perpetual self-criticism, you could "act as if" you are a wonderful person who simply needs some extra attention and self-care in order to feel good again. Start giving yourself *positive payoffs*, whether that takes the form of treating yourself tenderly and considerately—almost as if you're physically ill—or self-indulgently, with a few special treats, experiences, or excursions that you ordinarily wouldn't allow yourself. And if a period of self-indulgence begins to make you feel guilty, just remind yourself that it will also tend to help you move out of your depression much faster than self-denial will. Chances are, you've already tried self-denial. It hasn't worked, has it?

13.

Laugh and Relax

" . . . humor is one of the most creative forms of emotional survival."

Everyone needs an outlet of some kind to help relieve the stresses, tensions, and frustrations that build up in the course of daily living. It's particularly important for depression-prone people to have accessible and dependable outlets for relief. Why? Because people who are depression-prone tend to store up negative energy for periods of time, then turn it on themselves in destructive ways.

After a period of "working" diligently on your feelings of depression, consider setting your diligence aside and using (or cultivating) your sense of humor. Humor, laughter, whimsy, and a sense of the absurd are incompatible with depression. Consider the positive power of laughter; it's not easy to feel down while having a good belly-laugh.

I regard humor as an essential tool in my own "sanity and survival kit." In fact, I think that humor is one of the most creative forms of emotional survival. Humor can take the edge off anxiety and tension; humor also can transform a somber and potentially depressing situation into an interesting and perhaps even humorous moment or event. There's something so emotionally freeing about being able to translate potentially blue feelings into refreshing humor. Seeking out and finding comic relief in certain circumstances and situations can bring a new perspective, eliminate weighty somberness, and actually *relieve* some of the symptoms of depression. Humor can also place depression-prone thinking and reacting styles in perspective. For example, "playing out" an incident or situation to its extreme, ultimate, and *illogical* conclusion frequently releases tensions by helping us act out our worst fears and speak the unspeakable. With the use of humor, these irrational fears can be exaggerated until they evaporate.

Fortunately, the ability to *appreciate* humor isn't determined by one's genes. So don't think that "being funny" is a recessive trait and yours is the generation it missed! If you didn't cultivate your own sense of humor or an appreciation of humor in others as you were growing up, you can start doing both *now*; it's never too late to learn to look at the humorous side. Develop your humorous point of view and seek out enjoyable people who have a sense of humor and appreciate that quality in others as well. To be a bit more specific, why not try some laughter therapy: • watch comedies on television and at movie theaters • attend plays and other public presentations that you know will be light and humorous • listen to comedians and read books, articles, and verse by humorists or otherwise entertaining writers • familiarize yourself with comedy classics which, interestingly enough, often examine the lighter side of life along with its dark underside.

Wouldn't it be *wonderful* if we could always reason things out, transcending petty annoyances and the upsetting aggravations of life? Of course, no one has found a way to do that on a consistent basis. But rather than risking the psychosomatic illness or truly regrettable explosion that may result from stuffing frustrations and annoyances and being a "good sport" for days or even *years*, it may be helpful to arrange for regular opportunities to safely and effectively let off some steam. Whether you think you need this kind of outlet or not, build in "rage releases" or specific methods to discharge the excess tension or frustration that builds up when life simply doesn't go as you hoped it would. Regular physical exercise can be a very effective way to handle this need to let off steam. Also, on a regular basis—daily, if necessary—you could kneel on a couch and pound it with your fists (while yelling, if you want to) or hit a heavy pillow, sandbag, or punching bag. If you're inclined to do something useful with all that pent-up frustration, chop wood, clean the basement, mow the lawn. Do something physically active and feel the negative energy drain from your body and your mind.

Sometimes, however, you'll discover that you're not feeling frustrated, tense, and enraged as much as you're feeling fatigued, discouraged, and vulnerable. The latter symptoms are, in fact, more consistent with the symptoms of depression. Fatigue, discouragement, and vulnerability could make you feel like collapsing emotionally. And sometimes when you feel like collapsing, it can be useful to just give in to that feeling. Most of us just don't know *how* to fall apart gracefully when pressures build, or how to "collapse" for a while in order to allow ourselves time and energy to mend. Instead, we put our energies into maintaining the status quo—no matter *what* it is. Yet, if we're healthy, our minds will bend without breaking. Just as a fatigued body may tell us, in one way or another, "let me collapse for a while; I want to rest," the mind may tell us, in one way or another, "*I don't care; I'm going to blow it. I can't take it any longer; I give up!*" (These are times when we might panic, get upset, cry, or have a temper tantrum.) But, occasionally, this kind of regression helps to discharge and dissipate tensions created by holding up for so long. And the more freely we let go at times like this, the more quickly we may be able to bounce back.

Prolonged periods of beating your head against the wall won't increase your awareness of anything . . . except the wall and your head. Occasionally, though, when things build up so much that "rage releases" or "planned collapses" aren't enough, we should have something to run to; call it an "escape hatch." An escape hatch may serve as a quick exit for a strategic but temporary retreat when the battle of life gets too fatiguing or confusing. There will always be close-at-hand, simple ways to temporarily escape the pressures of daily life: hobbies and other enjoyable and fully engaging activities can serve to keep us energized and stimulated and can also help to alleviate the tensions and frustrations of daily living. But when we've been withstanding pressure for an extended period of time, it may be worthwhile to do whatever needs to be done to arrange for a physical, mental, emotional, and *geographical* retreat. Just the knowledge that a relatively complete break is somewhere in the future can ease us through some horrendous times.

In order to deal with pressures in my own life, I once spent a week camping alone in the mountains of Colorado. During that week, I did little more than play with the squirrels and watch the grass grow. But it was a wholly refreshing and rejuvenating experience.

Nowadays, I drive the hundred miles or so from my home to Madison, Wisconsin, twice a year to spend a weekend alone. There, I rent a motel room and spend my time reading science fiction books and articles, sleeping, probably eating too much, and simply watching the sailboats on the lake. Consider a little rest and relaxation now and then to alleviate battle fatigue, to recharge batteries, and to allow the emergence of some new perspectives for difficult situations.

As you seek out other meaningful ways of releasing tension and frustration, you may find that you are enhancing your life in the process. Consider, for example, investigating some specific tension-reduction techniques. Neurolinguistic programmers point out that when people are depressed, they tend to use internal visual and auditory sensory representational systems. In other words, they focus on negative images and formulate or review negative phrases and words that actually serve to *maintain* their depression; they become *stuck* in those feelings. But when people engage in vigorous physical exercise, they move into what is called the external kinesthetic representational system—a sensory mode in which they are not depressed.[1]

> A psychologist trained in Neurolinguistic Programming told me the story of a suicidal patient of his whose phone call happened to interrupt him in the midst of a session of psychotherapy he was conducting with another patient. He told the woman who called that he would see her in a half-hour, *but only on the condition that she ride her bicycle to his office.* So the woman peddled to his office, and a half-hour later was ushered in and invited to pour out her desperation and panic. To the woman's surprise, she was unable to remember exactly what she'd been feeling when she called the psychotherapist. The half-hour bike ride had essentially taken her out of one representational mode (internal visual and auditory sensory) and put her into another representational mode (external kinesthetic) that was not depressed— all the while distracting her negative thinking, dissipating her nervous energy and agitation, and energizing her body and mind through increased oxygen intake.

Other less direct but probably more familiar methods of reducing tension, stress, and fatigue include: • autogenic training • meditation • self-hypnosis • biofeedback • yoga • or just the simple but highly effective exercise of tensing, then relaxing muscle groups. [2] By carrying out any one of these body-mind disciplines twice a day, you'll almost certainly reap benefits on a continuing basis. Along with the temporary relief that comes with taking a break or "tuning out" from a hectic schedule, you'll learn valuable skills you can call on in the future to deal effectively with inner turmoil, negative obsessing, and muscle tension—whether you're in a full-blown crisis or are just momentarily upset.

But you needn't always do something that requires commitment, vigorous physical exercise, or training in order to relax and relieve stress. Activities like gardening, crafts, or reading—certainly not strenuous activities—can bring beneficial tension-reducing results. In fact, just watching the movements of fish swimming languidly in an aquarium has been proven to markedly reduce stress.

References/Notes

1. Neurolinguistic Programming is a comparatively new approach to psychotherapy developed by Bandler and Grinder and first presented in two volumes titled *The Structure of Magic*. After observing what they believe to be common techniques and approaches employed by such therapists as Friedrich Perls, Virginia Satir, and especially Milton Erickson, the authors describe elements for therapy that they consider to be particularly useful and important. They delineate specific rapport-building techniques which involve selectively responding to certain client behaviors through mirroring and pacing the behaviors. Step-by-step techniques are used to target specific behavior patterns. These techniques frequently involve the use of the trance and mental imagery. Knowing the client's most favored representational system helps the therapist shape interventions within the perceptual framework of the client. (Bandler, Richard, and John Grinder. *The Structure of Magic*, vols. 1 and 2. Palo Alto, Calif.: Science and Behavior Books, 1975.)

2. *Suggested readings on various methods of stress reduction*:

    Benson, Herbert. *The Relaxation Response*. New York: Avon, 1976. (*Meditation*)

    Davis, Martha, Elizabeth Robbins Eshelman, and Matthew McKay. *The Relaxation and Stress Reduction Workbook*. Oakland, Calif.: New Harbinger, 1980. (*Exercises in stress reduction, body awareness, relaxation, breathing, meditation, self-hypnosis, autogenics.*)

LeShan, Lawrence. *How to Meditate.* New York: Little, Brown and Co., 1974. (Meditation)

McKay, Matthew, Martha Davis, and Patrick Fanning. *Thoughts and Feelings: The Art of Cognitive Stress Intervention.* Oakland, Calif.: New Harbinger, 1981. (*Systematic desensitization, problem solving, combating destructive thinking.*)

Naranjo, Claudio, and Robert E. Ornstein. *On the Psychology of Meditation.* New York: Viking, 1971. (*Meditation*)

Powers, Melvin. *A Practical Guide to Self-Hypnosis.* North Hollywood, Calif.: Wilshire Books, 1976. (*Self-Hypnosis*)

Progoff, Ira. *The Well and the Cathedral.* New York: Dialog House, 1977. (Meditation)

14.

Accentuate the Positive

"Learn to shift your focus."

If you're like most people, you probably don't have much energy or enthusiasm for change in the midst of a depression. There are, however, a few important things you can do during a depression in order to launch an effort that will shift your focus from the negative to the positive. Think in terms of simply altering existing bad habits of thinking.

Do you tend to think negatively? Have you ever considered the possibility that you may actually feel more "comfortable" with a negative point of view? Depressed feelings may have become familiar to you, and you may feel resigned to seeing life in shades of gray. Thus, when you actually *do* have feelings of contentment or happiness, you tend not to trust those feelings. In fact, you may even catch yourself thinking or saying *"Things are so good, I'm nervous. I wonder how long this will last and how it will all finally fall apart again."* It's as if bad feelings are the *rule*, rather than the exception. There is a basic expectation that life events will be negative—or, at the very best, neutral. Good times, on the other hand, are fleeting, unstable, not to be hoped for, or depended upon. When misery-oriented people say *"You can't expect me to feel good all the time!"* I counter with *"Why not?!"* What so many negative-thinking people don't realize is that "down" feelings have become oddly solid and secure to them. At the bottom, there's no place to go but up, right? Depression-prone people tend to feel that life is precarious, any way you look at it. Therefore, someone on a "high" has that much further to fall and it's only a matter of time until the descent begins. With thoughts like this playing through one's mind constantly, any form of risk-taking would seem to be out of the question. Someone really in the pits might even think (or say): *"My life looks so much better now that I've given up hope."*

When depression-prone people are feeling happy, they may spend their time and energy watching and waiting for some disaster, rather than trying to keep the good spirits alive and well. In their anxiety about not knowing when IT will happen, they might even sabotage the happy situation by setting the stage for or actually *bringing about* the feared disaster. Other times, out of fear of losing the good feelings they have, depression-prone people may choke those feelings off by clinging desperately to them. When this happens, they're apt to conclude that "Feeling good just isn't worth it!" And then, there are those people who pride themselves on being prophets of doom. You know the kind of people I'm talking about— *"My grandmother had an inflamed mole exactly like that on her leg. Turned out to be cancer. Died in three months."*

When people feel badly about themselves, they're almost always tempted to indulge in negative feelings and self-pity. A good strategy for preventing yourself from ruminating over how bad things are is to distract yourself by doing something away from home: visit a friend; attend a movie; do a little shopping. When you're alone, you can short-circuit negative ruminations by forcing yourself to do some hard work or physical activity that requires relatively little thought. Another way is to become involved in lightweight mental activity that has nothing to do with the object of your obsessions. For instance, read a sci-fi novel, a romance, or detective story; do a crossword or jigsaw puzzle; undertake an enjoyable craft project.

In suggesting these activities, I'm not in any way encouraging you to *avoid* confronting major life issues and decisions that must be made. I'm simply considering the tendency of the depressed mind to gravitate toward the negative, then toss 'round and 'round within it regrets, guilts, frustrations, losses, past embarrassments, unfinished business, and unexpressed resentments. Consciously pulling oneself away from negative thoughts and feelings is not repression or denial; it is simply a shift of focus. Ideally, distraction through activity should have the effect of a brief vacation. You let your mind take time off to rest and think about nothing in particular. And then, when you return to the fray, things may not look so bad or hopeless or impossible. Even if a situation hasn't changed significantly, after a rest it probably won't bother you as much as it did before. So, whenever your mind begins to drift toward the negative, pull it away and zero in on something else that is positive and outside of yourself.

Try to activate a *positive mental attitude* as soon as you awake in the morning. Remind yourself of positive past events and think about things you can look forward to that particular day. Don't wake up and review distressing things that happened to you—whether they occurred yesterday or ten years ago. Also, make a conscious effort to not focus on the things you're dreading that day; you'll only tend to blow them out of proportion. Instead, consciously and deliberately look for several things in the day ahead of you that you feel fairly sure you'll enjoy. If you can't think of anything on your schedule that day likely to be pleasurable, create a couple of special treats. There's nothing wrong with dangling a "carrot" in front of your eyes to maintain a positive, forward-looking attitude. At almost any time in all of our lives, certain unpleasant things hang over our heads:
• disagreeable chores to be completed • negative prospects and options to be faced • confrontations with people. But if you look carefully, there are always positive things to be done, thought about, and encountered as well. *Learn to shift your focus.* For example, while eating breakfast, you could either dwell on a situation at work that bothers you and is beyond your control, or you could choose to notice how good your egg tastes and how pretty the sky looks. Occasionally, it's also helpful to give free reign to your fantasies and think about some of the supposedly "unrealistic" things you might want to accomplish. But how unrealistic are these things, really? Isn't there some way that you could actualize a fond daydream or two?

Take note: if you visualize yourself in different roles and situations, only to discover that you haven't included a *single thing* you're doing right now—or actively planning to do in the near future—you may want to consider some life changes. Ruts can be very comfortable . . . but, then, so are coffins! With practice, you can develop the self-discipline needed to catch yourself in the act as you begin to dwell on something negative—then consciously move your mind somewhere else.

Parts of us are like bright sunny rooms; other parts of us are like small, cramped rooms with gray walls and stale air. When you find yourself focusing on a negative part of yourself or on a depressing feeling, move your attention to a different part of yourself, or on to a different thought or feeling. *Just as you wouldn't want to linger in a dark room with bad memories, don't allow yourself to linger in a negative emotion or remain focused on a negative part of yourself.*

With experience and careful self-observation, you can sharpen your ability to recognize signs that point to the onset of depression. You can become alert to the vague, uncomfortable, and "blue" feelings people experience prior to slipping into a depressed mood. Even people who at first report that there seem to be *no* warning signs of depression eventually become attuned to the psychological and physical states that appear before depression begins. Through self-monitoring, you can sense when a depression is starting to creep up on you. You may have some or all of these feelings: • disappointment in yourself and/or others • feelings of not being appreciated • guilt • fatigue • emptiness • vulnerability. Then, at the now-acknowledged "choice-point" you can either say, "Oh, what the hell," and sink into your depression OR you can use the warning signs to alert yourself to mobilize all the tactics you can muster to combat the feelings before they gain momentum and *really* bring you down. Over the years, you may have chosen again and again to slide passively back into a depressed condition, saying, "*I just don't have the energy to cope*"; or "*I'm such a loser, I may as well go back into that hellhole where I belong*"; or "*People have to realize how hard life is for me.*" If you're tired of getting depressed time after time—and most depression-prone people certainly are—there are many things you can do on your own to stop this response pattern.

Depression-prone people I'm counseling occasionally ask this question: "*Will I always get this depressed? I want to reach a point where I will never become depressed again.*" I tell them that this question itself is essentially fear and perfectionism talking. My experience indicates that no depression-prone person *ever* becomes completely depression-free. After all, no one can claim absolute freedom from the blues. What *can* realistically happen, though, is this: depression-prone people can develop effective personal strategies and techniques for combating depression. The characteristic early symptoms need not signal an inevitable, impending depression. Instead, think of these early symptoms as flashing signals at the *gate* to depression; the individual chooses whether or not to open the gate and enter into a state of depression. If a person does not *choose* depression at this point, then skills are mobilized to fight or otherwise divert or deal with the potential depression. As people become more successful in halting episodes of depression before they take hold, the feelings of helplessness are replaced by alertness and activity, and the episodes of depression are shorter and less frequent. Indeed, some episodes are neutralized before they can take hold.

If you want to reduce the potential for future bouts of depression, you will need to devise a system of techniques and strategies for dealing with impending depression. You will also need to identify and confront the sources of your depression-proneness. If you can see no possibility of reward, appreciation, or fulfillment in your present life, then you need to *change* your circumstances in some way. Or, as is more often the case, if you determine that you are the main source and solution of most of the problems that cause your recurring depressions, then you need to change certain things about *yourself*.

But trying to design a system for depression prevention or depression management *while depressed* is like planning a fire drill while sitting in a blazing building. (How important is it to worry about who or what started the fire?) Once you've come through a depression and you're feeling better, you might find it helpful to take a look at what may have caused it in the first place. When you're feeling better able to cope with your life and the world again, you can take confidence in the fact that you now know, firsthand, that you can take control of your feelings and your life. Then, energetically and creatively, you can begin to make those changes in your life situation, thinking style, and personality that will ultimately reduce depression-proneness and short-circuit future bouts with the blues. *Chapters 15-23 address the life changes you can begin to make whenever you are willing.*

Long-Range Techniques to Help Reduce Depression-Proneness

Once you've come through a depressive phase, you'll be more interested in taking positive action and you'll feel more capable of making some permanent changes in your life as well. Some of these changes can make you considerably less depression-prone. Compared with the short-term tactics presented in Chapters 4-14, the following long-range techniques will take more time to implement and fully integrate into your life. These techniques will also require more sustained effort than the short-range tactics, because they require that you identify, analyze, and perhaps even alter certain beliefs, attitudes, reactions, or behavior patterns that are likely to be related to your depression-proneness. Short-term tactics will prove ineffective in the long run if underlying feelings, convictions, and self-defeating behavior patterns continue unchanged—and unchallenged.

Try not to let the suggestions in this section overwhelm you. Let me assure you that you don't have to change *everything* when writing a script for a healthier lifestyle, and you can work on one change at a time. *Focus on the fact that the essential you is really okay;* it's the bad habits you've acquired in thinking, feeling, and relating to others that have contributed to your depression-proneness. Certainly not all of your personality characteristics make you depression-prone. Some of these characteristics need to be slightly modified; others may contain hidden strengths for you to build on. If you try to change too many things at once, you'll soon feel oppressed, scattered, and terribly weary. Concentrate, instead, on one change at a time. If, after a few weeks, a new behavior begins to feel like a comfortable and established habit, you might begin trying to integrate yet another new behavior into your life at that time. Start by selecting behaviors that would be likely to have the most far-reaching, positive, and immediate effects. But if you don't feel like tackling a pervasive, tough-to-change behavior at first, zero in on a smaller one instead. *Small changes in the right areas at the right times can bring significant life changes.*

If you sense that your depression-proneness doesn't reside within you as much as it resides within your interpersonal relationships, you may want to read Chapters 24-27 prior to reading this section. And if you sense that deeper personality conflicts and problems exist beyond the range of the suggested techniques that follow, you would be wise to seek appropriate professional help (see Chapters 28-29).

15.

Alter Your Personality Style

Divide and conquer.

What follows is perhaps a gross generalization, but I'll risk it anyway: most depression-prone people are *sensitive, vulnerable, kind, good-hearted, passive, and non-assertive.* Depression-prone people also tend to be quite *demanding and critical of themselves, keenly aware of the feelings of others,* and *concerned about how other people view them.* The depression-prone person is also likely to have extremely *high expectations* of himself/herself and others, and a *strong conscience.* Many of these characteristics are perceived as positive and work together to produce a well-socialized individual, in the traditional sense. But many of these same characteristics seem to be very closely related to depression-proneness.

It is possible to reduce your depression-proneness by altering your personality style. But before you start tinkering in any way with your personality, ask yourself the following questions:

• What personality characteristics do I most admire in myself?

• What personality characteristics do I most admire in other people?

• What personality characteristics comprise what I believe to be the ideal personality?

Let's say, for example, that you value your own characteristics of kindness and thoughtfulness, but someone who knows you suggests that you should be "tougher" and "more assertive." If this is the case, you might be concerned that you'd have to give up things about yourself that you value most in order to alter your personality. But let me assure you that it won't be necessary to compromise your identity or your values when you alter your personality style. One important consideration in learning to become less depression-prone involves learning *how to consciously structure your behavior based on external circumstances.* As you develop this skill, you will learn to nurture those characteristics about your inner self that you value most.

It seems to me that many depression-prone people choose to behave in ways that are perceived by others as sensitive, thoughtful, and non-threatening. Of course, these human qualities are commendable. But the relative value of a certain personality characteristic is to some extent determined by the needs and demands of a specific situation. As a matter of fact, *any* positive personality characteristic used inappropriately can be self-defeating. For example, in an intimate situation, it's entirely appropriate to be self-revealing, vulnerable, and tender. But the person who can be *only* self-revealing, vulnerable, and tender will almost certainly run into problems with, for example, a disrespectfully aggressive salesperson. Some situations clearly call for firmness and assertiveness—and in the case of particularly objectionable sales tactics, the situation may call for downright belligerence!

If you are consistently kind, thoughtful, and sensitive to the needs of others, you probably know all too well that these personal qualities can be completely lost on people who are exploitative, stingy, and manipulative. It's one thing to be kind and sensitive, another thing to be a compliant and self-effacing doormat; it's one thing to be open and honest, another thing to be dangerously gullible and/or to allow yourself to be abused by others based on their knowledge of you.

On the other side of the coin, I'll risk another generalization: most of the people I have known who are strong-willed, active, decisive, assertive, and forthright tend *not* to be depression-prone. Furthermore, because people tend to group personality characteristics together that don't necessarily *belong* together, sometimes these strong personality characteristics are mistakenly associated with insensitivity and thoughtlessness. But I know many people who could be called "tough"—they're real survivors with personalities that are certainly strong and decisive—who are also sensitive and kind. An individual can be thick-skinned and know how to stand up for himself or herself and still be very compassionate.

Conversely, many people I would describe as "thin-skinned"—in other words, quick to be offended or otherwise hurt by others—have emotional constitutions of cast iron. And some of these same "sensitive" people are actually unfeeling and insensitive to others. (In some cases, these people have been exploited by others and have subsequently withdrawn emotionally in order to protect themselves.)

Think about it: aren't direct and forthright people sometimes stereotyped as aggressive and lacking in thoughtfulness and sensitivity? Actually, the opposite is often true. If these direct and forthright people handle situations appropriately, they are generally *more open* and *less defensive* in their communication. It follows, then, that they are more likely to be empathic and sensitive when the situation calls for it than people who are veiled, circumspect, and engaged in withholding their true feelings in order to be "nice." The following example from an employment situation illustrates just how wrong negative stereotypes of direct, forthright people can be:

> Chuck, a friend of mine, asked me to assess a management situa-
> tion that troubled him in the business he owns. He sensed there
> were serious communication problems developing among the
> staff. In order to assess the situation, I attended some of his staff
> meetings and carefully observed interactions among the people
> there. It didn't take long to see that one major problem was the
> ongoing conflict between two managers with very different inter-
> actional styles: Alice, a 48-year-old woman who had worked for
> the company for fifteen years and Fred, a 31-year-old man who
> was relatively new to the company. Indeed, it seemed that Fred
> and Alice were on opposite sides of nearly every issue discussed
> at the staff meetings.
>
> On the surface, Alice was a congenial person who was ob-
> viously quite cautious with other people and their feelings. In-
> deed, Alice never directly disagreed with her subordinates be-
> cause, as I later found out, she felt that to do so would embarrass
> them or otherwise make them feel uncomfortable with their
> peers. (I sensed that Alice was quite aware of being the senior
> member of the staff and that she also had some awareness of her
> tendency to be controlling.) Alice attempted to compensate for
> her controlling nature by making a conscious effort to always be
> diplomatic and never too forceful. I noticed that she'd always
> qualify or temper her remarks so they wouldn't sound the least
> bit critical, and she was oblique in her comments and judgments
> so as not to, as she put it, " . . . catch someone off-guard and make
> him or her look bad or feel awkward or uncomfortable." I sus-

pected that Alice was projecting her own thin-skinned nature onto others and treating them very carefully not because *they* needed to be treated that way, but because *she* needed to be treated that way!

I subsequently recommended that Chuck speak separately and in confidence with Alice and Fred regarding his concerns about staff communication. I also recommended that he suggest to Alice that she give Fred "some of his own medicine"—that she try to be direct with Fred in order to "smoke out" the underlying hostility she sensed in her interactions with him. Chuck also told Alice to begin "laying her cards on the table" by challenging some of Fred's ideas and countering with some of her own.

It was not surprising to Chuck or to me that Fred handled the change in Alice's behavior very well. In fact, Fred seemed to appreciate Alice more as a co-worker when her interactional style was more direct and open. And Alice began to enjoy this active give-and-take with Fred; she relaxed even more when she discovered that the open, much freer exchanges between them resulted in better communication and productivity, and more positive feelings about each other and their work. As it turned out, Fred was honest and direct, not aggressive and ego-invested. When Alice had an idea Fred believed was better than his own, he'd discard his original idea and support hers instead, feeling free to expand on it. In time, a mutual respect between Alice and Fred developed—primarily, I believe, because Alice learned through experience that it was possible to be direct and forthright without being controlling, intimidating, and insensitive.

Another erroneous belief people have about personality characteristics relates to the thinking/feeling dichotomy: if we value sensitivity and emotional responsiveness, we may devalue or otherwise overlook the qualities of rationality and logic. In fact, we may actually come to see all rational people as "rationalizers" and all logical people as cold and detached. *But, be assured, we can value feelings and emotions without decapitating ourselves!* Furthermore, it is important to recognize that pulling oneself out of a depression may indeed require rational thinking—the kind of thinking that allows a person to accomplish some important things: objectively examine misperceptions, distance oneself from confused feelings, and proceed systematically to change behavior.

When we erroneously group personality characteristics together and use them to label people, we are also likely to engage in all-or-nothing thinking. For example, if a person is direct and forthright, we might then assume that he or she is direct and forthright *all of the time and in all situations*. Actually, as whole and healthy people we need to develop the capacity to exhibit a *wide range* of behavioral responses. *But this doesn't mean that we must always appear on the outside exactly the way we feel on the inside.* Our feelings need not be completely consistent with the behavior "required" by a situation. I think it's important to understand that acknowledging and accepting some inconsistency between outward behavior and inner feelings is not hypocracy, but an *essential survival skill* that we can employ voluntarily and consciously.

For example, if you feel that you're being taken advantage of by someone, you don't necessarily have to *feel* perfectly confident on the inside in order to stand up for yourself effectively; you merely have to *appear* firm and reasonably self-assured as you take your stand. Try not to sabotage your first efforts to change some aspects of your behavior with negative (and powerful) internal monologues like, "If I don't act the way I feel, I'm being dishonest . . . "

Whenever we human beings experiment with new feelings, perceptions, and behaviors, we will experience some discomfort and doubt. But remember, almost everything we do—from learning to ride bicycles to comforting friends who are grieving—seems awkward, and perhaps unnatural at first. Whether you undertake a significant change in your personality or simply choose to alter subtle nuances of feeling or attitude, the task may seem *formidable* at first. For this reason, it might help to use the "divide and conquer" tactic: *identify specific behaviors and new skills to learn within a broader change you wish to make.*

For example, let's say you always feel extremely nervous and stiff and unnatural in social situations and you decide that your goal is to be comfortable and adept in those situations. Now, it's doubtful that just making this decision will enable you to climb out from under the sofa where you've been hiding and do a song-and-dance routine on the buffet table at the next social event you attend. If, however, overall improvement of social skills is your goal, there are some specific things you could do prior to a social event that will productively ease you toward that goal. Consider these suggestions in preparation for a social event: • talk to the person hosting the event and learn something about other guests who will be attending • consider common (or diverse) interests and experiences you might comfortably share with one or more of the guests • think about some conversational openings and topics you might be comfortable discussing—perhaps you could review some interesting stories and experiences of your own or others you know, or you could review some interesting books and articles you've read recently • an hour or so before you leave for the event, lie down, play some soothing music or a meditation tape, and relax • use mental imagery to create in your mind's eye some likely scenarios that could occur at the party • picture yourself at the party and at ease—interested, interesting, and generally confident in your interactions with others • rehearse these positive interactional scenarios in your mind • allow yourself plenty of time to get ready for the party so that you don't feel rushed. *In short, break down that lofty goal of "I want to be comfortable and adept in social situations" into small, manageable pieces of behavior, then systematically implement them.*

This "divide and conquer" tactic has the effect of making alterations in personality characteristics less intimidating and therefore more attainable. Vague and lofty goals like "I want to be more successful socially" seem out of reach when they are conceived as completely finished, absolutely perfect "end-products." Starting with a few *specific behaviors* and building upon those behaviors once they've been implemented and practiced is a much more sensible way to arrive at the broader goal of a personality "overhaul" in a certain area.

But be on guard for other forms of erroneous thinking that seem to be fairly common in depression-prone people: all-or-nothing thinking and/or negative self-labeling.

Don't fall into the trap of feeling/saying, *"Either* I become cold and hard, *or* I let myself be used" or *"Either* I go with my feelings, *or* I become a heartless robot." This kind of thinking also makes it very difficult to focus on specific behaviors to be altered.

Also, rather than thinking of each of your personality characteristics as *traits* firmly rooted in your psyche, focus instead on *specific behaviors that together constitute a personality characteristic.* (Some of these behaviors actually make a person quite vulnerable to depression, whereas other behaviors might be particularly useful in staying grounded and vital.) Focus on changing only those aspects of your behavior that seem to be making you depression-prone. By focusing on *specific behaviors*, you can avoid the danger of using an overall label like "wishy-washy" as a given and long-standing characteristic within your psyche and feeling that change is impossible because "That's just the way I am." Try not to label yourself; instead, redefine the problem you perceive *as a skill deficit—an as-yet-to-be-learned aspect of what you do, rather than a long-term character flaw in who you are.* The first approach focuses on a skill to be learned; the second approach focuses on what you perceive to be a missing part of your human machinery. The first approach will enable you to see solutions and then either identify or *create* learning situations for yourself. For instance, instead of referring to yourself as "wishy-washy," consider yourself—at least for the present time—*deficient in decision-making skills.* Or, instead of labeling yourself as "passive," you could identify a specific deficiency in your assertiveness skills.

As you work to overcome some of your skill deficits, it will be helpful to identify the *erroneous beliefs* that may be reinforcing the very behavior you want to change. You are likely to find that many of these beliefs are actually broad and incorrect generalizations about human behavior: "Once an extrovert, always an extrovert"; "People never *really* change on a *deeper* level"; and "There's nothing they can do about it—some people are just born losers." Or, you may have beliefs about the basic unchangeability of your own so-called character flaws—"I'm just naturally passive"; or "I've always been disorganized."

Indeed, some erroneous beliefs seem to take on a life of their own. In many cases, these beliefs were automatically internalized years before, then almost forgotten. At one time in our lives, these beliefs may have been beneficial and appropriate: "Always share" (your toys); "Always be concerned about other people's feelings" (don't kick your friend again). But now, when you find yourself questioning why you have to do something a certain way, just pause for a moment and think about what your answer might be. Sometimes the answer might be as simple as this: "Because that's the way I've always done it." Chances are you wouldn't "feel" right doing things differently. But if you really want to alter certain aspects of your personality style, at least *practice* doing some things differently. In time, these new ways of doing things will take hold and become natural to you and your life.

Don't wait until you *feel* ready to practice new skills and behaviors—life is far too short to postpone improvements and positive steps toward enhanced self-esteem.

16.

Build Self-Esteem . . . Actively

Emphasize the word "Actively."

Consider this: people spend *hours* each year maintaining their automobiles, yet they expect their self-esteem to maintain itself. Indeed, some people seem to feel as if self-esteem is an aspect of their lives completely beyond their control. Some people live their lives with an erroneous belief that they either feel good about themselves or they don't feel good about themselves, not because of how they live their lives, but because of genetics, environment, chance, or fate. Along with this, they may also believe that self-esteem is foreordained and irrevocable. *But this just isn't so.*

Self-esteem isn't the sum total of diverse experiences that filter into our life systems through our pores and it isn't an ethereal quality that transcends daily life. Simply stated, self-esteem is pride in and respect for oneself. And we build self-esteem *when we stop undermining ourselves with criticism, when we seek out positive feedback from others, and when we decide what we need to do or accomplish in order to feel better about ourselves, then do it!*

To work on building self-esteem, you need to make a realistic self-appraisal and you need to take an honest and careful look at your life. First of all, it is exceedingly useful to take to heart the wisdom contained in what is almost universally known as *The Serenity Prayer*. (I sometimes call it the Mental Health Prayer:)

> *God, Grant me the serenity*
> *To accept the things I cannot change,*
> *Courage to change the things I can,*
> *And wisdom to know the difference.*

Progressing toward the ultimate wisdom contained in The Serenity Prayer will take time and close scrutiny of your natural traits, assets, life circumstances, and decision-making abilities, along with plenty of trial and error experimentation in habit modifications and changes. But the goal certainly is something worth aiming for!

There are many specific and practical things you can do in order to begin developing a more positive self-concept and thereby enhance your self-esteem. For starters, you could:

• Make a list of your personal strengths and then make specific plans for ways to actively expand and enhance those strengths.

• Set up realistic goals that you want to accomplish, then systematically work toward those goals each and every day.

• Examine some of your undeveloped or unexplored interests and potentials, then design a plan for actively pursuing and realizing some of them.

• Explore your "wants"—the elements you sense are missing from or being neglected in your life—and consciously work to bring those elements into your life more consciously and frequently.

• Decide how you wish to alter your personality and/or your lifestyle, then plan how you might initiate and sustain those changes. Consider developing a "life-support system" through friends and family, specialized support groups, psychotherapy, special training and education, self-help literature, and/or travel.

Setting up a "life-support system" that will enhance your self-concept and self-esteem requires a multifaceted approach, including some realistic goal-setting and attention to accomplishments. It also requires that you break some habits of self-criticism and self-punishment that you may have formed. Instead, learn to compliment yourself for jobs well done, and concentrate on building solid friendships with at least a few people who care about you, accept you, and are willing to give you positive but honest feedback. Building a support system to enhance your self-esteem means *actively designing a life that helps to support and nurture a positive self-concept.*

The first step in a program of self-esteem development is to take a careful look at personal *strengths.* What is uniquely positive about you? Although this step probably seems obvious, many people quickly dismiss their most notable strengths with a shrug and a comment like "Well, I know I'm intelligent (or kind or honest, or have a good sense of humor), *but I'm not self-disciplined* (or articulate or organized or assertive). By focusing on our weaknesses and deficits, we defeat ourselves before we even get an esteem-building activity off the ground. Conversely, by simply focusing on what you *are* rather than scolding yourself for what you *aren't*, you can set in motion a positive change in your life and break a bad habit at the same time. Then, once you've made a realistic self-appraisal from a position of strength, what can you do in order to establish and *maintain* a high level of self-esteem? Obviously you're not going to be able to do this by indulging in new self-criticism—that will only increase the depression-proneness you may already be suffering from. Instead, make a bold move toward healthy self-acceptance by doing three specific things:

> • Identify the ways you regularly put yourself down. For example, everyone who puts himself or herself down is probably familiar with negative self-talk: *"I'm a fat slob." "I look so old." "I'm ugly." "I'll never learn." "I'm just a nobody." "I'm not likeable." "I can't do anything right." "I have no will-power." "I'm so selfish." "I make everyone around me miserable." "I'm a clumsy oaf."*

> • Replace any and all self-talk that is negative—even if it is thought or uttered in humor—*"I'm dumb,"* and *"I'm so awkward,"* with positive statements like *"I am a bright and creative person,"* and *"I feel graceful and coordinated."*

> • Ask for positive feedback from others. But a warning here— until you begin to really open up to these positive expressions, you probably won't be prepared to let compliments in completely.

Asking for positive feedback isn't easy for most of us, so I'll expand on it a bit: the tendency to block or otherwise discourage positive feedback from others is certainly a barrier to the cultivation and enhancement of self-esteem. Some of us have become highly skilled (and effective) in discouraging compliments from others and in blocking good feelings that would come to us naturally from jobs well done.

The ability to accept compliments and expressions of gratitude are essential skills in building self-esteem. And by "accepting," I mean *letting the words sink in—really feeling them, basking in them until they actually make you feel warm and glowing.* If you're so hung up on humility and unselfishness that you cannot allow yourself to bask in the glow of positive feedback, remind yourself that *genuine* humility is based on an accurate perception and evaluation of oneself and that accepting a compliment is a positive experience for you as well as for the person offering the compliment. It can and should be a mutually enhancing experience. Self-deprecation grows out of an underestimation of oneself and a *false* sense of humility. And, statements of self-deprecation in response to a genuine compliment make an unmistakable non-affirming statement to the person who has given the compliment.

But *receiving* compliments is, of course, only half the story. One of the best ways to indicate to others that you'd like positive feedback from them is to learn to be comfortable in offering compliments to them. In fact, some people seem to have just as much difficulty offering compliments as they do receiving them. In this way, our society almost seems to encourage polite restraint. Too often, we assume that people know how we feel or we're concerned that we might embarrass someone or make him or her uncomfortable with a compliment. But we all need to know that we are cared about, admired, and appreciated. *Practice giving and receiving compliments even though doing so may initially cause you some discomfort and anxiety.* Give others honest praise whenever the opportunity presents itself. In time, you'll be comfortable with this new behavior. The positive and affirming responses you receive from others when you are genuinely supportive and positive will help to enhance your own self-esteem.

Obviously you won't go far in terms of building self-esteem if you constantly undermine yourself by playing negative roles in your relationships with other people. *Stop being a victim.* Isn't it strange that people seldom do anything for long that causes them physical pain, yet choose psychological pain repeatedly with no apparent reward? It's hard to believe that otherwise intelligent people would knowingly and willingly make victims of themselves and suffer for no good reason or reward.

So *what's the hidden payoff in suffering?* This question—and, I think some useful answers—remind me of a divorced woman in her mid-thirties who was in a therapy group I once led. This woman was desperately unhappy, completely alienated from herself and others, and at times frightened to the point of panic. To complicate matters, this woman also had a crippling fear—a phobia, really—of appearing awkward to others or of being humiliated. For this reason, she also struggled with self-imposed isolation. But despite this woman's profound sadness and her defeated and frightened look, other people in the group could see something exquisite and appealing within her. Sensing her honesty and her genuine willingness to change, I asked her to stand in front of each of the other eight people in the group and, in turn, spontaneously finish the sentence, "If I ever let go of my suffering" . . . with whatever thoughts came to her mind. As it turned out, the payoff in this woman's suffering was revealed in each of the eight sentences:

"If I ever let go of my suffering . . .

I would feel empty."

"If I ever let go of my suffering . . .

I would feel scared."

"If I ever let go of my suffering . . .

I would feel unworthy."

"If I ever let go of my suffering . . .

people wouldn't feel sorry for me anymore."

"If I ever let go of my suffering . . .

I would lose my humility."

"If I ever let go of my suffering . . .

people would think I was proud and arrogant."

"If I ever let go of my suffering . . .

    I would feel lust."

"If I ever let go of my suffering . . .

    I would have to be successful."

In a seemingly simple but really very powerful exercise, this woman was honest enough to acknowledge and confront many of the payoffs inherent in her suffering. Because of her tremendous suffering, this woman didn't have to deal with her loneliness; she filled up her feelings of emptiness with *pain* instead. Her pain, in turn, gave her "permission" to feel that she deserved special consideration and sympathy from friends. Her pain also protected her from confronting her subconscious feelings of superiority and related feelings of guilt. Her pain also served to distract her from the normal sexual desires that made her uncomfortable anyway. She came to rely on pain as an excuse for not trying new ways of thinking and behaving. It seemed quite clear to me that this woman was using depression as a *payoff for her suffering*—an artificial, temporary solution to psychological problems. Sometimes, feelings of depression actually provide temporary relief from guilt and self-punishment; other times, feelings of depression provide an escape from the struggle of life or the overwhelming burdens that result from having unrealistic expectations of oneself.

Some depression-prone people may consciously or subconsciously use their depressed states to control and manipulate others. They may have learned that when they're depressed, they can get people to rescue them, take care of them, and give them what they could give to themselves if they only knew *how*. A depressed state of mind might also be a hide-out—a protection of sorts from the demands and expectations of other people. Sometimes the "payoff" of depression is found in the heightened sense of guilt about not overcoming insurmountable obstacles or not reaching unrealistic goals. This payoff is clearly revealed when someone tries to convince a depression-prone person that he or she shouldn't expect so much of himself or herself. The response is that he or she "should" have been able to accomplish the impossible . . . if only he or she had tried a little harder. In response to this, an arrogant perfectionism like this may surface: "Well, maybe *you* wouldn't expect as much of yourself, but *I* do." In this case, extremely high goals are set up, identified with, and sometimes even flaunted. Pride is taken in establishing and carrying out superhuman goals—and eventually in harsh self-judgment. *And* the suffering and unhappiness continue on . . .

Sometimes, suffering, self-pity, and negative self-indulgence actually become *substitutes* for the satisfaction of accomplishment or for healthy involvement in the simple pleasures of life. When people deny themselves relaxation, joy, emotional expression, and the satisfaction of a job well done, emotional needs become distorted and eventually become counterfeit. For example, feelings of self-pity are substituted for joy; in other words, negative self-indulgence becomes a substitute for indulgence in positive feelings. Some people have such low self-esteem that they actually feel they don't deserve *anything* and consequently feel guilty over the smallest of self-indulgences. Other people actually derive a certain sense of satisfaction from feelings of deprivation—viewing themselves as superior to those they judge to be materialistic, superficial, or self-indulgent.

When people are feeling numb, empty, or depressed, they may discover that pain is actually preferable to no feelings at all. Pain can be sharp and bright and serve as evidence that one is still alive. Pain is also stunningly *real* and can give a person a clear sense of still being in touch with himself or herself; pain also has the effect of filling up the void some people feel inside themselves.

One of the most pervasive and self-defeating reasons people have for assuming the "martyr" role is their belief that they can actually gain a sense of identity through suffering. They may feel that suffering makes them more sensitive, deeper, more responsive to others, somehow more deserving, and that suffering makes life more worthwhile. The suffering that occurs through this kind of self-denial is really a form of masochism—certainly a negative self-indulgence. Sometimes the reasons for this kind of suffering have to do with personal relationships. For example, people who are fearful of intimacy may actually prefer the sympathy of others to the love of others. By placing themselves in a subordinate position, people distance themselves, thereby interfering with both physical and emotional closeness. Or, because of low self-esteem, these people feel that they just aren't good enough or that they don't deserve *real* love, so they systematically arrange to maintain that deprivation. Other people are so shy and non-assertive that they feel they're completely unable to stand up for themselves. Fearful of potentially painful confrontations, these people withdraw from others emotionally.

If you ever realize that you are, even for a moment, playing any of the victim/martyr roles characterized above—look very carefully at what you're doing. Ask yourself straightforward questions that go to the very heart of the issue you are facing—Do I really *want* to live a life like this? (*Of course not!*) So, resolve to arrange things in your life in such a way that you will no longer get "rewards" from your performances. When you become aware of what you're doing, act decisively to circumvent the payoffs of suffering by doing the following things: • remind yourself that self-imposed suffering is just another form of self-indulgence • interrupt the flow of sympathy and pity you get from others by telling those offering it how you, yourself, set the stage for your own disappointment and disillusionment • consider carefully that for every situation in which you are in the "victim" role, you have played at least a small part in setting yourself up (unfortunately, many people cling to the belief that they are helpless victims of circumstances beyond their control at the very same time they're actively engaged in sabotaging themselves).

Remember, very few self-confident, successful people get that way by chance. Most fulfilled and self-actualized people have mastered life skills that give them the self-assurance they now have. Chances are very good that there is plenty of careful work—*not luck*—in the stories of the people you most admire.

17.

Banish Self-Doubts

Self-esteem resides within

Naturally, most young children look to their parents for evaluation and approval of their behavior. Then, when they're older, many children begin looking to other parental figures in their lives— siblings and other relatives, teachers, coaches, and counselors—for evaluation and approval. But as the healthy, self-actualized person matures, it becomes increasingly evident that approval from others is one thing, self-esteem is another. Self-esteem is not an external quality "awarded" by another person, but an internal quality that develops and is maintained and enhanced within oneself.

Noted psychiatrist, Silvano Arieti, suggests that many depression-prone people have, as a result of childhood messages and training, come to rely on the approval and nurturance of others in order to develop and maintain self-esteem.[1] Those individuals whose parents somehow blocked the development of their self-esteem or robbed them of their self-esteem are, indeed, likely to become depression-prone. As adults, these people feel—at least subconsciously—that their parents actually have the power to *confer* self-esteem upon them and that they must "return" to their parents emotionally in order to establish or recapture that self-esteem. Even as middle-age adults, these people are likely to continue to seek the approval of the parent or "parentized" person who they perceive can give them the self-esteem they lack.

It's true that many depression-prone people have or had parents who were either very critical—overtly or covertly—and/or offered love and approval on a conditional basis only. Becoming aware of these early parental messages and communication styles actually can help you understand how you might be feeding your own self-doubts and depression.

First of all, it seems to me that adults tend to question, undermine, and criticize themselves in ways that are almost *identical* to the ways their parents questioned, undermined, and criticized *them*. If your parents are alive, make a special effort sometime to objectively consider what it is they say and do that triggers your own feelings of guilt or self-doubt. A few years ago, I suggested this particular exercise to a client of mine who had successfully worked her way out of a depression.

This woman was doing well until the day she told me that her mother was coming to town to spend the weekend with her. As she told me about her mother's upcoming visit, this woman seemed to grow more uncomfortable. She even seemed to know how the weekend would proceed: "My mother will say, 'Oh, why did you arrange the furniture *that way*?' or 'I see you still have *that* rug,' or 'Have you really *tried* to lose weight?' And I just know I'll get depressed all over again."

I told this woman I thought it was great that her mother was coming to town. "But all this time, we've been working to-gether," I said, "we've more or less been guessing how and why you make yourself depressed. Chances are very good that you put yourself down in the same way your mother puts you down, so this weekend is an excellent opportunity for you to learn all about how you create your own depressions." I told this woman to try her best to be objective and to not discourage her mother from making critical comments. Instead, I suggested that when-ever her mother said something that had the effect of making her feel guilty or unsure of herself during their visit, she should write it down. As it turned out, this woman's weekend with her mother was quite pleasant. But each time her mother said some-thing that made her feel guilty or unsure of herself, she'd rush out of the room and capture the comment in writing so she'd be able to examine it closely later on. As she excused herself from the living room time after time to run into the bathroom and record every subtle nuance, every insidious little remark—nota-tions that would eventually provide her with important insights into her own depression-proneness—her mother sat there on the couch, worrying that her daughter had a bladder infection!

Depression-prone people who grew up with parents who were *explicitly* critical and demanding frequently discover that, overall, it is relatively easy to identify the childhood "shoulds" that contribute to their depression. These people—as children and as adults—can then decide whether or not to accept, reject, or rebel against these specific parental objections, expectations, and parameters.

In contrast, parental criticism and demands that are difficult to deal with and sort out later on are those that are vague and diffuse, those not explicitly "owned" by the parents: "We know you'll do the right thing," or "We trust you to do what you think is best." Then, when the child follows through in a way not acceptable to the parents, the parents act hurt or cold or aloof, or they *subtly* convey the message that the children did something bad or wrong, or in some way disappointed them. Then when the child reacts against a parent's veiled disapproval, the parent says: "How can you accuse me of that? I told you to do what *you* wanted to do." The parent essentially denies the implicit message, and expresses hurt feelings and disapproval over the child's unfair "accusation."

Indeed, if you had parents who somehow required you to *guess* or *imagine* what they wanted based on subtle cues only, all the while insisting that you "do what is right," these cues may have become powerfully negative forces in your life. Parents who furnish their children with implicit, indirect criticisms, or respond to "wrong" behaviors and decisions with subtle disapproval undermine the developing self-esteem of their children. If these same parents also appear to be kind and indulgent and they are not overtly punitive, the children are then left with poorly-defined feelings of insecurity, dissatisfaction, guilt, and self-doubt. When these children grow up, they tend to question everything they do. These are the children who, as adults, are likely to spend time and energy *reading* other people's reactions and responding to them *in order to gain approval*— just as their parents "taught" them to do through their own behavior.

Parents who are vague and non-specific in their expectations also lay something of a "trip" on their children with statements like *"We're confident you'll make us proud."* Messages like this leave to the child's imagination and interpretation just what level of performance or what choices the parents would be satisfied with. As a result, the child's self-doubts may be as diffuse and all-pervasive as the approval the parents withheld. Parent-child relationships characterized by this vague communication are likely to produce adults who think of themselves as being damaged or lacking in some fundamental way, people who feel they're "different" from other people or that important elements are missing within them, people with feelings that they possess some deep and mysterious character flaw, people who feel stupid, insensitive, dull, naive, or immature. Also, chances are pretty good that in most areas of life, these people ask themselves questions like this over and over again: *"Am I really an okay person?" "Am I overlooking something important?" "Am I really doing this properly?"* In other words, *"Don't trust yourself."*

When self-doubt is perpetuated in a person's childhood by parents or others, that person, even as an adult, is likely to continue to look to parentized friends and "significant others" (sponsors, friends, professional helpers) to tell them that they really *are* okay, to assure them that they *are* doing the right things, and to support their choices or actions. I've worked with many depression-prone adults who have ongoing conflicts with parents and friends over many issues. What always strikes me is that *even when these people are clearly right, and logic is overwhelmingly on their sides, they still tend to become very flustered and unsure of themselves and they maintain the conflict.*

When depression-prone clients say to me, "I *knew* I was right, but *they* kept disagreeing with me," I usually respond to them in this way: *"But why must they agree with you?* Once you explain your position to those you're in conflict with, why don't you just move on and do or think what you feel is right for you?" At this point, the client usually looks at me as if such an idea had never even occurred to him or her. It's as if these people cannot *feel* they're right until parents or parentized friends/associates agree with them. When these depression-prone people *do* follow through on something without the approval of a "significant other," they are likely to exhibit anger and resentment toward the other person for not seeing their point of view or conceding to them entirely. Furthermore, they simply cannot understand that there's really no need to *convince* other people that they're wrong. (In reality, of course, the "significant other" doesn't even have to understand or care about the issue in order for the depression-prone person to be right; and, after all, who says a person has to be right in order to do what he or she chooses to do?!)

I realize that it can be very difficult to work through the need for external approval and the accompanying tendency to doubt oneself. But it's essential to do this if you want your self-esteem *to reside within you*, rather than allowing it to be totally dependent upon approval from others and conferred upon you by others. Remind yourself that most people are unsure of themselves and doubt themselves *at least some of the time*.

The following incident in my own life clearly illustrates, I think, the *subjective, irrational,* but also *universal* aspects of self-doubt. Back in 1969, the year after I received my doctorate, I was living in Riverside, California. One day I saw a poster there that advertised a two-day workshop on contemporary psychotherapeutic techniques that was to be conducted by a famous Los Angeles psychoanalyst. I was in awe of the depth and variety of this man's professional background. At the time, I remember thinking to myself that if I had that kind of training, I'd be so self-confident that my feet would barely touch the ground. Because of my own professional self-doubts at that time, I subsequently signed up for yet another training program in Los Angeles. At the first workshop I attended there, the group leader was working with a man who was obviously very nervous and depressed. This very distressed man apparently was struggling with self-doubts even more profound than those I'd experienced. He was saying things like this: "I live in fear that someone will think I'm a phony and that people won't have faith in me anymore; I'll be ruined!" I thought to myself, That poor guy. Even in my darkest hours, I've never struggled with such gut-wrenching self-doubts. The next day, this poor fellow—who was by then feeling much better— asked me where I lived. When I told him I lived in Riverside, he said he planned to conduct a two-day workshop there the next month. The same man who had expressed such extreme self-doubts was the famous psychoanalyst with credentials that in my fantasy, would eliminate my own self-doubts forever!

Self-doubt just perpetuates self-doubt, and the more you indulge in it, the more powerful a force it will become in your life. *The point is to go about the business of living, in spite of self-doubts.* (Before you take action in spite of self-doubts, however, you would be wise to consider whether or not there is any validity in the hesitation you feel.) We can be cautious without being slaves to caution. Taking risks and following through frequently promotes relief from depressive tendencies by requiring people to get involved with the demands of the action itself. Also, attending to the action itself distracts people from useless brooding and obsessing. And if the action is sensibly planned, there's a good chance it will result in *positive change*—an excellent tonic for depression-prone people!

References

1.   Arieti, Silvano, and Jules Bemporad. *Severe and Mild Depression*. New York: Basic Books, 1978.

18.

Stop Trying So Hard

"Goals are most often achieved 'in spite of' rather than 'because of' perfectionism."

I've seen perfectionism almost take over people's lives when the pursuit of it becomes central to their personalities. Some people identify so strongly with the state of perfection that they actually build their identities around it. The drive for perfection seems to give these people something to focus on and take pride in. Indeed, some people find meaning in life through the constant striving to meet the elusive goal of perfection. These people may feel—if only subconsciously—that *any* compromise of their lofty standards would reduce them to complete worthlessness. For these people, it's as if extraordinarily high standards somehow compensate for natural limitations. I often wonder if this is the reason perfectionists tend to become dramatic and defensive when someone suggests they become more realistic in their self-expectations. When advised to be more realistic about their performance standards, they're likely to exclaim: "You mean you just want me to give up on myself?"

If you want to stop being a perfectionist, or want to know how to avoid becoming one in the first place, you need to distinguish between *achievable goals* that represent realistic standards and possibilities, and *unattainable goals* that are related to compulsive efforts and perfectionistic standards. Achievable goals represent high potential for enjoyment in the process of striving and deep satisfaction in the final accomplishment; unattainable goals almost certainly create anxiety, threats to self-worth, self-doubts that drain energy, constant fear of failure, and inevitable disappointment when the goal of perfection isn't achieved.

Psychoanalyst Karen Horney theorized that sometimes out of feelings of self-doubt, worthlessness, or failure, people construct a comprehensive system of self-demands that becomes embodied in an idealized image of themselves.[1] This image then comes to represent an unrealistic, subconscious picture of one of two things: what these people desperately feel they *must* be, or the fear of what they feel they are failing to be.

This idealized self-image may be totally unrealistic, or it may contain realistic elements that are all but concealed by perfectionistic standards. Some people identify so strongly with this idealized and illusive image that they seem to believe—most likely on a subconscious level—that perfection actually resides *within them*. In response to their quest for perfection, depression-prone people are apt to do one of two things: either they focus on the gap between the idealized image and their real selves and behaviors, frantically work to measure up, then fail and collapse in despair, or they focus on the realities of themselves in terms of observable characteristics and behaviors, compare the realities to their idealized images, judge themselves as terribly inferior, then begin hating themselves. In constructing this idealized image, depression-prone people take a giant step away from themselves. They become like the "Wizard of Oz"—vulnerable little people cowering behind a massive image that is actually an unrealistic and elusive projection.

I once had a student in a college class I taught who was perfectionistic to the point of being almost completely immobilized. For example, when this student, Will, received a term paper assignment, he'd begin by doing exhaustive research and writing lengthy notes on each of the many articles and books he read. He'd actually *delay* writing the paper until it was too late to meet the deadline. Will seemed to have a compulsive need to read almost everything related to his research before he could write a single word. And, inevitably, by the time he completed his research, he had enough material to write a full-length book!

I decided to set up an experiment that I believed would help Will recognize and alleviate two sources of his perfectionism: his self-doubts and his high level of anxiety. (These factors came out of his compulsive thoroughness in research and his procrastination in writing term papers.)

First, I assigned Will a topic, "Modern Behavioral Counseling Techniques," and told him to research it as thoroughly as he could for the next two weeks. Then I asked him to report to me on his progress at the end of the two week period; in fact, I asked him to set aside three hours for our discussion about his term paper. When Will arrived at my office two weeks later with dozens of books and note cards, I told him that I didn't intend to talk with him about his paper at all. Instead, I asked him to go to the library and spend the next three hours writing the paper. And I told him that no matter how good (or bad) the paper was, I would give him an "A", *even before I read it.* Will seemed to feel relieved, excited, and yet a bit guilty that he could get off so easily. Nevertheless, he left for the library and diligently worked under *self-imposed* pressure, but with very little real anxiety. When he returned to my office exactly three hours later, I took his hastily-written term paper and immediately placed an "A" by his name in my grade book and also at the top of his paper. Then I told Will to take all of his books and note cards home. I told him that for his final grade in the course, he was to write the most perfect paper he possibly could in the next nine weeks. Will's anxiety really seemed to kick in with this assignment!

At the end of the nine-week period I had specified, Will turned in a perfectly typed paper. (In the meantime, I'd arranged to have someone type the handwritten paper he had completed in the library nine weeks earlier.) When Will and I sat down together and read the two papers, he was absolutely *astounded* at how little real improvement nine weeks of compulsive, anxious refinement and perfecting contributed to the overall quality of the paper. In this painful but memorable exercise, Will learned that anxiety and self-doubt had interfered with his performance substantially. He also learned that when external pressures were removed—by my telling him that he'd get an "A" regardless of the quality of the paper—Will found he was able to relax somewhat and put his energy into doing the best job possible in the shortest time possible. Will also learned from the experiment, however, that even with the *absolutely guaranteed* "A" he'd received from me, he still struggled with extreme self-doubts and put substantial pressure on himself. Will discovered that internal, self-imposed pressures—not external pressure from the real world—created most difficulties for him. To his delight, he also discovered that he had some control over those internal pressures.

The lack of perspective and constant inner struggle that is common in perfectionists may lead them to believe that successful people achieve their goals easily, with supreme self-confidence, little anxiety, and few errors. When perfectionists see a truly successful person who experiences pure joy in striving and freedom from self-doubts, they tend to misinterpret those qualities as effortlessness. The truth is, successful people expend their energies on tasks and on healthy striving, rather than on the control of anxiety generated by the threat of failure.

Simple introspection reveals that perfectionism does not bring happiness—perfectionists can *always* find something to undermine their own satisfaction—and that if some kind of perfection *is* achieved, it seems to engender boredom or complacency. When achievements come so easily that there is no longer any challenge or struggle, perfectionists are likely to abandon the activity for something that requires effort and offers a new challenge. On the other hand, when perfectionists achieve near-perfection in a few tasks and restrict themselves to those tasks, this is what can happen: they become adept at avoiding failure by avoiding the risk represented by new interests and skills; consequently, the narrowness of their lives may undermine any happiness they might experience through their achievements.

If you carefully examine all of your activities, you may be surprised to discover that the relative amount of satisfaction you derive from one particular activity has little connection with how "perfect" you are in carrying it out. Actually, routine activities that most people have little ego investment in—and probably no perfectionistic standards for—may produce surprising pleasures. For example, a prominent surgeon I knew never felt that his professional work fully measured up to his perfectionistic standards, but he felt great pleasure and pride when he discovered he could hang a door *reasonably* well.

Goals are most often achieved "in spite of" rather than "because of" perfectionism. Also, you may find that other people will respond to you more positively when you drop your perfectionistic stance. When you blunder or fail at some challenge you've accepted and brace yourself for criticism, you'll probably find others surprisingly accepting and empathetic. These people may even admit that they're relieved to know that your primary aim isn't superiority. Chances are pretty good, also, that they'll feel closer to you when you acknowledge that you are as humanly imperfect as they are.

But perfectionism is difficult to overcome for many reasons:
• you may get so many praises and rewards for a job well done that the
striving all seems quite worthwhile • because of insecurity and self-
doubt, you may believe that if you relax your standards *at all*, you will
feel completely worthless and unacceptable • a great deal of
underlying anxiety might conceivably be contained and managed
through compulsive attention to detail • exacting standards can help
take the uncertainty out of one's activities.

But regardless of the many reasons and rationalizations involved
in justifying perfectionism, try to remember this: *life is too short for all
that fussing!* "Anything worth doing is worth doing well" is an old
adage that probably should apply *only some of the time.* Unless an
activity is a high-priority endeavor, it is possible that nothing will be
lost if you do it in a hit-or-miss manner, just to get it done. This way,
you'll then have time for some other enjoyments and things worth
doing very, very well. When you think about it, not everything we do
in life *has* to be done well. And if you discover that there are too
many things demanding your attention and perfectionistic standards,
admit your imperfection in at least one area—*your ability to set
priorities!*

Long-term perfectionists are seldom, if ever, able to overcome
their perfectionism entirely. But insight into your perfectionistic
tendencies can help you set up your life in ways that will *protect* you
from these non-productive tendencies. For example, an
undergraduate student once told me he was majoring in psychology
because he loved music. My stupefied expression must have indicated
that I needed clarification. "If I majored in music," he explained, "it
would be *work.* My ego would be on the line because I would identify
myself as a musician and would have to be the best damn trumpet
player in the world. And then playing the trumpet just wouldn't be
fun anymore!"

In my own life, one of the primary reasons I haven't chosen to
pursue further art training is because I sensed that it might interfere
with the pleasure I derive from "dabbling" in art. If I received formal
education and/or professional training in this field, my goals would be
such that I wouldn't enjoy the finished product unless it met certain
exacting standards of quality. And, the process of learning itself

might also lose its happy spontaneity for me because I know that in formalized training situations, I would tend to be more consciously controlled and tense.

Try to gain a clear understanding of *your* "should" system and how it operates. When you're feeling overwhelmed during a depression, perhaps you will only *dimly* recognize the pervasiveness of your self-demands, sensing that there may be thousands of inner expectations. At times like this, it is important to recognize that some of these shoulds may not be impossible—all of the shoulds together certainly *are* impossible!

Using a "divide and conquer" technique, confront your "shoulds" head-on, rather than letting them randomly rattle around in your head, using precious time and energy. For starters, put these shoulds in writing. One way to do this is as follows: list the major areas of your life—marriage, children, job, friendship, relatives, activities, and career. Then, create a list summarizing your roles in life: employee, employer, spouse, mother, friend, son/daughter, brother/sister. Under each of these headings, list your self-expectations and the rules inherent in each of these expectations. (For example, "*I should always put my husband's needs first.*" "*I should never show my temper in front of the children.*") If the rules aren't clear, look at your *behavior* and abstract the rule from it. For example, you might *feel* that you have the right to get some of your own needs met, whereas your behavior manifests a subconscious self-imposed rule that you meet everyone else's needs first. True, you may attempt to take care of your own needs later, if there's any time and energy left. But that seldom seems to happen. List all your shoulds on one side of the page and then list your wants on the other side of the page. Then ask yourself this question: *What do I really want from each area of my life and from each role?*

Initially, you may come to the painful realization that you don't have any clear wants. Once you find out what you *should* do, feel, want and need, as well as what you imagine others expect you to do, feel, want and need, there doesn't seem to be much left for determining what it is *you* want.

When you've become alert to your predicament, it may require time and effort on your part to discover what it is you *really want*.

Start by paying attention to your feelings when you look at your own life and out at the world around you: • take special note of the types of characters you identify with in novels and screenplays • try to catch the *heart* of your fantasies as you daydream • keep a journal of your dreams • notice especially any "wish-fulfillment" dreams you have • analyze what elements are conspicuously missing from your dreams • keep a private daily journal and jot down fleeting desires, longings, and regrets, as well as in-the-moment thoughts and feelings.

Once you have a clearer sense of what you really want, enter these wants on the opposite side of the page from your list of shoulds. It may be instantly and dramatically obvious to you that your shoulds have no real connection with your wants and/or that your wants and shoulds are in conflict with each other. In your efforts to achieve perfection and receive approval, then, you haven't done much to meet your own real wants and needs. So many small, unmet needs contribute to overall vague feelings of deprivation. These feelings of deprivation frequently emerge from attitudes of self-denial and related self-talk with common themes: *"We'll make do." "We can't afford . . . " "I should be able to do without." "I can't take the time to do that."* Hopefully, the "should/want" exercise will help you identify neglected and unmet needs and wants.

Next, you'll need to convince yourself that a depression-prevention program must include a system for identifying and fulfilling unmet needs. If you monitor the time, energy, and financial resources you expend on low priority items in your life, you may find the wherewithal to identify many long-neglected needs and wishes— shopping for a new appliance, taking occasional walks in the woods, organizing the family album, picking fresh strawberries, writing a poem, having your back rubbed, asking for and receiving hugs, looking up old friends, visiting your hometown. The challenge is to identify these unmet needs, prioritize them, and resolve to do something every day to work toward fulfilling them.

If, somehow, this should/want technique doesn't help you ease up and let go of your shoulds, give in to your should demands and try the go-for-broke technique. This technique is more likely to work if you prepare a "should list" of the things you believe you really must accomplish in the next two weeks. Don't forget all those tasks that you've been putting off and feeling guilty about but that must, nevertheless, be carried out. Also, include *all* your regular shoulds. Then divide those shoulds into a fourteen-day period. For each of these fourteen days, you must work until you complete every should on the list for that day, even if it takes you until the next morning. At the end of a two-week period (if you and your family last that long), you'll be in a much better position to assess just how realistic your shoulds are. By this time, of course, you'll be exhausted, possibly physically ill, and sick to death of "shoulds." *And then you'll also have some notion of the price you're paying for attempting perfection!*

Reference

1.   Horney, Karen. *Our Inner Conflicts.* New York: Norton, 1966.

19.

Consider Your Thinking Style

Many errors in thinking come into our consciousness as specific sentences.

You wouldn't think that perfectionistic people could get so messed up with their thinking, *but they do.* And confused, regressed, and negativistic thinking creates, contributes to, and perpetuates depression-proneness. For this reason, any good depression-management program includes the identification and correction of erroneous thinking.

David Burns, a student of Aaron Beck, pioneer in the psychiatric treatment of depression, states that our thoughts create our feelings.[1] For example, if we incorrectly *think* we're being rejected, we will react with the same negative emotions that occur with actual rejection. Then, because we *think* we're being rejected, we inadvertently respond in ways that, in fact, do tend to make others withdraw from us. Or, if we misinterpret cues from another person and thus anticipate rejection, we might—out of a need to protect ourselves—reject the other person before he or she has an opportunity to reject us. In situations like this, inaccurate feelings and inappropriate behavior follow from incorrect thinking.

Beck and Burns cite a number of characteristic errors in thinking that appear to create, catalyze, and/or perpetuate depression.[1], [2] As I summarize (and somewhat exaggerate) these errors in thinking here, consider whether or not they are consistent with your own thinking and personality styles.

• *All-or-Nothing Thinking* — You see your personal qualities in rigid categories. You are either one way or its polar opposite: either brilliant or stupid; perfectly coordinated in every way or the clumsiest person ever to come down the pike. You get one "B" grade with several "A" grades and you consider yourself a complete failure.

• *Overgeneralization* — You draw a general rule or conclusion on the basis of an isolated incident, then apply that rule across the board. For example, you ask a friend to go to a movie, he declines the invitation because of a previous commitment, and you say to yourself, *"Nobody likes me. I'm doomed to be lonely for the rest of my life."*

• *Mental Filter* — You select a single negative aspect of a situation or circumstance, and dwell on it to the exclusion of any positives; subsequently, the entire situation seems negative. For example, you have a wonderful weekend with friends, remember only a teasing comment from one of them, and conclude that not one person enjoyed your company for three days.

• *Disqualifying the Positive* — You overlook, trivialize, or reject positive experiences and outcomes by insisting that they lack importance and you negate evidence supporting positive conclusions. For example: *"My 'shrink' likes me because he's paid to like me." "My family likes me because they have to like me." "My friends like me because they don't really know me."*

• *Jumping to Conclusions* — You automatically and arbitrarily make negative assumptions that do not follow from the facts of the situation. For instance, you might arbitrarily conclude — without checking any facts — that someone is reacting negatively to you.

• *Magnification or Minimization* — You distort the importance of things by blowing them up out of proportion or shrinking them. Magnification is looking at a small error and reacting to it in this way: *"My God, this is terrible!"* Minimization is dismissing a substantial achievement in this way: *"It's no big deal. Anyone could have done as well if they had worked as long and hard as I did."*

• *Emotional Reasoning* — You assume that if you feel a certain way, that is necessarily the way things are. For example, if you feel guilty, you assume that you must have done something.

• *Should Statements* — You use shoulds and shouldn'ts to motivate yourself, with guilt frequently the result. You apply shoulds to other people and become frustrated and bitter.

• *Labeling and Mislabeling* — You engage in overgeneralization and take it to an extreme. Instead of identifying an isolated error

("I made a mistake"), you attach a strong negative label to yourself: "*I'm a failure.*" Mislabeling is, for example, referring to yourself as a "pig" when all you've done is eat a bowl of ice cream.

• *Personalization* — You perceive that you are accountable for a negative external event that is well beyond your control. You may erroneously believe that what happened was your fault or reflects your inadequacy, even when you had no control whatsoever over the situation or occurrence. You tend to confuse influence with control. For example, if your son gets pneumonia after camping out in cold weather, you say "*I'm a bad parent. I should have been able to prevent this from happening.*"

Many of these errors in thinking present themselves in our consciousness as specific sentences and they clearly *do* contribute to depression. The cognitive theorists call these involuntary thoughts that suddenly pop into our minds "automatic thoughts." Everyone has these thoughts from time to time, but depression-prone people just seem to have more of them and they fail to recognize them as problematic. The best time to identify these thoughts is at the very moment they occur. But when things happen so fast that you don't have time to think about them and you find yourself getting depressed, do this: set aside fifteen minutes at night to replay and review an event or series of events during the day that may have triggered automatic thoughts that disturbed you in some way. What follows is an example of an automatic thought actually *triggering* a depression.

> When I first met Jack, a 30-year-old client of mine, he was dis-couraged and had been thinking about quitting a very good job. Jack complained that within a period of five days, his boss had asked him to recheck his figures for three projects he was in the process of completing. When Jack did this, he found only a cou-ple of minor, insignificant errors. In reviewing the situation in counseling, it didn't seem to me that Jack's level of despair was warranted. Although his boss seemed irritable, it was a very busy time for the company and the entire staff was working long hours.
>
> When Jack told me that he believed his boss wanted to fire him, I asked, "Do you have any evidence to support your

hunch?" A quick review of the situation on Jack's part seemed to reveal the opposite. The boss, who happened to be a hard-driving, demanding person, seemed generally pleased with Jack's work. As he recounted several similar incidents, Jack remembered that even though he felt okay about the encounters with his boss at the time, he would go back to his desk and start to think. And that's when the troubles began. An automatic thought intruded repeatedly: "I am not competent to do this job." When I inquired whether or not anyone in his family had ever said anything similar to him, Jack replied at once: "My God, when I told my dad I had landed this job, he said to me 'This might be too much job for you, boy.' "

I indicated that I was surprised that his father would question his competency rather than congratulate him for getting the job. It didn't take long to conclude that Jack's father was a man who had not received a formal education; he was a self-made man who had worked his way up by himself. It's just possible that he might have been somewhat envious of Jack's good fortune in landing a superb job immediately upon college graduation. Realizing that he might be projecting feelings about his father onto his boss, Jack decided that his insecurities might stem from ambiguity in his work situation. Thus, Jack asked his boss for short, biweekly feedback sessions to review his performance. When Jack began having these performance updates on a regular basis, his automatic thoughts stopped because they were no longer being verified in any way.

This "Where's the evidence?" technique helped to identify the inaccuracy of Jack's depression-inducing automatic thought by testing the validity of the conclusions inherent in it. A similar technique—which begins with the same first step of describing the situation in detail—involves defining the problem. "Exactly what is the problem?" By asking this question, you can sometimes break through the murky clouds of negative feelings and erroneous beliefs to the realistic issue of what the problem really is. Frequently, we develop "feelings about" a problem before we're even clear in our minds exactly what the components of the problem are. In Jack's case, the real problem was not the automatic thought, "I'm not competent," nor was it the accompanying feelings of discouragement or despair. Through an analysis and blow-by-blow description of the events, the evidence did not confirm that Jack's boss wanted to fire him. The "problem" was only that Jack was asked to recheck his figures.

Though automatic thoughts frequently have their origins in early parental messages or self-messages, certain kinds of current incidents are more likely to stimulate automatic thoughts than others. Since irrational thoughts usually don't operate in a vacuum, we should clearly describe and analyze the present-day recurring situations that trigger such thoughts. In Jack's case, several components contributed to the problem and ultimately to the solution as well: 1. The boss's request for Jack to recheck his figures. 2. Jack's automatic thought, "*I'm not competent.*" 3. Recognition of the source of the automatic thought in his father's words: "*This might be too much job for you, boy.*" 4. Similarities between the personalities of Jack's boss and his dad. 5. Lack of on-the-job feedback that gave free reign to Jack's insecurities and the resulting automatic thoughts.

It does help to locate the source of an automatic thought (in Jack's case, the comment from his possibly envious father) and then set up a situation that reduces the potential for recurrence of this automatic thought (with Jack, the biweekly feedback sessions).

Here's a good exercise that helps most people see the irrationality of the conclusions made from automatic thoughts. Begin by taking a piece of paper and dividing it into three columns. From left to right, label the columns A, B, and C. Then write down an automatic thought in column A; in column C write down the inferences and conclusions you make based on this particular automatic thought. Then, in the middle column, B, write down your "evidence." In the situation just described, Jack's automatic thought process would look like this:

(A)	(B)	(C)
Automatic Thought	**Evidence**	**Conclusion**
"I am not competent to do this job."	"The boss told me to recheck my figures for 3 projects in a 5-day period."	"I am incompetent. My boss wants to fire me."

If you are clear and explicit in what you write down about your own automatic thoughts, you'll most likely be struck by the fact that given the evidence (B), C simply doesn't follow from A and B.

Realizing this, you might want to go a step further and list evidence *contrary* to that which supports your automatic thoughts. You may discover that your support "evidence" is scant, compared to the list of contradictory incidents. In Jack's case, for example, his boss had given him a good six-week evaluation and had, in fact, made several positive comments to him about projects he had completed in recent weeks.

When we write down our thoughts, essentially we are making an internal subjective process *more objective*. Errors exhibited in the various stages of thinking are much more apparent when we write them down—errors from implicit assumptions and falsely projected "meanings"—to inadequate verifications and illogical conclusions. Also, by *writing down* thoughts, secret insecurities, vague fears, angers, and irrational beliefs, depression-prone people may begin to feel that they have some power. At first, this power may reside only in the process of *revealing* these "secrets." But that's a beginning—an action step.

There is much to be said about keeping a completely private journal with daily entries, if you can manage that. The habit of doing this enables you to deal more effectively with problems as they come up. Somehow, "rerunning the film" of prior disturbing events in your own mind, inspecting it "frame by frame," then describing on paper what you see and remember, will begin to give you a sense of *control* over your own life. And seemingly vague thoughts, feelings, and beliefs recorded in black and white will help you step back, distance from a problem, and, as a result, analyze your whole mental process in more objective terms.

Once you have objectively identified a problem, solutions may spontaneously emerge. In Jack's case, logical solutions to the real problems became apparent through the process of identifying what, in fact, actually transpired in his job situation that led up to his feelings. *Clearly and objectively identifying the problem helps to uncover obvious solutions.*

For example, Sue, a single woman in her twenties, had a very demanding job at an advertising agency. Because Sue had little time during the week to "play," she really looked forward to recreational activities on weekends. Sue and her best friend, Val, usually spent a great deal of time doing things together on weekends. But, not infrequently, Val would cancel out of their planned activities at the last minute. When Sue expressed disappointment, Val would say, "Well, Sue, I do a lot of things with you. You shouldn't be so upset when I cancel out of our plans now and then." Sue would then feel guilty; she acknowledged in subsequent counseling sessions with me that she felt she was "too demanding, possessive, and inflexible" and that it really was "selfish" of her to expect Val to be available "all the time."

In helping Sue identify the problem clearly and objectively, I asked: "Are you, in fact, demanding, possessive, inflexible, and selfish?" Sue, who was depression-prone and tended to blame herself for everything and call herself names, answered "Yes" to my question. But, interestingly, Sue could give me no clear or specific examples of demanding, possessive, or selfish behavior on her part.

I pressed Sue further: "What, specifically, about Val's canceling out is disturbing to you? Is the problem that you fear she doesn't like you or is rejecting you?" "No," Sue responded. After I asked that question several additional times, Sue was finally able to define the real problem: It wasn't the fact that Val canceled out, but that she canceled out too late for Sue to find a "stand-in." Because of Val's last minute change in plans, Sue often faced the choice of going somewhere alone or just staying home.

When Sue finally realized that it was the lateness of Val's cancellations, rather than her own demands, possessiveness, or selfishness that was the real problem, a number of possible solutions to the problem spontaneously emerged. Sue explained her predicament to Val more objectively and Val acknowledged that she was rather disorganized and tended to overbook herself. In fact, Val admitted that sometimes she'd get so confused that she'd mistakenly schedule two appointments for the same night! And other times, her week became so harried because of her own lack of planning and mismanagement that she was too tired to go out at all on Friday evenings.

Once Sue understood the problem clearly, it seemed appropriate that she negotiate with Val in order to avoid problems in the future: When Val agreed to do something with Sue, she would give her plenty of notice if she subsequently had to cancel out. Val would attempt to plan her week ahead of time, but if she didn't want to go out at the last minute because she was too tired, she'd try to solve the problem *herself* by taking a nap and going out a little later, or by going out at the mutually agreed-upon time but perhaps not staying out quite as late. Sue came to see the overbooking and late cancellations as Val's problem, not hers.

Even when you learn to get to the heart of the problem and the solution, be watchful for thinking that regresses into the distorted patterns of the past. For instance, even after clarifying a problem that has depressed you, sometimes you may continue to rigidly narrow your thinking in "either/or" ways that typify depressive-style thinking: *"Either I keep my mouth shut, or I get fired. Either I say no to everything, or I get taken advantage of. Either I feel guilty, or I blow up."* As a reminder, return to the list of errors in thinking on page 133-135. Then, correct the course of your thoughts and try again to seek a rational solution to whatever problems you're facing.

In a depression, people frequently maintain that they've tried everything, but "nothing will work." It's possible that halfhearted efforts made while believing that they wouldn't work doomed them to failure from the start. But when people are severely depressed, they rarely get to the point of actually *attempting* a solution. More often, they ignore obvious solutions because they appear too simple, or they dismiss creative solutions because they "feel" unworkable, or they convince themselves that they have really "tried everything"—which means just running possible solutions through their minds, then rejecting them outright.

Whenever you find yourself thinking in negativistic terms and playing the *"Yes-But"* game while searching for solutions to problems, you might benefit from the *"Solution-Objection-Modification"* exercise. Divide a piece of paper into three sections. Your task is to come up with a list of solutions—*no matter what*. In the first section, write a solution to a problem; in the second section, write your objection to the proposed solution ("It will never work because . . . "). Since you *must* make each solution workable, in the third section modify the solution in light of your objections in order to *make* it work. Sometimes this added pressure forces you to reconsider hastily rejected solutions or solutions you dismissed before you even *attempted* to modify them.

For example, a woman I once worked with complained that her husband controlled the finances and that he wouldn't even allow her to have money in her purse for emergencies. When she confronted him on this issue, he said, "You don't know anything about budgeting!" Other times, she would press him and he would say, "You want money? Then *you* take over the bills and the checkbook." And then he'd toss both to her. This woman would then retreat because she was aware of the fact that she knew very little about finances. Since this woman's husband didn't sound like any financial wizard himself, I suggested that she try the *"Solution-Objection-Modification"* exercise. What follows is the outcome of her exercise:

Solution

Take over the finances.

Objection

"I don't know anything about finances or budgeting. I don't have a head for figures. I'm a terrible money manager."

Modification

Take over the finances after: 1. going to county social services department and getting counseling about budgeting, 2. reading books on budgeting, and/or 3. taking a course on money management at the local vocational school.

The absence of information, knowledge, and skills isn't the same thing as the lack of ingenuity for *acquiring* information, knowledge, and skills. In this case, the woman who "didn't have a head for figures" did, indeed, complete a course on personal financial management. She subsequently became better informed about money management than her husband and agreed to take complete responsibility for all household finances. An increase in self-esteem that resulted from acquiring a new skill helped her deal later on with the real issue: *her husband's need for control in their relationship, his tendency to put her down, and her pattern of passive acquiescence.*

In applying the mind-sharpening strategies suggested here, it's not necessary to believe the hypothesis that thoughts *create* feelings. It *is* clear, however, that thoughts influence feelings and behavior, just as emotions and actions affect our thinking. The relevant point is that depression-prone people can apply such strategies directly to their thoughts or feelings, or they can directly change their behavior—depending upon what seems most appropriate and efficient at the time. It *is* important, however, to *believe* that you can make positive changes in your life by changing your thinking style.

References

1. Burns, David D. *Feeling Good.* New York: William Morrow, 1980.

2. Beck, A.T., A.J. Rush, B.F. Shaw, and G. Emery. *Cognitive Theory of Depression.* New York: Guilford Press, 1979.

20.

Break Out of the Worry Cycle

"... catch the negative thought process of worry when it first begins, before it has a chance to gather momentum."

Along with their views of past and present, the way people choose to relate to the future also affects their vulnerability to depression. If you're depression-prone and, therefore, almost certainly a worrier, you probably look to the future with at least some anxiety and dread. This anxiety may be focused on specific concerns or it may be "free-floating"—experienced as a sense of impending doom or as a vague feeling that something ominous is lurking just around the corner. Many of us waste so much energy worrying about incidental issues and things over which we have *no* control, that in the end we have no energy left for the vital issues over which we *do* have some control. Psychologist Donald Tubesing said it all so succinctly: *"Putting ten dollars worth of energy into a ten-cent problem is like pole-vaulting over a mouse turd!"*

At times, you may rationalize the pain that accompanies worry by convincing yourself that worry keeps you alert to possible dangers and serves as protection from false moves and serious errors. Letting go of worry may, at first, seem roughly akin to dropping your shield on the battlefield. In fact, you may have come to believe that worry is an essential part of coping, and that you simply cannot eliminate it from your life without risking disaster. You may even go so far as to justify worry as a coping skill! In other words, you've somehow convinced yourself that because you worry about alternatives, fuss over things again and again, cover every angle, and sweat every step of the way, you are successful at accomplishing positive things—and avoiding failure besides. When things turn out badly, you conclude that you just didn't worry *enough*. Some of us really *do* manage to talk ourselves into believing that worry *is* productive (*"Well, I have to worry about the future and anticipate what might happen!"*).

At first glance, it seems that at least some of this worrying pays off. But if we look closer at our thought processes, we'll see that the truly productive aspect of "worry" is not worrying at all, but *planning*. In simple but realistic terms, there are two kinds of problems in our lives: those we can influence or control in some way and those we can't. Worrying about situations we *can* influence or control is distracting and unproductive, an energy-waster that frequently takes the form of trying to predict the unpredictable and dwell on possible but improbable negative outcomes. Worrying about situations that we *cannot* change is even less productive and helpful!

There is a useful distinction between worrying and *rational planning*. You'll know that you're engaging your energies in plans rather than worry when you do the following: • analyze a problem • generate alternatives and solutions to the problem • project potential solutions in the future • attempt to rationally predict consequences • proceed ahead, based on your analysis • set your goals and objectives • map your plans and strategies.

If you're thoughtful, oriented to productive planning, and genuinely *concerned* about a problem, you don't need worry and anxiety to motivate you to evaluate it and develop a solution. For example, instead of anxiously worrying about a fire breaking out in your home, you can actively work on home fire prevention and you can work on special measures to provide and ensure home safety measures in case of fire: • buy smoke alarms and fire extinguishers • have experts from the fire department inspect your home for fire hazards on a regular basis • plan escape routes for all family members • have everyone living in the house participate in fire drills. And, think about it, you can do each and every one of these productive activities *without worrying*!

Of course, it's just plain reckless and foolhardy not to plan in order to avoid or minimize *real* risks and dangers. First-aid kits, burglar alarms, attack whistles and sirens, lightning rods, and disaster supplies serve as necessary equipment to alert us to and/or help us meet actual problems and emergencies. Worry and anxiety, on the other hand, interfere with effective planning and problem solving because they interrupt concentration, sap energies, and distract us from clear-headed evaluations of problems. Worse yet, worry and anxiety seduce us into believing that we are doing something active and productive.

Depression-prone people are notoriously good at playing the "What If" game. "What if I . . . ?" (. . . flunk the test . . . don't heal . . . get audited . . . have cancer . . . drop the ball . . . throw up.) In other words, they tend to indulge in fantasies about dismal circumstances and dire consequences. Instead of dwelling in the here-and-now, depression-prone people spend a great deal of time *waiting* for the future—which, in the midst of a depression, *always looks bleak*. They may even "test" themselves to see whether they would be able to tolerate some future catastrophe. They may ask themselves: *"If I'm this depressed over nothing, how could I ever deal with my mother's death"* or, *"If I feel this lonely when my spouse is with me, how could I survive if something happens to him/her?"*

It's as if depression-prone people anticipate dire circumstances as a way of "preparing" themselves for a future catastrophe. To make matters worse, they seem to believe that unless they constantly remind themselves just how *terrible* everything could turn out to be, they'll be caught "off-guard" and ill-prepared in the event the worst thing imaginable occurs. Usually, this anticipation consists of negative words, negative thinking, and negative rehearsals that eventually exhaust them and may even increase the probability that something catastrophic might occur—as if to make all the worry worthwhile, after all. In moments of maximum vulnerability and dependency, they project themselves into the future, begin to "catastrophize," then collapse from the anticipation of a crisis that is nothing more than fantasy.

Obviously, though, one cannot adjust to the future until one is *in* the future. Of course the best way to affect the future is to do something in the present—plan, strategize, formulate—to set into motion positive dynamics that are designed to produce favorable outcomes. But, given this simple formula, why do people opt instead to do nothing active and spend their time imagining the worst? Maybe they secretly believe that they can *scare* themselves into overcoming obstacles. Or maybe they feel that by preparing themselves for the possibility of failure, they won't be caught off-guard when they *do* fail. Or maybe by imagining worst-case scenarios, they feel relieved when things turn out to be only *somewhat* bad—so that they somehow feel they're being "let off easy." (What a consolation prize.) All that anxiety just to experience a little relief!

Admittedly, I may be one of the world's most experienced worriers. I used to worry about everything. Finally, I was able to gain insight into my worrying, then curb it, by constructing a "worry list." Given my own experience, I highly recommend this activity. A few weeks after I made my first worry list, I prepared a new worry list, then I prepared yet another one a few weeks after that. What I discovered was that all of the things I'd dreaded and wrenched my guts over a month earlier were completely replaced two weeks after that with another set of terrible dreads. And— you guessed it—two weeks after that, I had yet another set of horrendously upsetting issues on my list. *I began to realize that it wasn't the content of my worrying but the process of my worrying that was the real problem!* The contents changed completely from list to list. The specific issues couldn't have been that critical or I wouldn't have been able to replace them so swiftly with other issues. Thus I saw that because I was a "worry addict," worry was a never-ending process for me, a string of trivial dreads and self-initiated upsets that made me feel I was doing something active to make my life better.

But I began to see that I had carefully cultivated a lifelong worry habit; in fact, I even took some pride in being a good worrier! After all, I told myself, worriers by nature are responsible, dutiful, solid folks. They care! (Obviously, I had a real investment in maintaining my worry skills.) But in order to break the worry cycle, I finally managed to fake out my psyche, and this is how I did it: I decided not to stop worrying, but simply to become more efficient at worrying. Until that time, I seemed to worry constantly, and I was very haphazard about it as well. At times, I was only half-worrying, and other things like food or television were competing for my attention. I decided that I needed to become a worry "purist" in order to appease my subconscious need to worry. Instead of spending all day worrying inefficiently and halfheartedly, I would put off worrying until I could give it my undivided attention. I would set aside an hour each evening to devote entirely to efficient worrying. I found it much easier to postpone worry during the day when I had promised myself an intense worry "binge" that night. Sounds like a crazy idea, doesn't it? Well, how rational an idea is worry?

Since worry is—for the most part—irrational, some of the methods useful in breaking the worry cycle may actually appeal to our irrational needs and appease our erroneous beliefs. But this method worked for me; it had the effect of cutting way down on the time I spent worrying. And it also helped me begin to take control of an activity which, up to that point, had completely controlled me. I found that I could turn worry off temporarily by promising to give myself time to bring my worries out later. And I learned that when I fully gave in to worrying for my dedicated "worry hour"—rather than struggling to resist, repress, deny, or rationalize away my worries—I could more quickly think over things and dismiss them from my mind for yet another day. When I began to feel some control over the process of worrying, I found that I had freedom to choose to cut down my worry time to a half-hour, or even less. Eventually, I began to feel that maybe I could put off my worry sessions for increasingly longer periods of time and maybe even here and there postpone a session or two indefinitely. Once I had the knowledge that I could gain some control over the worry process—that I could stop worrying at will, postpone worry, or actually decide when and how long I would worry—it became much easier to engage in rational planning sessions. In these sessions, I could prioritize concerns, determine which issues I could actually do something about, put my energies into active problem-solving and decision-making, then dismiss worries regarding things over which I had no control. There's only so much we can do to organize and plan for the future. Really, all we can do is our best at any given time. Thus, I recommend "Cleve's Paradoxical Principle of Power and Surrender": Use your power to struggle, scheme, strategize, plan, decide, and work. Once you have done all you can and it's out of your hands, let go! No amount of caring or worry will change the course of something over which you have no control.

There are some people, though, who find that they are completely unable to "turn off" the worry process. But behavior modification practitioners report success with a technique called *thought-stopping*. To employ this tactic, you must learn to recognize the first signs of worry and interrupt your negative thought process immediately by shouting (perhaps at times only inwardly) "STOP!" The trick is to catch the negative thought process of worry when it first begins, before it has a chance to gather momentum.

But, over and above all of the techniques you can use to stop worrying, remember that life is a *process* that will always include problems. Live with each problem as a transient, temporary bother, a source of ongoing worry and anxiety, or as an opportunity for learning to deal more effectively with whatever life has to offer. Above all, steer clear of my old maxim: *"There's nothing to fear but life itself!"*

21.

Confront Your Past

"We cannot change the past, but we can interpret it differently, respond to it differently, and choose to make it a positive force in the present."

To live fully and productively in the present, we must learn to appropriately remember, interpret, and use the past in our lives. This is an important skill to learn, because the way people *choose* to view and use the past in their present lives ultimately affects the extent to which they are depression-prone. The way people relate to their past can also enhance or undermine their appreciation of the present. Some people have only dim recall of the past and rarely relate to feelings tied to earlier experiences in their lives. (This is not to say, however, that they have not been shaped by those experiences.) Other people are actively and frequently in touch with the past. It seems to me that many depression-prone people tend to regret, become upset or depressed over, or even *indulge* in past guilts, longing, privations, or traumas.

If you are depression-prone, it is vital to assess the various negative effects your parents or a painful past may have had on your childhood. Keep in mind that you are not responsible for having parents who may have been demanding, rejecting, inconsistent, or insecure at a time when you were vulnerable and defenseless. And you are not responsible for creating within yourself the resulting scars, fears, and self-doubts that can deeply affect your current feelings and behavior.

The past cannot be relived or changed as you "replay" it in your mind. Actually, grieving, regretting, resenting, keeping bitter memories of the past alive, or continuing to feel shame or guilt about events of the past will only maintain a *bridge* to an unhappy past. It seems that one reason people keep a painful past alive is to avoid or distract themselves from a fearful or uncertain present. Clutching the past gives a person something tangible to wallow in and brood about. And, of course, one cannot *do* anything about the past—and that makes it safe! The present, however, is another matter. The present isn't nearly as safe as the past, for in it lies the potential for change and the challenge for a better future. But some people find the prospects of change and challenge so threatening, they actively seek ways to avoid dealing with them. In the meantime, they risk nothing by wasting their time brooding over people and events of the past—elements of their lives they absolutely cannot change.

A common way to indulge in and thereby remain stuck in the past is by playing the *"If Only"* game. For example, five years after the death of her father, an elderly woman continues to torment herself with this brooding reflection: *"If only* I had been a better daughter." Two years after a divorce from his wife, a middle-aged man continues to voice his self-doubts: *"If only* I had tried to work things out with her." *"If only"* we had been . . . kinder, firmer, more foresightful, more loving, more assertive, less demanding, less selfish, and on and on. Ironically, many people frequently regret or long for a past that may have been intolerable at the time and offered far fewer opportunities for positive change than does the present.

But pay attention to the past when it sweeps over you. Your perception of the past can give you hints not only about what you *might have done*, but also about what you *can do* now. It can also serve to suggest what might be missing in the present. These messages of the past, however, will become obscured if you *indulge* in the past and use the "lost opportunities" it may represent to punish yourself in the present.

Perpetual indulgence in the *"If Only"* process can keep a person stuck for years, blocking growth rather than encouraging or enhancing it. When you think about it, very few opportunities are "once-in-a-lifetime" events. It is quite possible that more realistic and satisfying opportunities exist in the present. Guard against immersing yourself in the past to the degree that you immobilize yourself in the present. People *make* their opportunities by assertively seeking them out and living life with the assumption that it contains endless possibilities if only they are open to seeing them, then acting upon them.

When people feel good about themselves and things are going well in their lives, they are more likely to fully engage in and enjoy the present. But when people are depressed and feeling bad about themselves, they tend to look to the past with regret and/or great longing. A person may say, *"I'm not happy now, but I realize that I've never been happy."* Or conversely, *"If only things were as they used to be."* Well, things aren't as they used to be—and they never can be!

There is no reason to avoid, repress, or conceal your past from yourself or others. Feel free to sympathize with yourself—if you want to—for lacking in some areas, for having scars and "hangups," and perhaps for having to expend more energy in dealing with insecurities than people you perceive had more wholesome, secure and/or privileged childhoods. But remember this: few people are damaged so completely by negative childhoods that their psychological equipment is totally dysfunctional. *Never doubt your capacity to assume more responsibility for yourself—for your own feelings and actions, for your own future—than you are presently assuming!*

Most people can justifiably place much of the responsibility for how they developed *up to a certain point in their lives* on their parents, their upbringing, their abilities and innate limitations, and/or on the context in which they were raised. But then, when people reach a certain age, they are mature enough and most of them have the necessary intellectual and psychological equipment to begin to assume responsibility for themselves. If you're an adult, one thing is clear: it's a cop-out to spend time and energy rationalizing current self-defeating behaviors by blaming parents, teachers, siblings, and a traumatic past. To use the past to justify your problems in the present serves only to "confirm" and reinforce your feelings of helplessness and passivity. The game of blaming the present on the past also arms you with excuses for not assuming responsibility for yourself and for continuing to avoid—and therefore not confront and alter—what you are and what you're doing in your current life.

How we remember, interpret, and experience the past is, to a great extent, determined by our feelings about ourselves, other people, and the world around us. For instance, if I feel happy about myself and my life in the present, I can look to the past and say that having had a neurotic father and a dysfunctional family life "deepened" me, made me more self-aware and growth-oriented, and helped me understand other people better. If, on the other hand, I feel unhappy and dissatisfied in the present, I can look to the past and declare that having had a neurotic father and a dysfunctional family life damaged me irreparably, making me incomplete and incapable of dealing with current crises and that, furthermore, these facts of my past will continue to have a negative influence on me, making me miserable for the rest of my life. Both these viewpoints are *interpretations* of the same past! Thus, one day we can use traumatic past experiences to torment and depress ourselves, justify current misery, and excuse ourselves for not assuming responsibility for our own behaviors and feelings. Then, the next day, we can use the very same traumatic past experiences to accomplish a number of things: gain new insights into ourselves and our relationships; congratulate ourselves for progressing as far as we have despite troubled beginnings; gain awareness of our current blind spots; and develop objectives and goals for aspects of ourselves that perhaps need to be examined further and changed.

It is clearly self-defeating to hang on to the past and in it find excuses and "justifications" for not growing in the present. On the other hand, to *reject* or deny your past is to reject or deny an important part of yourself. You can examine and learn from your past, using it to gain insight into who you are and how you feel and function *now* by examining where you've been. With a clear understanding of the past, you can begin to see current blind spots, perceptual distortions, inappropriate attitudes, repetitive, self-defeating behaviors, and the characteristics of depression-proneness.

Feelings of the past tend to remain active and potent in the present when people actively repress, deny or avoid painful experiences, or when they choose to use the painful experiences of the past as a payoff of some sort in the present (sympathy from others; an excuse for continuing to act helpless). A person might say, for example, that he or she is unable to reach out to others because of past hurts or because a painful and deprived childhood left him or her lacking in social skills. But that proclamation is more accurately an excuse for not reaching out to others in the present because of a fear of being hurt or for not being willing to take risks and to learn and practice social skills. Some people carry feelings of the past with them in the present because they have perpetuated the *conditions* that elicited the feelings in the first place. For example, a person may feel emotionally deprived because of a mother who rejected him or her, but that person then maintains those feelings of emotional deprivation in the present by maintaining emotional distance from others.

Of course, it's impossible to rewrite the past, deleting "expletives" and rearranging scenes, characters, dialogue, and outcomes. But many unfinished issues from the past can be put together in the present. Many of the things you didn't say or do can be said or done now. You can make a "contract" with yourself now to behave and live differently from the way you may have lived and behaved in the past. If past regrets, resentments, and grievances are still affecting you, they are affecting you in the present—and therefore can and must be *dealt* with in the present. Work to become more aware of how feelings from your past are interfering with your current life. *We cannot change the past, but we can interpret it differently, respond to it differently, and choose to make it a positive force in the present.*

Confronting your past also involves learning to grow through your losses. As we become adults, we "put away the things of childhood" and assume adult accountabilities. We also lose the sense of being taken care of by others. There are gains and losses with the passage of time in each stage of the life cycle: In adolescence *we gain* a degree of maturity, freedom, and integration and *we lose* the security, protection, and simplicity of childhood. As a marriage continues, *we gain* new growth in companionship and commitment and *we lose* some of the freshness and romantic passion that characterized the relationship in its early stages. When a child leaves us to attend school for the first time, *we gain* some new freedom and *we lose* that child's absolute dependence upon us. Indeed, everyday events bring many different kinds of loss to our lives: when a dear friend moves out of town, when the old rocking chair breaks, when a very nice summer comes to an end, and when, because of a promotion, we have less contact with the "old gang."

It is natural, healthy, and *necessary* for us to grieve over the loss of things, people, and situations that have been important to us. Generally, if you give yourself permission to mourn losses and refrain from criticizing yourself for grieving, you will eventually heal. Denying or suppressing the reality of loss or attempting to escape the feelings of loss through compulsive activity are techniques that only serve to postpone or disrupt the grieving process. Grief not experienced and expressed may "hang on" and actually expand within, eventually becoming unmanageable, possibly taking the form of severe depression. Grief cannot be rushed or pushed, either. You must be patient and accept the natural need to grieve on your own terms and in your own time. Psychiatrist and author David Viscott suggests that people confront their losses very directly. [1] For example, if you know or fear that you are about to experience a loss, you might figure out what may occur and devise a plan to help you cope with the loss. If you are hurting because of a loss, you have to go through the pain *and* try to keep from losing more than is necessary. If you are still angry over a previous loss, you should confront that anger and accept it now.

By fully experiencing a significant loss, you learn its "dimensions"—its breadth and depth in your life—and thus have a clearer understanding of its impact on you and what you must do to deal with it and get on with your life. However, you must first experience the many ramifications of the loss, noting all the areas of your life—the "nooks and crannies"—that may be affected by it. Grieving can actually become a positive growth experience, for when you are forced to say goodbye to someone or something and allow yourself to feel the vulnerability, frustration, anger, and loneliness that come with loss, you may get in touch with deeper levels of yourself. You may discover other areas to be examined, re-evaluated, changed, and renewed. You may even view a trauma later as an experience that strengthened you and helped you become a more complete person.

I once worked with a 38-year-old married woman named Jane, who came in for counseling because she'd been having difficulty sleeping and was unable to concentrate. As Jane talked about her life in vague, general terms, I caught sparks of energy and an interesting sense of humor emerging occasionally from an other-

wise low-key, rather vacant rambling about life in general. I suspected that the onset of Jane's depression was relatively recent.

As usual, when I listen to a person who is dealing with loss,
I sensed in Jane a kind of fragility and I, myself, felt vaguely sad
and heavy as we talked. When I asked her if she'd recently experienced any losses—for example, the death of a friend or relative—she initially responded that she hadn't. Then she suddenly
remembered that an uncle of hers had died a month or so earlier.
But except for very few visits with him, she'd hardly known him
at all. I decided to trust my feelings and play detective. We subsequently went over her current life very carefully. What
emerged was a coincidental series of occurrences reflecting
"mini-losses." I felt that no single one of these losses would have
been sufficient to trigger a depression.

But it turned out that even though Jane hardly knew her
uncle, he was the much older and favorite brother of her de-
ceased mother. In fact, after Jane's mother died, this uncle had
purchased the house in which Jane had grown up. At the time of
his death, her uncle was the only family member still living in her
hometown. On Jane's infrequent visits back to her hometown,
she had stayed with this uncle. And she remembered saying to
herself upon hearing of his death: "Well, there won't be any reason for me to go back to Bayville again." Though she only visited
her hometown a few times after her mother's death, she'd had a
happy childhood and enjoyed growing up there. The death of
this uncle—her last surviving relative—made it "unnecessary"
for her to visit the town anymore. And now, all of the relatives
that had been around during her happy childhood were gone.
At some level, her uncle's death seemed to cut Jane off from her
roots. Quite literally, she "couldn't" go home again.

Because her past had taken on considerable significance for
Jane, I suspected that her difficulty with and repression of the
loss might have something to do with things that were presently
missing in her life. As we examined her current life, we discovered that a good friend with whom she'd had almost daily contact for a long period of time had recently married a man with
two children. Although Jane and this friend maintained contact
with each other, things weren't the same as they'd been before.
The phone conversations were a little rushed, and her friend was
getting considerable support from her new husband and was,
therefore, less in need of conversation with Jane. And since Jane
had no children herself, she had some difficulty relating to her
friend's new and demanding roles as wife and mother. About the

same time her best friend got married, Jane's husband took a part-time job. Although the job was not particularly stressful, it meant some reduction in their quality time together because he was busier and somewhat distracted.

I was surprised how quickly Jane moved from insight to behavior change. First, dismayed by her apparent over-dependence on her friend, Jane quickly moved to re-establish several other friendships that she'd been neglecting in recent years. Second, with her husband's cooperation, the two of them found more time for each other within their busier schedules. They began getting up earlier in the morning to have a leisurely breakfast together; they made lunch dates on a regular basis. And then, Jane's newly married friend began to call her more frequently. She told Jane that she missed contact with her and that her life was beginning to settle down. She had established herself as a stepmother and was beginning to find the role less time-consuming than she had at first. Now she needed time off from her family responsibilities and time with her old friend, Jane.

These changes alone made Jane feel better, but she decided to do something else as well. Through an exploration of current feelings about her childhood, she decided that a solid connection with her past provided her with a kind of personal continuity and connection with herself. She determined that memories of her happy childhood provided her with a reassuring sense of security and confidence in her current life. Times when she felt anxious or self-doubting as an adult, she'd simply reflect back on some wonderful childhood experience and say to herself, "With that solid background, I should be able to handle almost anything!" By touching base with the foundation of her own emotional health, Jane was able to confront her life with renewed confidence and strength.

This realization of the continued importance of her childhood and family history motivated Jane to re-establish connections with her past, a past she had started to neglect. She drove to Bayville alone, and for three days casually explored and rediscovered forgotten details of her childhood territory. She visited the school she attended as a child; she also visited the house that she grew up in and excitedly showed the older couple living there the "secret" passageway in the sub-basement, a cave at the end of the property, and a wild strawberry patch the couple knew nothing about. Coincidentally (or was it?) the older woman now living in Jane's childhood home had known Jane's mother in grade school and they talked at length about her mother and the town.

Jane learned and re-learned many things about the area. She'd also brought her high school yearbook with her to Bayville and actually found that a few old friends still lived there. With one of these childhood friends, she visited a high school teacher who had long since retired, then hiked to a lake where they used to swim as children. To this day, I think Jane still has vivid memories of that visit and of the "lost" memories recovered and enhanced by her journey.

On many occasions, I have suggested to people I'm counseling that they look through old family albums and perhaps even return to their roots through a visit to their hometowns. Sometimes I make these suggestions when unresolved issues emerge in counseling. Since Jane's childhood had been so happy and she was doing so well, I didn't immediately think of suggesting such a visit. Jane's initiative in undertaking the journey herself underlines two important guidelines: *Each person is an expert on himself or herself, and if that person listens at a deeper level, he or she can sense what is needed to resolve issues and reinforce existing strengths. Regardless of the expertise and insight of the therapist, a person must ultimately decide what is best for him or her.* A therapist is a consultant and guide, not a guru, sage, seer, or final authority on anyone but himself or herself.

In Chinese, the word "crisis" has two meanings: danger and opportunity. Dealing effectively with a crisis that accompanies loss may result in mobilizing yourself and changing your life so that it becomes more meaningful and you become more resilient. There's a difficult psychological state recognized these days that carries with it this potential for positive evaluation and change: the mid-life crisis that usually affects men and women sometime between the mid-thirties and fifty. At this time of life, perhaps more than any other, a person is apt to review the past, re-examine the meaning of his or her life, confront mortality, and work through the "unfinished business" of earlier years. Depression—perhaps even severe depression— sometimes accompanies this crisis state, which may last from several months to several years. Especially at this time of life, neglected or abandoned hopes for individual accomplishment may be renewed and suitably shaped to accommodate reality.

One of the most difficult "losses" we must discover and deal with, quite commonly at mid-life, is what psychologist Helen DeRosis and writer Victoria Pellegrino call our "Lost Dream." [2] We all have certain dreams that may have been all but forgotten on a conscious level, but that continue to influence us. At age seven, we may have wanted to grow up to be firefighters, doctors, cowboys or cowgirls. Then, at the age of twelve, perhaps we wanted to be astronauts, teachers, or major league baseball players. In our early years we probably "knew" that we were special and, deep inside, we had dreams, likely spun from unachievable goals and ideals. Hopefully, out of the raw material of hopes, dreams, and values, in later adolescence and early adulthood we were able to weave the right amount of reality, fantasy, and ambition into a reasonably practical "dream" that reflected realistic goals and was based on genuine potential and an accurate self-image. We had to catch a glimpse of "the possible" to fashion the short- and long-term goals that, if achieved, would transform our dreams into reality. To do this, however, we needed to have a fairly accurate assessment of our potential, based on actual capabilities and skills, as well as a set of *self-expectations* consistent with that potential.

Although self-expectations are made up of cultural ideals, popular stereotypes, a degree of idealism, and also the expectations of others, in the final analysis they are *self-expectations*. The parameters of our scope of choices must not be set directly by parents and grandparents or any "significant other." If we allow the expectations of others to determine our own personal goals, we may end up in the "wrong niche" for a lifetime because we aren't meeting *our own* needs and expectations. Yet, if we reject outright—without adequately working through—the expectations of the "significant others" in our lives, we may someday feel vague but pervasive dissatisfaction with ourselves. We will therefore be vulnerable to self-doubts and guilt whenever we meet with difficulties.

Things get a bit more complicated when we recognize that our self-expectations may have been based on an awareness of our real, innate abilities but that we revolted against having anyone else set our goals for us. And the adolescent or adult who vigorously broke with the *person* of the parent may experience extreme disappointment years later, when small failures make him or her vulnerable to painful introspection and "if only" thinking. Frequently, vague existential ruminations about the meaninglessness of a job, a relationship, or an entire life may be rooted in feelings of failure for not meeting parental expectations contained in one's lost dream.

Many people struggle for almost a lifetime with overriding discontentment related to their recognition that they will never achieve their earlier dreams. If years go by and these discontented people make no real, sustained effort to develop themselves, their grief over failed ambitions may take the form of severe depression. Everyone has a different lost dream; the dream itself is unique and always connected with one's self-image. When anxiety over conflicting or failed shoulds becomes too painful, it is often masked by depression. But in the subconscious mind, these goals and expectations endure, even when we're not consciously aware of them.

What can we do about our lost dreams now? First, we must explore what the dream involves, in detail—including all the conflicting shoulds that may be woven into it. Second, we must determine what part of the dream is really *our own*. Third, we must take a realistic look at the price of trying to achieve the dream *for ourselves now*, not to satisfy a significant person of our past (or present). We may discover that attempting to fulfill our lost dream now, belatedly, may require giving up some of the things we like and need: maintenance of a particular lifestyle, extra time with family, contact with friends.

> As an example of past dream/present reality, let's consider Kate. An only child, Kate was expected by her ambitious and demanding father to become a competent and prominent trial lawyer, as well as a good wife and mother. (Her father may have needed not only to bask in her professional success, but also to see her give to her husband and family what his wife and parents perhaps failed to give to him.) Having fulfilled half of her father's plan for her, Kate began thinking again about a halted "glamorous" legal career as her children grew older—particularly when she felt depressed and housebound.
>
> Kate's father still wants her to be a lawyer, but does *she* really want to be one? When people are depressed, they tend to believe that only the achievement of lofty goals will truly satisfy them; these goals, of course, seem well beyond reach when they're depressed. But what if they weren't depressed? Would

they feel less compelled to do something magnificent? Kate asked
herself these questions, then decided that while still very interested in law and pursuing a legal career of some kind, she really
didn't need or want to become an exceptional trial lawyer, particularly at the present time. She decided that being an excellent
paralegal could satisfy her needs IF she could abandon her father's unrealistic, contradictory, and ego-inflating dreams for her.
Putting the dream into realistic perspective, attending law school
is not practical for Kate right now. Aside from the time and energy required for law school, Kate does not feel she's in a position
to invest money in a lengthy and expensive legal education at this
time.

But, Kate has decided that as she continues to manage her
household, she will begin considering practical steps toward the
realization of an appropriate future goal that is consistent with
her wants and needs. Taking an occasional course in law and
reading law books may keep her interest in law active and help to
alter her lost dream in favor of a more realistic future dream. She
feels that part-time work in a law office might help her get a taste
for what she would find enjoyable and challenging; the nature of
the work would also give her a welcome relief from household
chores. In the future, she might even go to law school—if that is
her choice at the time. Through careful attention to her own
needs and desires, Kate has been able to recapture and alter her
lost dream.

Your lost dream—if you still find it alluring and consistent with your
needs and desires—may be altered to fit your present circumstances.
You can also opt to view your lost dream not as a hopeless prospect,
but as a temporarily postponed goal that can be worked on in the
present, even if it is worked on in less-than-ideal or limited ways.
Working on your lost dream requires attention to goal-setting,
another important long-range technique in combating depression-
proneness.

References

1. Viscott, David S. *Risking*. New York: Simon and Schuster, 1979.

2. DeRosis, Helen A., and Victoria Pellegrino. *The Book of Hope/How
   Women Can Overcome Depression*. New York: Bantam, 1977.

22.

Revise Internal Messages

"Words don't merely reflect reality, they help to create it."

For better or worse, a person's self-image is supported and reinforced by words and sentences (self-talk) as well as by mental imagery. During our waking hours, words, sentences, and mental pictures flow through our minds almost constantly. While these internal sentences and images seem to be spontaneous and automatic, anyone can gain control over them; with practice, they can be converted into powerfully positive forces in our lives. Revision of these internal words and statements, along with utilization of positive mental imagery can bring positive change and progress in virtually every area of life.

Shakti Gawain, workshop leader and proponent of visualization techniques, maintains that we attract into our lives whatever we think about most, believe in strongly, expect on the deepest level, and/or imagine most vividly. [1] If we are generally positive in attitudes, expecting and envisioning productivity, pleasure, satisfaction, and happiness, we attract people and create situations that align with those positive expectations. On the other hand, if we're negative, insecure, or anxious, we tend to attract negative feelings, experiences, situations, and people. A person with a negative self-image tends to view the whole world—other people as well as himself or herself—in negative terms.

Self-image has so much to do with how successful we are in achieving our goals. Our interests, values, feelings, behaviors, abilities, potentials, and goals are often *consistent with* and also *limited by* a self-image that may have been narrowed by criticism, negative feedback, and low self-esteem that had its origins in childhood. Self-image sets *boundaries* for accomplishments. It's really very simple: we are what we expect to be, and we do what we expect to do.

People who have the most difficulty with depression often have a self-image that includes a belief that they are unable to handle that depression. Changing a negative self-image, then, is a vital prerequisite for dealing with depression effectively.

In my work with depression-prone people, I have found that many of them had parents, teachers, or other significant people in their lives who in some way undermined their confidence in themselves and, more specifically, their abilities to deal with challenges. These people then learned to perpetuate the self-doubt they grew up with by continuing to undermine their own self-confidence with a constant internal flow of negative statements. I've watched people throw themselves into a panic over their blue feelings with this brand of negative talk: *"This is terrible." "This is awful." "I can't possibly handle it." "I'll never break out of these horrible feelings."* And then this negative talk is compounded with comments like: *"I'm overwhelmed." "I'm overloaded." "I just can't cope."*

As people repeat old, time-worn commands already programmed into their nervous systems, they automatically activate patterns of negative response. The words become a kind of self-hypnotic induction. The relative power of negative self-hypnosis may seem a little far-fetched, until we look at case studies involving hypnosis. While in a truly hypnotic state, a person is so open and vulnerable to suggestion that words can actually by-pass the conscious mind, go directly to the nervous system, and essentially become reality there. For example, given the right conditions and the willingness of the subject involved, the subject might actually *feel* very cold and even begin to shiver when a hypnotist suggests that he or she is in the Far North. Subjects have been known to recoil in pain or even develop blisters when touched with a pencil that the hypnotist has suggested is red-hot.

Most of us don't fully realize that *words have power. Words don't merely reflect reality, they help to* create *it.* But we misinterpret reality and undermine ourselves with statements like this: *"I'll never be successful." "Why do bad things always happen to me?" "Why do other people have all the luck?" "It just won't work."*

Considering the power of words and hypnotic suggestion in light of everyday situations, think for a moment about the effects of sitting down to study for a test and repeating to yourself over and over again, "*I'll never understand this.*" Or, consider the effects of calling a friend on the telephone to ask her to do something with you, all the while saying to yourself, "*She's probably busy and won't want to get together with me anyway.*" Or, consider the effects of saying to yourself as soon as you wake up in the morning, "*I'm so tired; I know I'll never get anything accomplished today.*" Most everyone has, at one time or another, reacted to his or her everyday reality with negative statements like: "*It's a pain in the neck to do the laundry.*" "*I'm sick and tired of this cold weather.*" Remember that the brain is no *subtle* interpreter of such statements. When you say "*It's a big headache to clean the garage,*" think of your brain responding like this: "*So the guy wants a headache? Okay, one headache coming up!*"

To counteract the depressing effects of all the negative sentences you've stored in your mind, strive to replace them with *positive* statements. How to do this? First of all, try to become more aware of specific elements of your own negative programming. The more aware you are of individual negative statements that flow through your mind, the easier it may be to convert these statements to positive ones. As a matter of fact, each negative statement can be turned into a powerful *affirmation*. Simply replace deeply ingrained negatives, powerfully "hypnotic" statements, with positive suggestions and commands such as: "*I can do it.*" "*It will all work out.*" "*I'm strong; I can handle it.*" "*Take it easy.*" "*Keep cool.*" And "*Go with the flow.*" Following are some positive coping statements and affirmations that you can substitute for all-too-common negative statements:

"*I can't do this.*"
    coping statement: "*I can do this effectively.*"

"*I feel overwhelmed.*"
    coping statements: "*Take one thing at a time.*"
                       "*I can only do the best I can.*"
                       "*I can move slowly and systematically toward completion.*"

"*I feel harried and confused.*"
    coping statement: "*I am relaxed and clear-headed.*"

"*I'm stupid and incompetent.*"

affirmation: "*I'm bright and effective.*"

"*I'm selfish and self-centered.*"

affirmation: "*I'm self-nurturing and giving.*"

"I'm hopelessly neurotic."

affirmations: "*I'm whole and centered.*"

"*I'm healthy in mind and body.*"

"*I'm sensitive and compassionate.*"

The use of positive coping statements is one of the techniques I successfully used to combat my own past tendency to get colds. As I considered the succession of colds I'd had in a relatively short period of time, I noticed a pattern that is probably familiar to many people: I'd push myself to accomplish certain tasks and goals, then develop a cold and ultimately take a few days off for much-needed rest. As I traced the progression of specific experiences leading up to an illness, a predictable chain of events became clear to me: When I noticed I was beginning to feel tired and developing some early symptoms of a cold, I'd feel a little disappointed and blue and say to myself, "*Oh nuts; I'll bet I'm coming down with another cold.*" Sensing that illness was then inevitable, I could almost *feel* my body giving up and surrendering. Even though the illness was coming at an inconvenient time and I'd say to myself, "*I hope I don't get a cold,*" I'd still have a strong sense that the inevitable was about to happen. And sure enough, in a day or two, I'd have a cold.

After reading about illness styles and the important role that suggestion plays in perpetuating negative habits, I decided I no longer wanted to have colds. If I felt that I needed a rest, I would slow down and enjoy a rest as soon as possible rather than "earning" a rest by pushing too hard, then collapsing. And I had the belief that when I replaced my negative feelings and statements with positive ones, I could positively affect the outcome. So I experimented a bit: each time I felt overly tired and that a cold was coming on, I would work toward being completely relaxed and centered, then I'd say these words to myself: "*I'm fantastically healthy!*" "*I'm indestructible!*" "*I'm invincible!*" I'd stir up feelings of being robust, powerful, in charge, determined, and I'd focus on an image of my body glowing and pulsating with energy. Then I'd slow down, rest, and increase my intake of infection-combating vitamins. And I'd frequently call up these positive statements, feelings, and energies. To my delight, I found that these procedures alone—rest, slowing down, positive words, statements, and imagery—worked for me about 95 percent of the time. More than 5 percent of the time, however, my attempts to combat illness in this way were only halfhearted.

When I felt myself in some way "giving in" to impending illness I wondered if at some level, I didn't actually have a *will* to get sick. At those times, I learned to challenge myself directly, *"You want to get sick, don't you?"* Some of the time, I'd have to admit to myself that perhaps I *did* want to get sick. So I'd explore the reasons and pay-offs in doing so: What am I avoiding? How am I neglecting my own needs? Why do I need to make myself physically miserable? What function is the illness serving in my life at this time? Whether or not I come up with any good answers to these questions, they usually result in my renewed ability to repond with an emphatic "No" to the question *"Do I want to get sick?"* If the "no" feels strong and decisive to me and reverberates at a deeper level as well, the coping statements seem to take on added power and I really begin to *feel* that I am indestructible. At that point, I have decided at all levels that I *don't want to get sick.*

Fending off minor illnesses and getting through stressful situations is one thing, but changing self-image is another. Most people question how simple statements can really be effective in changing self-image. There is considerable evidence from research on hypnosis that simple statements and commands find their way to one's subconscious mind more readily than do complicated concepts and directives. An example of a simple but positive coping statement: *"Today, I will be relaxed,"* instead of *"Today, I won't fall apart."* Instead of saying *"I'll never remember the details of this subject"* before an exam, you could say to yourself *"I am clear-headed and intelligent."* Before a difficult confrontation, you could say to yourself, *"I am straightforward and confident"* rather than saying *"I'm defensive and frightened."*

Even if you don't completely believe the positive statement, the process of repeating it will tend to produce a calming effect in that your subconscious mind will hear the statement and will subsequently be influenced by it in positive ways. Positive coping statements can be formulated to reinforce a new self-image. Some examples of such affirmations are as follows: *"I accept myself totally, here and now!" "I love myself just as I am." "I am kind and generous." "I have everything I need to enjoy my life."*

Consider the likelihood that at first you might resist or reject positive statements and subconsciously negate them as well. Sondra Ray, author of *I Deserve Love/How Affirmations Can Guide You to Personal Fulfillment* has refined the use of *affirmation statements*; in doing so, she has identified techniques that help people anticipate and overcome objections and resistance to positive statements. Ray suggests that one of the easiest and most effective ways to use the positive affirmation technique while making allowances for subconscious objections is to write each affirmation ten to twenty times per day on a sheet of paper, leaving space on the right-hand side for responses to this statement. After you write the affirmation on the left-hand side of the page, record on the right-hand side any negative thoughts, reactions, resistances, fears, objections, or questions that come to mind. As you keep writing the affirmation over and over again, observe how your responses on the right-hand side change. [2]

A client of mine shared her responses to the affirmation statement: *"I deserve happiness."*

Affirmation	Response
I, Mary, deserve happiness.	
I, Mary, deserve happiness.	
I, Mary, deserve happiness.	*What right do I have to be happy?*
I, Mary, deserve happiness.	*I'm not a good person.*
I, Mary, deserve happiness.	
I, Mary, deserve happiness.	
I, Mary, deserve happiness.	*I deserve to be punished.*
I, Mary, deserve happiness.	*I haven't earned happiness.*
I, Mary, deserve happiness.	*I'm afraid to be happy.*
I, Mary, deserve happiness.	*If I was happy for a while, then lost that happiness, it would hurt too much.*

I, Mary, deserve happiness.	*I deserve to hate myself!*
I, Mary, deserve happiness.	
I, Mary, deserve happiness.	
I, Mary, deserve happiness.	*If only I could believe it.*
I, Mary, deserve happiness.	*If only I could forgive myself.*
I, Mary, deserve happiness.	*Is that possible?*
I, Mary, deserve happiness.	*Could I do it?*
I, Mary, deserve happiness.	*Do I really?*

This simple exercise serves to illustrate that positive thinking alone isn't enough. Sometimes old negative thoughts continue to undermine results, even when you're no longer consciously aware of them. This ongoing effect of negative thinking probably occurs because the conscious mind has readjusted, but the subconscious mind has not. But whenever contradictory thoughts arise, try not to put your time and energy into denying them or trying to hold them back. Consciously trying to combat or suppress these thoughts may give them a power they don't otherwise have. Just let these negative statements briefly flow through your consciousness, then promptly return to your positive statements.

A powerful affirmation will quickly summon up virtually all the negative thoughts and feelings stored in your subconscious mind; you will therefore have the opportunity to discover for yourself just what it is that's standing between you and your goals. Furthermore, in rewriting the positive affirmation over and over, deeper conflicts can be resolved by repeating the affirmation until the negative thought has been *replaced* by a positive thought in your subconscious mind. In the process of doing this, you may uncover some negative decisions you made or some erroneous beliefs you formulated earlier in your life. As I see it, there are several guidelines for formulating affirmations:

1. *Phrase affirmations in the present tense, rather than the future tense.* In other words, state an affirmation as if it's a condition that already exists. Instead of saying "I *will get a very good job,*" say "I *now have a very good job.*" Now, I'm not advocating delusion or denial. I'm advancing the theory that before something becomes an objective reality, it is created on a mental plane.

2. Phrase affirmations in positive language. Affirm what you *do* want, not what you *don't* want. Instead of saying, "I *no longer wake up tired in the morning,*" phrase it this way: "*I now wake up refreshed and full of energy in the morning.*"

3. Brief and uncomplicated affirmations are generally most effective; wordy, abstract affirmations lose their emotional impact. An affirmation should consist of clear, concise statements that convey strong feelings. Actually, the more feeling a statement conveys, the stronger an impression it will make on your subconscious mind.

4. When utilizing an affirmation, try to create a belief that it can be experienced and is therefore true. Temporarily—for a few minutes at least—suspend your doubts and hesitations and put your full mental and emotional energy into the statement. Then, whenever doubts, objections, resistances, or negative thoughts get in the way, go back to writing your responses in the right-hand column for a time.

Working on too many things at once, however, may confuse your internal programming and overload your subconscious mind. Thus, it is best to attempt no more than one or two new affirmations (internal sentences) at a time. Work on the affirmations until they begin to effect change, then gradually introduce new affirmations.

It *is* possible to move toward the core of subconscious feelings, beliefs, and attitudes and work to improve your perception of yourself and the world. And what a powerful difference a positive self-perception can make in all our lives. Consider the words of writer Ken Keyes: "*A loving person lives in a loving world. A hostile person lives in a hostile world. Everyone you meet is your mirror.*"[3]

References

1. Gawain, Shakti. *Creative Visualizations.* Mill Valley, Calif.: Whatever Publishing, 1978.

2. Ray, Sondra. *I Deserve Love/How Affirmations Can Guide You to Personal Fulfillment*. Milbrae, Calif.: Les Femmes Publishing, 1976.

3. Keyes, Ken. *Handbook of Higher Consciousness*. California: Living Love Center, 1973.

23.

Practice Positive Mental Imagery

". . . if you deeply believe that you can achieve a goal and you can clearly imagine it as well, you're already halfway there."

Internal visualization techniques can be very effective in combating depression-proneness. Perhaps one of the most powerful methods for changing one's self-image consists of pairing affirmations with *vivid mental images.* One of the early proponents of this technique was Maxwell Maltz, a prominent plastic surgeon and author. Maltz points out in his best-selling book *Psycho-Cybernetics* that the brain and nervous system constitute a "goal-striving mechanism" that operates automatically to achieve certain goals.[1] If we want to reach specific goals, we first must create a clear picture in our minds—*a goal picture*—upon which this automatic mechanism works. Maltz maintains that if this picture of ourselves and our behavior is clear, we will literally be *pulled* toward the accomplishment of our desired goal.

Thus, if you deeply believe that you can achieve a goal and you can clearly imagine it as well, you're already halfway there. This has been true in athletics, for example. For years, no one thought it was humanly possible to break the four-minute mile. And, for years, no one did. Then, soon after Roger Bannister broke that barrier in 1954, several other people did the same thing in fairly rapid succession. Today, athletes must run the mile in less than four minutes just to *qualify* for some races. Just imagine—what used to be considered an impossible feat now is a minimum requirement for participation in some contests. Indeed, the very act of recognizing that something *is* possible helps to make it possible—so long as what is imagined is conceivably within the realm of attainment.

Research psychologist Alan Richardson demonstrated the power of mental imagery in a now-famous experiment conducted with high school basketball players.[2] Dr. Richardson divided the players into three groups: He asked the first group to refrain from practicing free-throw shots for a period of twenty days; he asked the second group to practice free-throw shots for an hour per day for a period of twenty days; he asked the third group to vividly *imagine* practicing free-throw shots for an hour per day for twenty days. He asked this last group to visualize throwing the ball correctly as clearly as possible. The individuals in this group were instructed to get the "feel" and sense of the proper body movements, as well as the correct way to shoot the ball. If the ball didn't go "into the basket," they were to correct for the error in their minds, then try again. This is what Richardson documented at the end of twenty days: the group that did not practice showed no improvement in their free-throw performance; the group that had practiced for an hour a day improved its overall performance by 24 percent; and individuals in the group that had "practiced" only in their minds—using mental imagery for an hour each day—improved by 23 percent!

How is it possible for the body to respond this way to mental imagery? Adelaide Bry, author and psychotherapist, reports that anatomists have discovered pathways between the parts of the brain where mental pictures are stored and the autonomic nervous system.[3] This system controls so-called "involuntary" activities such as digestion. These pathways link the autonomic nervous system and the pituitary gland and adrenal cortex. The end result is that a "picture" in our minds can have an impact on every cell in our bodies!

Furthermore, the nervous system does not respond to words and mental images in the same way that a computer might respond to words and mental images. For example, when we let our minds focus on a sad experience that has long since passed, we actually *relive* it through our imagination; we become sad or depressed all over again. When we imagine a favorite food, we *feel* hunger pangs and we begin to salivate. Even *imagining* a metaphor can create a physical reaction. Consider "Sliding down the razor blade of life"; think of having a tooth drilled without an anesthetic; remember the sound of chalk squeaking on a blackboard. We may shudder as if we're in pain at the very mention of such things. The nervous system responds to images *as if they were reality.* What we have, then, is a powerful tool with which to reprogram our nervous system, to create positive pictures and successful experiences to draw upon. Through mental imagery, we can change beliefs, feelings, and behavior as well as the image we hold of ourselves.

About seven years ago, I decided that I needed to lose fifty pounds. As I reviewed all of the factors contributing to my weight problem, I realized that I couldn't imagine being slim. Worse yet, I really liked being large, though at that time, I could have modeled circus tents! However, I did realize that my sub-conscious mind would be fighting me every step of the way if I didn't have a clear picture of an ideal body image that included slimness. I looked through magazines and finally found a picture of a man who had a build that I felt I could reasonably strive to attain. I recall saying to myself, I'd even be willing to give up Twinkies to have that "bod." At that time, I simply added this vis-ualization exercise to my weight-reduction program; in fact, I be-gan visualizing myself with that body for several sessions per day.

I used visualization in other ways as well. When I got tired of salads, I stopped eating them for a week. Subsequently, I be-gan to visualize myself devouring salads again with such orgiastic delight that I felt I should have a mirror on the kitchen ceiling! So, in a relatively short period of time, I redeveloped a taste for salads. Then, when I began imagining eating lots of greasy, fat-tening foods, I began feeling bloated and nauseous. I discovered that I actually could affect my food preference; using this visual-ization technique, I even found myself craving low-calorie foods from time to time!

But the power of mental imagery was driven home to me most clearly with a very subtle change—the source of which had temporarily evaded me. For two years, I had jogged two miles each day during my lunch hour. I didn't jog very fast. Actually, because of my excessive weight, I called it "the elephant walk." And when people asked me why I was fat even though I jogged each day, I jokingly told them—for lack of any other response—that I always ate while I jogged . . . and broke even. Anyway, for no apparent reason one day, I pushed myself to jog *more* than two miles. I didn't actually decide to jog the extra half mile, I just *did* it. After awhile, I found myself pushing to jog three miles per day. I found my behavior annoying; the jogging was taking up too much of my lunch hour. (Nevertheless, I continued to jog the extra distance and still jog about three miles each day.)

As I was reviewing my weight reduction program with a col-league and the important part that visualization played in it, I confessed my puzzlement over my seemingly irrational push to jog further. I said, "I don't know why I feel compelled to run further. My run no longer fits comfortably into my lunch hour slot." My colleague thought for a moment, then asked this: "What are you usually doing when you are visualizing yourself slim?" "Jogging!" I replied. Without realizing it, in my conscious mind I had been visualizing myself gracefully jogging in a slim body with a smile on my face. At some level, my subconscious mind formulated longer runs as a goal and provided me with the necessary motivation—almost a compulsion—to achieve that goal. By the time I discovered the source of my "compulsion," I had lost forty pounds, was jogging much faster, and was willing and able to fit a three-mile jog into my lunch break each day. *Why argue with success?!*

But until we learn to effectively practice and control mental imagery, this very powerful tool can actually work *against* us. (Left to its own, an imagination can run rampant, with disastrous consequences.) For example, if we consciously dwell on past errors and feel guilty about them, *the error or the failure itself becomes the goal that is consciously held in our imagination and memory.* And the error is reinforced over and over again by dredging up and vividly reliving the painful experience. Therefore, we inadvertently *practice* the failure! We keep the feelings of failure, shame, and guilt alive and increase our *expectations* that negative things will happen again. If you have a tendency to think like a failure (or, more correctly, *imagine* like a failure), the first thing you might do is this: *begin to de-emphasize negative past experiences.* The minute you make the decision to stop giving power to the negatives in your past, those past negatives will lose their powerful grip on you. Assume that you do, in fact, have certain powers and talents. You can use these abilities if you go ahead and *act as if* you have them, instead of behaving in halfhearted, tentative ways.

In order to utilize the power of mental imagery to its fullest, you might try practicing visualization at one of these two times: • upon awakening from a dream—while your imagery-making mental system (the one that produces dreams) is still active, or • just before sleep, when your conscious mechanisms are "off-guard" and you are more in touch with the flow of inner experience. Relax as completely as possible by using breathing, meditative, or other relaxation techniques. Picture yourself actually *possessing* some quality or *accomplishing* a task. Since your negative beliefs were formed by *thought* plus *feeling*, you will thus generate enough positive *emotions* and deep positive feelings so that your new thoughts and images will cancel out the old negative ones. Dwell on the positive images and go over them again and again in your mind. *This process is really quite similar to worrying—except that you have changed the goal from negative to positive!* It is essential, however, that you really *want* what you visualize and that you put your *will* and *energy* solidly behind your visualization. This means that you must be open and committed to doing whatever needs doing to accomplish what you truly want to accomplish.

José Silva, developer of mind control techniques, advances a set of guidelines to help ensure the achievement of a goal:

- You must *desire* that the imagined event take place.

- You must *believe* that the event can take place.

- You must *expect* the event to take place.[4]

Now, the first two elements in this set of guidelines are relatively simple and passive, but the third element—involving expectations—introduces some dynamics. It is possible to desire an event, believe it can take place, yet not really expect it to occur. You may *want* your boss to be pleasant, you may *know* that he has the capacity to be pleasant, but you still may be far removed from expecting him or her to be pleasant to you. Remember, if you really want something to happen, you must *expect* it to happen.

Remind yourself that your built-in "success mechanisms" must have a clear goal or target. This goal must be regarded as *already in existence*, right now, either in actual form or as potential. Before he even bought his first hotel, Conrad Hilton said that he had a clear image of himself sitting in a big office and running a chain of successful hotels. Similarly, many skilled golfers claim that *before* they actually swing the club, they vividly imagine swinging the club with ease and watching the ball glide toward the hole. This process of clearly imaging the accomplishment of a goal operates either by *steering* you to a goal already in existence or by helping you *discover* something already in existence. Think in terms of the *end result*. The *means whereby* will often take care of itself. For example, when Hilton was working as a hotel custodian, he probably didn't spend a lot of his time and energy worrying about the exact means by which he would accomplish his goal. If he had, he'd have been stuck— perhaps for years—wondering where in the world he'd ever find the money to buy all those hotels. Then he probably would have gone on to dismiss his dream as unrealistic.

Vivid goals help alert us to opportunities that are almost hidden, as well as to previously "nonexistent" possibilities. Also, when we carry positive, goal-seeking self-images around with us, other people may respond to us as if we are or will be successful. Sheer *intentionality* seems to create opportunities or otherwise helps us tap into the flow of opportunity in life.

How to use mental imagery in our daily lives? As vividly as you can, picture yourself doing something of real significance that you regard as a key to your success, but that you also see as a troublesome barrier of some kind. For instance, imagine yourself walking up to the front of a room to make a speech. Go through every detail of the presentation imaging a lively and interesting talk, an interested and responsive audience, and a positive outcome—applause, enthusiasm, and genuine praise. If anything can be improved upon, it can be practiced again and again in your mind. Fantasize a positive *process* as well as a positive *outcome*. Get a vivid "feel" for how it is to *attain* the goal in order to be successful. As you visualize yourself delivering the speech, maintain a relaxed, positive attitude toward the mental imagery exercises.

There is no "right" way to visualize. Some people close their eyes and see vividly and in technicolor in their "mind's eye." Others "see" shadowy images, but may or may not sense the experience in any other way. Some people visualize with their eyes open by looking at a blank wall and projecting the images out in front of themselves, as if they were watching a movie. Some people use the sensory modalities in addition to vision and hearing: touch, taste, smell. No one way seems to be universally more or less effective than any other. I'd suggest that you experiment with different methods to come up with one of your own or a combination of methods that work best for you.

The degree of vividness of the visualization itself doesn't seem to seriously alter the effectiveness of the mental imagery exercise. Effectiveness seems to be influenced more by the *completeness* of the experience. You are more likely to get good results with visualization if you do the following:

• *Relax deeply*, so that the affirmation and image bypass the conscious mind and become translated into neural impulses that are sent directly to the brain.

• *Set a specific goal* that you definitely want, are open and committed to, and will take advantage of opportunities to attain.

• *Create a clear mental picture*—as if your goal already exists—which includes details in all sensory modalities.

• *Pair the image with affirmation statements.*

• *Put positive feelings and energy into the image and affirmations* by stimulating enthusiasm and excitement.

• *Create a firm intention* for accomplishment of the goal, desiring, believing, and expecting the wanted change to take place.

If you are depression-prone, chances are good that you often picture yourself as a tired, stoop-shouldered person with head down, a pained look on your face, and an inner voice that mumbles over and over again, "*I'm a failure, I'm a failure.*" Yet, if you can get in touch with these negative sentences, convert them to positive self-statements and affirmations, and pair them with a positive yet potentially attainable image of yourself, you can replace a negative self-image with a positive self-image. We all have much more potential than we might even imagine. Limitations are *always* self-imposed. By giving free reign to your imagination, your self-image loses its rigidity and becomes flexible and open to the possible. If you can *imagine* and then truly *believe* that your potential is limitless, *it is limitless!*

Even your relationships can be altered in positive ways by changing your self-image from negative to positive and putting your new attitudes and responses into action. Ready to confront the interpersonal world? Then proceed to the next section, *Improving Your Interactions with Others.*

References

1. Maltz, Maxwell. *Psycho-Cybernetics*. New York: Essandess, 1960.

2. Richardson, Alan. *Mental Imagery*. London: Routledge and K. Paul, 1969. (Springer Publishing.)

3. Bry, Adelaide. *Visualizations*. New York: Barnes and Noble, 1978.

4. Silva, José. *The Silva's Mind Control Method*. New York: Simon and Schuster, 1977.

Improving Your Interactions
with Others

Relationships are, of course, vital for everyone, but they're particularly important in the lives of depression-prone people for two primary reasons:

• Caring relationships with others have, within them, a remarkable potential for helping the depressed person. They can provide a much-needed and dependable support system and they can also aid and comfort the depressed person as he or she works through personal and interpersonal issues that may have contributed to depression-proneness in the first place.

• Ongoing relationships—with family, friends, coworkers, and particularly life-partners—are frequently conflicted and, if not conducted properly, can actually trigger, aggravate, or prolong a depression. Relationships tie in so closely with depression because the ingredients of the relationship itself reflect, contain, and perpetuate deep, unresolved problems of the past.

In the four chapters that follow, I'll touch upon many of the basic issues in relationships that characterize or affect a depression-prone person's social sphere.

24.

Nurture Friendships

". . . self-acceptance is a prerequisite for genuine acceptance of others."

Whatever their basis—familial, intergenerational, same-sex, opposite sex, occupational, or neighborly—friendships, when they are working well, enhance life in relatively dependable and highly satisfying ways. Many depression-prone people, however, have difficulty forming and sustaining healthy relationships.

People who feel depressed would actually do well to distract themselves from their depression by reaching out to others. Unfortunately, however, depressed people are apt to be highly sensitive, vulnerable, and fearful of rejection. So, just at the time when they need people most, many depressed people remain alone. Understandably, isolation can actually intensify feelings of depression. But depressed people often rationalize their withdrawal from others by masking it as concern for others: *"I don't want to expose anyone to my bad feelings."* They assume that others will become just as "bummed out" as they feel, or they fear that people will judge them as harshly as they judge themselves. Oftentimes, clients tell me that they fear reaching out to their friends when they're down because those friends might feel uncomfortable or overwhelmed and turn away from them. When I ask these same clients how *they* would feel if friends told them they felt depressed and wanted to talk, the response of the depressed person is usually something like this: *"Oh, I'd be flattered! I'd appreciate their willingness to seek me out . . . But that's different!"*

So even though we're perfectly willing to comfort friends when they're feeling depressed, we somehow *assume* they'll feel differently toward us if and when *we're* down. We project our negative feelings about ourselves onto others, assuming they'll be just as disgusted with us as we are with ourselves. At that point, we simply don't realize that *we* are the people who are depressed, not the friends we're turning to.

Now, our depressions no doubt *concern* our friends, but not to the point of immobilizing them. In fact, I think that most of us would find that our friends would feel perfectly comfortable responding to us by simply saying "Let's talk about it," or "Let's go *do* something to take your mind off your troubles."

Paradoxically, it seems that when our need for people is most immediate and intense, we create the greatest distance between ourselves and others. Most of us are so afraid of appearing weak and needy; or we fear that we'll become too possessive and demanding, thus driving people away. Also, the more depressed and lonely we feel, the more we begin to believe that contact with others will be insufficient to combat our loneliness. We feel that no one could understand the depths of our pain, so we just give up on other people. We might, at times, get angry with ourselves for not reaching out, for hiding our needs, for failing to ask for support. Other times, we ask ourselves these questions over and over: *"Don't they see how I feel?" "Why don't they care?" "Why am I the only one who wants to reach out?" "Why don't other people need me?"*

It is important to recognize and deal with feelings of loneliness, because loneliness is known to further complicate and aggravate depression. Oftentimes, it's not the loneliness itself, but our feelings about *ourselves* when we're lonely that are so painful. For example, we may feel that being alone or feeling lonely reflects our lack of worth as people, proves that no one wants or needs us as friends, and clearly demonstrates that we have been rejected or abandoned by others.

But when we use our feelings of loneliness to beat ourselves with, we only perpetuate those feelings. If you feel that being alone is a temporary situation and that feeling lonely is a natural result of the normal human need to be close to other people, you'll be more likely to accept loneliness for what it is. Simply feeling lonely—without negative encumbrances and without feelings of worthlessness, deprivation, and abandonment—may be good because it pushes us to reach out to alert a support system that will be available to us when we're depressed or to take risks in establishing a support system. Contact with other people and an ongoing support system are extremely effective defenses against depression.

Good and close relationships that have qualities of openness, trust, and satisfaction help people deal with stress by making it possible for them to share anxieties with others, thereby clarifying and diminishing them. Good and close relationships also lend effective support at those times when people feel confused or overwhelmed. It is therefore important to know where you stand with friends and to be sure you have a person or persons with whom you can be yourself and talk honestly about your feelings, in order to gain vital, dependable support from them.

But it's another story if you turn to friends only when you're down. If you present yourself to friends only when you're gloomy and upset, you deny them the other facets of your personality. And if your "depressed self" is the only side you offer them, contact with you may understandably become wearisome, even for the best of friends. If your depression isn't chronic or severe, there are certain things you can do to improve the receptivity of your friends. Most important, you can make special efforts to be with them when you're "up" and to share positive activities and feelings with them. And then, when you're "down" and they help *you*, you can express your appreciation for their availability and encourage them to ask for your support when *they're* in the dumps. In short, if you're depression-prone, make conscious efforts to develop a reliable support system in the form of a network of friends who can depend on each other when they're feeling either good or bad. Think and plan ahead, for your own well-being! Don't wait until you're in "desperate straits" to reach out to others, because at that time you'll have little to bring to the relationship other than your woes. If you've already spent time and energy helping someone else through a period of emotional trauma, you will feel far less hesitant about asking for support when you're in trouble yourself.

But a caution: in recognizing the value of relationships in combating depression, guard against becoming too eager in making friends. A healthy friendship isn't likely to spring full-blown from a few positive interactions. Long-term friendships—even those that *seem* to "spark" quickly—evolve from an ongoing investment of energy and concern. Deep and mature relationships are often low-key, non-possessive, and quietly satisfying. They're based on a sharing of interests, time, and mutual trust. The capacity for building these kinds of non-frenzied relationships seems to develop with personal maturity. On the other hand, immature relationships are characterized by insecurity, possessiveness, self-doubt, and neediness.

If you act anxious or needy, or in some way attempt to force intimacy in the early stages of a friendship, you may place the other person in an uncomfortable position. If you are overly dependent, the other person may become much too important to you. You may become precariously vulnerable if you raise your hopes and expectations about the relationship too soon—before you have a clear understanding of the trustworthiness, consistency, preferences, and needs of the other person. And out of your own desperate neediness, you may persuade yourself that the relationship is equally important to the other person as well, letting yourself in for a great deal of disappointment, perhaps heartbreak, if the situation proves to be otherwise. Dependency and desperation can generate emotional neediness that is so intense it makes other people wary of a person and his or her apparent desire for "instant intimacy." Implicit demands and obvious vulnerabilities create "stickiness" and awkwardness in relationships with people who need some freedom and autonomy for their own growth and motion. Extreme neediness restricts freedom, so that friends tend to feel suffocated.

> Linda, a 24-year-old client of mine, evidenced a very chaotic friendship pattern following her divorce. I suspected that before the divorce, Linda had experienced very few problems with her interpersonal relationships. I guessed that she'd probably been extremely open and gregarious, that her self-esteem was good, and that she hadn't been particularly needy or dependent. Friendships came easily for her and were maintained without much work or concentrated effort on her part. During her con-flicted marriage, Linda had neglected many of her friendships and instead put all of her energies into trying to make the mar-riage work. Then, when her marriage ended, she felt really isolat-ed for the first time in her life. She simply didn't have the variety or volume of daily contacts she'd had throughout her life to that point: she was no longer in college, she was living alone, and she had a job in a very small office. In fact, Linda's daily routine put her in contact with very few people.

Up to that time in her life, Linda had never been in a position to have to consciously try to make friends. People were always around her and she regularly attended classes, clubs, and school events. And, because Linda was vivacious and enthusiastic, friendships more or less just "happened" for her. Daily contact with people led quite naturally to familiarity with them, comfort, a sharing of mutual interests and, eventually, friendship. But after her divorce, contact with people became at once more important and more difficult for Linda. At that time, ironically, the opportunities for new friendships were few and far between.

Linda began to leap at any chance she had to make friends with a person. But at this point in her life, her vivaciousness and energy subtly conveyed a certain desperation to others. The few people Linda did meet at this time in her life apparently felt a bit uncomfortable around her; in fact, it seemed that people were *avoiding her.* Thus, for the first time in her life, Linda was having to approach the process of making friends consciously and somewhat systematically. Once she dealt with the disconcerting realization that she could not depend on her spontaneity or trust herself to be "appropriately" open with others, she began to map out some specific strategies for herself and her quest for new friendships. She supplemented the support she was getting in individual psychotherapy with a group counseling experience. In this group, she felt understood and supported and was able to appropriately share her emotional neediness. Linda not only developed a few friendships in that group, but she also felt good about her ability to be helpful to other group members as well. And group members began to seek her out and offer positive feedback. With increased self-esteem, confidence, and the resulting renewed energy she felt, Linda began to explore other potential sources for friendship in the community.

Still sensitive to rejection, Linda made the decision to join some organizations comprised of people who were also seeking friends: groups for single people, groups for divorced people, and the like. As she began to make some new friends in these special groups, she also began to spread her dependency around, consciously choosing to limit her contact with any one person so as not to "scare" anyone off. As Linda got some of her needs for contact with others met and experienced an increase in self-esteem, she began to feel less needy. Then she began to take occasional classes in subjects she'd long had an interest in through a college extension program and a vocational school. As Linda met more and more people in the process of doing things she en-

joyed doing, her opportunities for new friendships increased pro-
portionately. And as she began to feel less emotionally needy and
desperate for friendships, she also began to be more selective and
to take her time nurturing potential friendships that looked most
attractive and promising to her. Eventually, she again felt casual
about friendships, and learned to trust her spontaneity and liveli-
ness. So it was that after a temporary setback in the area of
friendships in her life, Linda was able to turn things around and
again it was "business as usual."

*Good, healthy friendships are not demanding or possessive, but
spontaneous and free.* And people need a variety of relationships that
vary in tone and depth. Having only extremely intimate relationships
would be exhausting. As a matter of fact, it's nice to have some casual
friendships that don't require intense conversations and sharing.
Strive to build some relationships that allow you to temporarily
"forget" some of the important issues in your life and simply have a
good time! And it may sound trite, but *choose your friends wisely*!
Depression-prone people may tend to befriend people who respond
very quickly to them in their quest for supportive associations. This
can result in sudden and intense relationships in which the depressed
person seems to have no "work" to do—an appealing situation to
someone with little energy to contribute to the building of
relationships. Such involvement, however, could actually become
detrimental if the "rescuing" partner in the association is attracted by
the opportunity to provide advice and "concern," which often turns
out to be controlling, manipulative, and/or coercive. Early in the
friendship, it may not be apparent that these people, possibly because
their lives are lacking in some important ways, tend to become overly
involved with others.

   At first, these overly involved people may be particularly
appealing, because they seem to be so "people-oriented" and are so
willing to talk about feelings—*especially your feelings.* A depressed
person is most likely to get "hooked" at this stage, when the new
friend seems so warm, interested, and accepting. But this strong
personal investment in you is likely to become rather intrusive,
demonstrating that the other person has a real stake in how you live
your life and what decisions you make. And you may actually feel

guilty when you *don't* take his or her advice. People like this may ultimately indicate that they resent the amount of time they "give" you, since you clearly aren't "profiting" from their advice and concern—by doing things *their* way.

Though seemingly open and honest, the feedback given by the kind of newfound "friends" I've just described may become increasingly negative, particularly if you somehow fail to follow their detailed instructions of guidance or you miraculously "snap out of" your depression. This dissatisfaction can be prefaced with words like this: *"If I weren't your friend, I wouldn't say anything, but . . . "* or, *"I'm only telling you this for your own good . . . "* Depression-prone people generally accept "constructive criticism" because they believe that this person is "just trying to help." While they're appreciative of this other person's concern, that concern ultimately leads to more depression.

Because depression-prone people are self-critical, they often select companions who are critical as well. In other words, instead of relying on themselves to be self-critical all the time, depression-prone people find someone else who will conveniently do it for them! And since depressed people are usually hypersensitive to criticism as well as socially and emotionally vulnerable, this makes for a rather bad combination of personalities! Depression-prone people often accept criticism from others because they labor under the illusion that they need to hear the worst about themselves in order to improve. They feel that they must seek out, invite, or at least put up with negative feedback, as if they're *obligated* to take all the criticism they "deserve"—most likely because of low self-esteem and the need to receive punishment for perceived defects and failures. Thus, they seem to say to others, *"Go ahead and tell me what's wrong with me; I can take it!"* But of course they really can't; few people could, and no one with a healthy ego *would*.

If the foregoing sounds at all like you and some of your relationships, you need to remind yourself that negative feedback from critical people is *always* distorted. Critical people rarely criticize others "for their own good"; they criticize others because something about the other person annoys them—something that may be perfectly acceptable to a person who is less critical. (As they say, with friends like that, who needs enemies?!) And in analyzing the fault being criticized, it might well turn out to be a repressed fault of the person doing the criticizing, one that has simply been projected onto the depressed person, then distorted in meaning and magnitude. You'll find that much of what's supposedly "wrong" with you in the eyes of the super-critical friend either falls away naturally or can be dealt with far more easily when you've come through the depression and are feeling better about yourself.

I'll repeat: *choose your friends wisely.* Be wary of any tendency you might have to attach yourself to critical people—or to new friends who seem to have an extraordinary amount of interest in helping you out of the dark pit you're in . . . but ultimately may succeed in keeping you there. Both kinds of supposed friends—the intense, "overly involved" variety and the "overly critical and/or brutally honest" variety—can be toxic, especially when you're feeling self-critical and depressed. Instead, surround yourself with people who are accepting of both themselves *and* you. They'll be interested in your life—but they won't be overly involved in trying to influence you and they won't be easily influenced by your moods and behaviors. Sharing some of your bad feelings about yourself should bring affirmation that you really *are okay* and that you're being too hard on yourself.

It's always reassuring to discover that others feel far better about us than we do about ourselves. Frequently a comment like "*Wow, you're sure being hard on yourself!*" brings our self-criticalness to light. Also, when we're too close to a problem, a friend's objectivity can help us put big "upsets" back in perspective. Hearing words like "*Gosh, I'd be upset too*" helps us feel that our response to a disturbing situation is *in fact* warranted and that we aren't being foolish, neurotic, or crazy to have become depressed over it. And, of course, when you spend time with less critical, more accepting and nurturing people, naturally you're going to feel more accepting of yourself. Since you feel good when you're with these people, you'll be more apt to show your best side. It just stands to reason that when you are spontaneously more lively and responsive to others, you will be a more enjoyable companion.

But unrealistic expectations can seriously interfere with the formation of close relationships, because these expectations undermine our acceptance of others and set us up for constant disappointment that perpetuates depression-proneness. Acceptance of others depends, to a large extent, upon our *self-acceptance*. As a matter of fact, self-acceptance is a *prerequisite* for genuine acceptance of others. If we are extremely self-critical, we will invariably be critical of others at some level. But we can't really accept others as they are until we can accept ourselves as we are. We fool ourselves by not seeing others as they really are, at least for a time. We attach to them some answer to an unmet need of our own, then expect them to satisfy that need for us; in fact, we get very upset when they don't meet that need. Or, we find, then reject in others some quality that we cannot accept in ourselves. And since we deny that particular quality in ourselves, we feel that we don't have to change . . . *but they do!* These are unfair *projections* of our own inner feelings onto other people; they're also forms of unrealistic expectations that must be recognized and dealt with if we are to build and maintain quality friendships.

Sometimes we're hurt by people we care about because, without even realizing it, we place vague or unspecific demands on them, then become upset when they don't respond as we expect them to. Even though we haven't conveyed to them the ways in which we feel needy and vulnerable, we somehow expect them to be sensitive and thoughtful. Or we may expect to receive something from them— emotionally or materially—after giving to them without alerting them to the "strings attached." Remember, we *choose* to do things for people, make efforts to get close to them, and share things with them. Those choices, however, don't give us the right to turn around and demand that the recipient do the same things for us—unless, of course, there is some sort of mutual agreement to that effect. But in a close relationship in which there *is* explicit commitment that is mutually understood, we do have a right to certain expectations that are reasonable and possible. Ongoing supportive relationships must have at their core a base of reasonable consistency and predictability regarding the other person's behavior; otherwise, we may feel that we cannot count on the relationship. Regarding close and intimate friendships, we must know that if we ever *really* need support, our close friends will come through for us. We need to know this in our hearts, even if the belief is never tested.

There *are* people in the world who will continue to like us and accept us once they know us well, and will enjoy being in our company and meeting our needs. It is far less stressful to cultivate relationships with nurturing people like this than it is to cultivate relationships with people who are more inclined to be critical or withholding. Rather than expending energy adjusting and readjusting our feelings and behavior to earn the approval or continued acceptance of a critical friend, you may want to concentrate on building friendships with people who make you feel good and to whom you're acceptable *just as you are*.

Depression-prone people should carefully examine their expectations about friendships and evaluate troubling relationships to determine whether they are unwise or unhealthy to continue. For example, there's a great difference between a close friendship or intimate relationship and an association that has developed primarily for a specific purpose, as that between business partners, a boss and his secretary, or a teacher and a student who share common interests. One involves an *emotional* transaction, the other a *functional* transaction. Many relationships contain both of these elements in varying degrees. A father, for instance, would have a deep emotional connection with his child, but would also be concerned about providing financial support for the child and teaching that child the rules of behavior. Sometimes individuals within these associations lose sight of the primary nature of the relationship and confuse personal ingredients with functional ones, all the while building up expectations that cannot be met. This confusion can lead to the kind of frustration that is known to trigger depression.

Frequently, we maintain relationship roles out of habit, seeming necessity, convenience, or simply because our passivity or lack of foresight resulted in slipping into an unwanted association. It is wise to periodically examine our relationships and work to eliminate any roles that are obsolete, irrelevant, burdensome, or stress-provoking. Then, too, people and their basic needs change over time. Rather than clinging to old, outmoded relationships, seek out people whose interests and feelings are currently more compatible with your own. And as you do so, notice that your expectations of others are no longer as unrealistic as they used to be; for this reason, your relationships are less likely to fall apart at the seams or come crashing down. Instead, you are seeing people more as themselves, not as you would like them to be. And you are also feeling far surer of yourself—less desperate or wary—and much more capable of forming relationships that are based on the equal give and take of real human needs.

25.

Be Assertive

"You have a right to your feelings."

Depression-prone people tend to be highly vulnerable to the negative words, behaviors, and manipulations of others. And, all too often, they're unable to handle this vulnerability adequately when it's most important for them to do so. In order to avoid a destructive build-up of hurts that could lead to depression, it is important to learn to be assertive.

Granted, it takes work to "unlearn" habitual ways of denying ourselves, guarding our feelings, or controlling our behavior. Some of us may even behave as if we feel guilty and apologetic for just being *ourselves*. It could be that consciously or unconsciously, we've decided *not* to be assertive. There may be an element of conscious manipulation in trying to appear unassertive, particularly if we've somehow been rewarded for that kind of behavior in the past. We've learned to be friendly, appeasing, diplomatic, and self-denying to the point that over the years, we've perhaps even lost touch with our own true feelings, wants, needs, and beliefs. We may have become chronic other-directed people-pleasers . . . and, as a result, we're vulnerable to disappointment, guilt, hurt, *and depression*.

How does one break old habit patterns of passive and possibly even manipulative behavior? And how does one begin to practice active, responsible assertiveness? The following considerations may help you *decide* to be assertive:

   • *You have a right to your feelings.* Feelings need no rational justification. They need not be reasonably defensible, nor do they necessarily have to be clear and easy to articulate. As long as you don't engage in blaming others for your feelings, you have a perfect *right* to feel confused, ambivalent, and inconsistent. Feelings are not right or wrong, good or bad; feelings just *are*.

• Give yourself permission to feel things—even if they are negative, seemingly inappropriate, or embarrassing.

• Take responsibility for your feelings. Use "I statements" like "*I feel*," not "*You make me feel*." Don't spend time and energy explaining feelings away with rationalizations and excuses.

• Make an honest, active attempt to get in touch with, acknowledge, explore, magnify, and expand a feeling rather than avoiding, denying, or suppressing it.

• Be willing, at times, to spontaneously express feelings without censoring or monitoring them. But express feelings for the purpose of *expressing* them, not in an attempt to impress, attack, or change another person.

• Be willing to risk rejection in order to experience and verbalize unacceptable, unpopular, or negative feelings. (The possibility of rejection decreases, of course, when you honestly *own* the feelings you are experiencing and expressing.) There is ultimately more security in honesty than in dishonesty and manipulation.

• Always remember that you have a *right* to your beliefs and values—as much as anyone does. And you have a right to express and act on those beliefs and values, as long as they do not exploit or jeopardize another person's rights, beliefs, and values.

• Recognize the fact that conflict and confrontation in a relationship, if dealt with properly—directly and honestly—can be an enhancing experience for both people involved. If a person you have a relationship with cannot tolerate an open confrontation intended to relieve conflict between the two of you, take a serious look at your relationship. You may be unable to develop within its confines by restricting yourself to beliefs and behavior "acceptable" to the other person, thus denying parts of yourself that may be important for you to acknowledge and express.

Keeping these basic guidelines in mind, let's look at specific instances in which assertive behavior may be required. When someone hurts your feelings, acts thoughtlessly, puts you down, makes insinuations, or tries to make you feel guilty, don't withdraw from him or her and brood in silence. In situations like this, guard against being extremely forgiving and/or rationalizing the insensitive behavior in some way ("*He probably didn't realize what he was doing,*" or "*That's just the way she is*"). There's *always* a danger that after rationalizing why you shouldn't be upset or act assertively, you'll turn the negative feelings back on yourself and become depressed. In any case, accepting objectionable behavior from others demonstrates to the offending people that they can do this kind of thing to you (and others) and get away with it. Also, if you let annoyances smolder, you may eventually dump on someone else anyway, then feel guilty if the person you finally dump on is not the one who really merits your anger.

Are you one of those people who perpetually plays the "nice guy" role, letting small hurts, annoyances, and concerns go by? If so, by now you probably know that *these things don't just go away, they build up*. Without knowing it, you may be gunnysacking many "injustices," and when that sack gets too heavy or too tight and you can control it no longer, it just explodes. And you then "justify" your "out of the blue" blowup by saying (or thinking), "*There's only so much a person can take.*" Take note of your "unfinished business" with people. Failure to assert yourself sufficiently or in a timely way can lead to enormous frustration, suppressed anger, and guilt. So, keep *current* with people. It's much easier to express small hurts and annoyances than it is to wait until they build to a blind rage. If you don't express feelings as they occur, you may expend a great deal of energy being resentful or hurt and ruminating over what you "should have" done or said. You may go over and over the upsetting incident and even *rehearse* the response you *wish* you'd given—but possibly never will.

> The so-called "nice guy" role brings to mind George, a 45-year-old client of mine who seemed an unlikely candidate for depression. George, a salesman by profession, was energetic and mobilized. In fact, when he bounded into my office and greeted me with a hearty handshake, I almost expected him to try to sell me something rather than share his personal problems. But in the course of several counseling sessions, George explored the roots of his vague feelings of unhappiness, emptiness, and self-dissatisfaction.

George had been a successful salesman for twenty years and really hadn't given himself much thought or consideration during that time. He just seemed to roll with the punches and would kiddingly say, "A moving target is the hardest to hit." In recent years, however, several factors contributed to his becoming more introspective, more questioning, and less self-assured. In his job, he had become a part-time manager. As he listened to young salespeople talk about some of their frustrations, George learned that his "pat" answers weren't helpful to them; he discovered that the years of second-guessing others, being super-vigilant, and accommodating them had left him a psychological chameleon. The very skill that made him a good salesman—his ability to step into another person's shoes—was coming back to haunt him at this time in his life. Painfully, George began to realize that he had no "shoes" of his own.

At this time in his life, his children were young adults and he no longer had a ready-made father role to keep him busy. His wife had launched a new career and was becoming her own person. Their two teenagers still living at home were challenging George with many "Why" questions and issues related to values. When, during family discussions, George's children demanded to know what Dad thought about an issue, he'd feel uncomfortable and verbalize his appreciation for both sides of the issue/argument. His teenagers would then confront him for being "wishy-washy" and express a general lack of respect for him.

Thus, a personality style that George had viewed as a strength was, at this time in his life, being called into question. George insisted that his style evolved *necessarily* because of the demands of the sales profession, but that just didn't ring true to me. As we reviewed his early family history, George's personal style become clear to both of us. George was the eldest of four children and served as an arbitrator during family squabbles and as a buffer during conflicts between his parents. His mother had been self-denying in the family and his father was well-known for being a "swell guy." In high school and college, George was well-liked. He had no real enemies because he was agreeable and generally avoided making waves. So it was that George's identification with his parents as well as his family role predisposed him to a people-pleasing style.

But the pressure George received from the sales personnel he supervised, his wife, and his children made it uncomfortable for him to continue to maintain his lifelong personality style. Fortunately, George was basically a bright, healthy individual who was not an angry person. So I encouraged him, for the practice, to take a stand on *everything* for a time. When offered a drink he wasn't to say, "I'll have what you have" or "Whatever is easiest." Instead, he was to ask what was available and make a definite *choice*. When he saw a movie or a television show, read an article, or heard an opinion, he was to decide what he basically liked or didn't like about it, then verbalize those opinions. After a period of extreme discomfort, he discovered that he not only had opinions of his own, but that people often genuinely respected those opinions and him—even when there was disagreement. George eventually felt stronger and more confident, and for the first time in his life, the inevitable anxiety associated with the "people-pleaser" role subsided.

The longer you put off expressing a feeling, the more foolish you'll feel if and when you finally *do* express that feeling. In fact, the person you're explaining the feeling to can rightly ask: *"Why in the world didn't you tell me sooner how you felt?"* If unexpressed negative feelings toward someone are bothering you because you didn't do anything about them earlier—at the time something actually happened—find ways to express those feelings NOW! Unreleased and unexpressed feelings create stress and have the effect of poisoning your system with resentment and anger. By being genuinely assertive—and I don't mean hostile or pushy—you'll feel more confident, powerful, and in control of yourself and the situation; you'll also be far less likely to get depressed.

Suppose someone is upsetting you by teasing or questioning you. How might you deal with this? First, allow yourself to become aware of your annoyance, rather than concealing it from yourself or draining it off through "barbed" humor or rationalizations like *"He really didn't mean anything by that."* Postpone your immediate, reactive response, perhaps by *acting as if* the stimulus provoking the annoyance is unclear. You can say, *"I'm unclear* (or confused) *about what you just said. Could you please say something more about it?"* If the person didn't intend to upset you, he or she will then have an opportunity to modify the remark. And if a "dig" *was* intended, he or she will then learn from your reaction that you don't intend to let provocative words from him or her slide past you easily. If the person doesn't alter his or her approach at this point, you could gently ease into a confrontation by saying *"I feel uncomfortable with what you said,"* instead of bellowing, *"I'm insulted, outraged, and ready to kill!"* If you *own* your feelings through "I" statements and don't condemn the other person for "making" you feel bad, you can often keep current and express feelings *as they occur.*

Also, if you *own* the part you might be playing in a misunderstanding, an inaccurate perception, or overreaction, the other person will tend to feel less threatened and will therefore be less defensive because you have given him/her a chance to save face and modify or explain away his/her comment, or examine its effect on your reaction. This technique will also enable the other person to reveal his/her intentions to you. If the individual is genuinely concerned and apologetic, the problem is likely to be resolved immediately. But if the person acts quite annoyed or insists that he/she was "just kidding," or accuses you of being hypersensitive, you're being tipped off that the original intent *may* have been to hurt you in some way. At this point you can say, *"Well, it may be kidding to you, but it bothers me and I want you to know that."* But try to focus on the *result* of the hurtful remark rather than on the probable *intent* behind it—which never can be proven anyway, unless the person admits to it. And, since the offending remark cannot be erased from the record, a modification of future behavior should be your goal. You have been warned that this person is apt to resume making upsetting comments to you; you have requested that he/she refrain from repeating behavior that clearly annoys you, *regardless* of intent. Either way, you will have the satisfaction of taking action *when the incident occurs,* but safely short of bashing someone in the face to express your irritation.

Guilt-prone people are particularly affected by the "passive-aggressive" behavior of others. By "passive-aggressive," I mean behavior which on the surface appears benign and innocent, but underneath is accusatory and critical. Around an "expert" passive-aggressive person, we may feel vaguely guilty or annoyed and not know why. The passive-aggressive person doesn't get angry or demanding; he or she invariably appears cooperative and controlled. A more careful look, though, may reveal that this person's teasing or "innocent" remarks or questions tend to make others feel guilty or just generally inadequate, such as: *"You aren't going to do it that way again, are you?"* or *"I don't know how you could possibly feel that way."* Other verbal cues of passive-aggressive behavior: *"That's okay, I don't mind"*; *"Don't worry about me. You do whatever you want to do"*; *"Mary has such wonderful children. And they never get dirty when they play the way yours do."*

People who are self-critical but not guilt-prone may be able to ignore insinuations, vague innuendos, and subtly implied criticisms from the passive-aggressive person. But the depression-prone person—who is usually overloaded with guilt and self-critical feelings already—makes the perfect target, so to speak, for the passive-aggressive person. So if you tend to be guilt-prone, keep the passive-aggressive people who wander into your life under strict surveillance. *Don't let them get to you!*

When you begin feeling depressed about the way someone treats you, examine the nature of what he or she has been saying, even though you can't quite put your finger on particular incidents or comments. If much or even some of the content is implied criticism or judgment, you're probably onto a closet passive-aggressive person who may even be unaware of this tendency in himself or herself. There are three things I recommend that you *not* do when interacting with a passive-aggressive person:

1. Don't permit any *vagueness.* Find out as specifically as you can what he or she is saying. To be effective, the passive-aggressive person needs ample room (and ambiguity) to operate in. Indefinite innuendos and statements with implied, not explicit, criticism should be immediately explored. When passive-aggressive people think they can get by with upsetting remarks, they'll continue. But don't attempt to stop them with direct confrontational remarks such as: *"What do you mean by that?"* They often weasel out of their remarks or beat around the bush. While you pursue the passive-aggressive person for clarity, *assume* nothing and play dumb: *"I'm not clear on what you are saying"*; or *"I'm not sure what you mean."* And give him or her a puzzled but inquisitive look. If, as you try to get an explanation, he or she suggests that you're being overly sensitive or taking things too seriously, pay no attention; he or she is in the process of discovering that you're going to make him or her work on those "opportunities" to be critical of you!

2. Don't let yourself get sucked into the passive-aggressive's game, with its insinuations and innuendos. Don't tell yourself that you're not going to give the passive-aggressive person the satisfaction of knowing he or she is getting to you. This only gives the passive-aggressive room to operate in and places you in the victim role, besides. It's a game that would be hard for you to win unless you play by the rules of the passive-aggressive person and just happen to beat him or her at the game. But then you wouldn't feel all that good anyway, because you would have merely reinforced and perpetuated passive-aggressive behavior.

3. Try not to blow up at a passive-aggressive person. Anytime you *do* get angry, he or she will act hurt—as the victim of your oversensitivity—making you, in turn, feel guilty, foolish, and even more angry. A particularly good technique to use if you find yourself getting angry is to respond by openly admitting to hurt or depression and simply "collapsing," rather than acting angry. Passive-aggressive people can question your right to be "unjustifiably" hurt or depressed, but they cannot deny your feelings. You can even say, "*I know you probably didn't mean any harm, but I feel very depressed and would prefer not to talk with you anymore right now.*"

If the passive-aggressive person is your parent, has no real insight into his or her behavior, and evidences no willingness to change, you may need to explore other approaches. If, for example, during a phone conversation the subtle passive-aggressive comment of a parent upsets you, you might say to him or her, "*I'm suddenly feeling very depressed; I'm not sure why. I guess I want to get off the phone.*" If the parent then asks, "*Is it something I said?*" you could respond with, "*Gosh, I'm not sure. I hadn't thought of that. Do you think it could be something you said?*" By throwing the issue back to the parent, you've made him or her aware that some element in the conversation disturbed you enough so that you want to terminate it—and possibly that you won't be happy within your relationship *unless* this kind of communication stops. If this parent was always inclined to be passive-aggressive, you already have absorbed enough subtle negatives to overcome during your lifetime; resolve not to collect more of them.

As I see it, the "compulsive giver" who is always bending over backwards for others exhibits a variation of passive-aggressive behavior. He or she overdoes giving in very self-sacrificing ways. Learn to trust the evolution of your feelings when you befriend one of these wonderful people who give *so* much and demand nothing in return—overtly, of course. Your first reaction is often gratitude, then comes guilt and, finally, anger. *Why anger?* Because when we receive gifts and favors from these folks, there's usually an implicit obligation to return the favor or gift. When you accept the gift or favor, you feel obligated to the other person and guilty if you don't reciprocate in some way. Whenever you feel that you're being pushed into doing more for a person than you want to do or have time to do, you may discover that you are consciously controlling your anger.

If you're exhausting yourself by having to deal with a compulsive giver, make it clear that your life is such that you simply are not in a position to do much for other people. You have family obligations or a busy schedule and don't want to be responsible for someone else's disappointment when you don't reciprocate. Either decline gifts and favors offered or, if it's uncomfortable, let the compulsive giver continue on until he or she wears out, abandons you, or finds someone else to work on.

It is not your responsibility to change *other* people. However, it *is* your responsibility to protect your self-concept and self-esteem from the subtle undermining of passive-aggressive people. They're not all bad; in fact, they often have characteristics you appreciate, which is one reason why you may choose to keep some of them around you. In the case of parents, of course, you can't just cross them off your list because of an occasional "misunderstood" comment. What you *can* do, though, is find effective ways of being direct and clear with people you come in contact with and encourage others to do the same. Take steps to master the assertiveness necessary to prevent personal interactions that lead to bad feelings and even depression.

26.

Work Through Your Anger

" . . . there are more options available than just
'taking it' or 'blowing up.' "

Because repressed anger is regarded as a major source of depression,
exploring the sources of past and present anger and ways that anger is
customarily handled are vital steps in learning to combat depression-
proneness.

Irritations, annoyances, resentments, and anger inevitably crop
up in all of our lives; sometimes these negatives accumulate and
become a rather powerful force. But dumping anger at its apparent
source doesn't add to our understanding of how the guilt-resentment-
anger cycle works, nor does it provide us with the opportunity to do
anything more productive than to just "get mad." For example, we
may frequently have a blowup totally out of proportion to the
incident that triggered it, then feel ashamed and guilty because we've
unfairly let loose on an inappropriate target or have exposed a
volatility that we usually keep well hidden.

I believe that some psychologists are overly simplistic in their
notion that we can *choose* not to get angry. If the underlying
psychodynamics and ways of dealing with anger-provoking situations
don't change, the element of choice is diminished. And if the buildup
occurs, undetected as usual, we will probably continue to blow up
because we didn't exercise our "choice" earlier—at the point when,
realistically, we could have done something to handle our initial
reaction.

> Emily, a 48-year-old woman with whom I worked, was at one
> time a good example of a person with a "passive-explosive" per-
> sonality style. Emily had learned two things as a child that af-
> fected her negatively as an adult: that if she stood up to her dog-
> matic father, he would devastate her; from her mother, she got
> the message that she shouldn't be like her father. In arguments

with her mother, Emily would attempt to control herself. When she became aware of being manipulated by her mother, she would explode. Her mother would then say to her, "You're just like your father!" Then Emily would feel frustrated and guilty. Through all this, Emily learned that if she passively gave in, her father wouldn't verbally assault her and that if she exploded in her mother's presence, she essentially "lost" and felt guilty about acting "just like Dad." Deep within Emily was this feeling: To be angry is to be like Dad.

As an adult, Emily actually was quite submissive and placating. Many people took her for granted and just assumed that she would put up with their moodiness or thoughtlessness. And for long periods of time, Emily did just that. Eventually, though, her frustration would surface and she'd explode. She would then feel terribly guilty and keep the lid on until the next explosion. As we explored the current roots of Emily's style, an interesting, subconscious pair of self-imposed "rules" emerged: • Never choose to give up control of your anger and • You are only justified in getting angry when it builds up to the point where it is completely out of your hands. These weren't actually rules in Emily's head. Instead, they were logical "guidelines" reflected in the sequence of feelings and behavior before and after an explosion. Emily always felt less guilty when she exploded after she let the rage build up to the point where it was out of her control. In this way, she could disassociate from her anger and not own it as hers. In other words, she didn't have to take responsibility for her own anger. She could continue to feel that others made her angry, that the anger wasn't within her, that she wasn't "just like Dad," after all.

Fortunately for Emily, this behavior style was so painful and unworkable that she became motivated to change. Step by step, she became less passive and stronger. Instead of waiting until matters were "out of her hands," so to speak, she developed a style in which she was firm, forthright, and fair. She learned that there are more options available than just "taking it" or "blowing up."

Frequently, angry confrontations can be averted when there is insight into the internal and interpersonal factors that *promote* anger. If you believe that much or even *some* of your depression-proneness is related to repressed or misdirected anger, you will find it helpful to carefully examine situations that have provoked anger for you and circumstances which make it difficult for you to hold your temper. This includes anger that festers within you in the form of the guilt, self-blame, and self-punishment that characterize the depressed state.

As I have pointed out, self-criticalness, guilt, low self-esteem, and the accompanying need for approval from others make depression-prone people very susceptible to criticisms and slights from others; excessive hypersensitivity makes them highly vulnerable to *hurts*. But it's difficult for many people to admit outright that they feel hurt, or to allow themselves to experience the vulnerability and feelings of weakness that come *with* that hurt. Frequently, before they are even in touch with this hurt, they've lashed back or exploded. Anger diverts us from the more painful feelings of vulnerability, and it gives the illusion of strength. Of course, an angry reaction may trigger negative feelings and anger in the other person, so that both people become engaged in self-defense and aggression rather than communication.

It helps to recognize the times when you're feeling particularly vulnerable so that you can immediately become aware of your hurt feelings. If you have the courage to admit to hurt—first to yourself and then to the person who actually hurt you—your interaction with that person will be much more productive for both of you. In fact, your acknowledgment of vulnerability will be far more disarming and may encourage sensitivity rather than defensiveness or retaliation on the part of the other person.

Sometimes anger comes from feelings of *over-responsibility*. If you feel responsible for everything and everybody, you may feel guilty for things you have no control over, things you have no responsibility for at all. As an example, an overly responsible mother may get angry at her cold and wet teenager for failing to bring a raincoat with him to school, but essentially she feels guilty because she feels it was her responsibility to remind him to bring his raincoat. If he catches a cold, she may become angrier still, resenting him for "putting" her in the position of feeling guilty. If she had left the responsibility for dressing appropriately where it belongs—squarely on the shoulders of the teenager—the mother would not have felt guilty and, therefore, would not have become angry.

Concentrate on taking responsibility for your own behavior and duties *only*. This will reduce your tendency to feel guilty, blame yourself, or blame others. And if you aren't busy taking responsibility for others, you'll have the energy to take responsibility for yourself. *As often as you need to, remind yourself that you can only be responsible for and have control over your own feelings, thoughts, and actions.* Sometimes we get angry at people because we sense that they're disappointed in us. What's the source of this kind of vulnerability? When we feel depressed, we become very self-critical, we whittle down our self-esteem, and we mistrust our feelings. This lowered self-esteem then increases our need for the approval of others. Mistrust of our own feelings makes us rely on others for constant positive feedback. Thus, other people have a great deal of power over us—in our eyes, not necessarily theirs. So when we're depressed and down on ourselves, we may feel that other people are just as unhappy with us as we are with ourselves. We project our own negative feelings about ourselves onto others and then may feel angry with *them* for thinking badly of us. We may also imagine that others have the same high expectations of us that we have for ourselves, we feel guilty for not meeting those expectations, and we resent them for expecting so much of us!

Our own negative feelings about ourselves and our need for approval from others will make us more susceptible to the actual expressed or unexpressed expectations, demands, or requests of others. Our neediness makes others powerful to us, and makes us guilt-prone and subject to manipulation by people who may want us to feel guilty. When we feel helpless and believe someone is trying to make us feel guilty, use us, or control us, we may respond with an act of desperation—anger. For instance, a child may say, "Mom, can I bake a cake?" Mom, who may be tired and harassed and doesn't feel like having a mess in the kitchen, replies, "No, dear." The child persists: "Please, Mom!?" Mom explodes. Why the explosion? Possibly because Mom is feeling that if she were a good mother she would be willing to let her child experiment in the kitchen, then clean up the mess for him or her. *Already she's feeling guilty.* Because of the guilt and the feelings of helplessness, she may believe that the child is "making" her feel guilty and trying to manipulate her into letting him or her do something that will inconvenience her. In other words, if we're guilt-prone, we tend to get angry at someone for asking us to do something because we know that we'll feel guilty if we say no.

Remind yourself that you have rights, too. You don't have to passively comply with everyone's requests or demands. You can congenially but firmly refuse—without feeling guilty or believing that you have to "throw a fit" in order to be heard or to get your way. You can simply state that you aren't willing to do whatever is being requested. Hold your ground rather than getting angry, out of desperation, because you think the other person is trying to make you feel guilty. Even if guilt is your Achilles' heel, you don't have to give in to it. *Despite* the feeling of guilt, you can rationally choose to hold your temper and calmly maintain your position!

You can stop *anyone's* efforts to manipulate you by simply saying, "No." Why bother getting angry over someone's *attempt* to manipulate you? If the other person is unable to manipulate you, there's no real reason for anger. The other person has a right to *try* to get what he wants from you . . . just as you have a right to *refuse* the request and look after your own needs. Let's say another person is trying to get you to do something. You can simply say to him or her, "Sorry, I won't be able to do that." (No explanation needed.) If the other person asks for an explanation, you might say something like this: "*I don't care to explain myself now*," or "*It's too complicated to explain*." When you don't evidence any need to explain yourself and firmly state that you aren't able to do something, the other person will be less apt to press you about it. But when you seem uncertain, uneasy, conflicted, and guilt-prone, people interested in manipulating you sense that they might change your mind and get you to do what *they* want you to do.

When you're feeling good about yourself, it's much easier to stay on top of things and block other people's efforts to influence you. But when you're down in the dumps you may, in fact, be easy prey for people who tend to dump blame on those who don't fight back. It's no accident that people who assume the victim role are most frequently victimized. If you carry around a big guilt bucket, you'll always be able to find people who are quite willing to make a generous donation!

Sometimes people set themselves up to be "taken advantage of." For instance, you may bend over backwards for others, thinking this will ultimately help you to feel better about yourself. You give so much that there would be no way another person could adequately repay you. Others may not have the time or inclination to pay you back, or they may see your "giving" nature as bribery. What's worse, the non-givers may eventually take your giving for granted and even *expect* you to give a great deal. Because you're so "good-hearted," they may ask more frequently or come looking for more of your handouts. If you aren't assertive in limiting your responses to other people's requests for time, effort, or material goods, you may eventually become very resentful and blow up at them. Or you may get depressed because you feel that people take you for granted. *But whose fault is that?*

Whenever you feel exploited, the first question you should ask yourself is this: *"How am I setting myself up to be used by others?"* After all, we *do* have the ability to control how much we *choose* to give to others. Therefore, we always have a hand in setting ourselves up to be taken advantage of. The best evidence for this principle is the fact that some people are always being taken advantage of, whereas others almost never are. Let's look at some general guidelines for successfully dealing with interpersonal anger.

Although basic personality changes require work and a lengthy period of modification, it *is* possible to alter behavioral effectiveness rather quickly with the use of some simple communication and interpersonal skills. For example, you can learn to modify external situations and limit the "opportunities" for anger long before you're able to become genuinely tolerant and patient. You can do this by altering your responses to anger-provoking situations, just as you can develop assertiveness techniques in dealing with problems posed in relationships.

Interpersonal anger usually involves three components: 1. physical arousal, 2. self-statements, and 3. behavioral response. All three seem to operate almost simultaneously in a blowup. We feel physically tense; we hear an internal statement in our head such as *"You're out to get me"* or *"I'm not going to let you get away with this"* and we respond impulsively. In order to deal effectively with our anger, we should work on all three of these components. Therefore, before we respond behaviorally, we should have control over the physical upheaval, we should interrupt and modify the self-statement, we should be aware of all the components of the situation, and we should formulate a response that we can live with later. Among the things that often torment depression-prone people are vivid remembrances of times when they discharged their anger immediately and inappropriately—perhaps wildly—and, as a result, felt shame and guilt.

Although counting to ten may only appeal to mathematicians, it's a good method for postponing an anger response so we won't have regrets later on. Instead of counting through our anger though, it's more effective to take a couple of slow, deep breaths, consciously relax any muscle tension or physical responses like clenched fists or gritted teeth, and attempt to remain calm. Dr. Donald Meichenbaum, an innovator in the cognitive-behavioral management of anxiety, anger, and pain, suggests that we can help the body further by talking to it: *"Stay calm." "Just try to relax." "Slow down."* (1)

When working through anger-producing situations, learn to speak to yourself in the same gentle way a concerned friend might speak to you: *"I have plenty of time to respond"* . . . *"As long as I keep cool, I'm in control here"* . . . *"I'm not going to let this get to me."* You may be able to talk to yourself calmly in dealing with the situation by *modifying* self-statements that have upset you in the past; for example: *"There's no need to doubt myself; what she does doesn't matter to me that much anyway"* . . . *"I'm not going to let myself get pushed around, but I'm not going to go haywire, either." "He would probably like me to really get angry. Well, I'm going to disappoint him."*

You can prepare yourself for a confrontation with a potentially provocative person by using internal self-statements geared to elicit specific behavioral strategies and responses: *"Don't assume the worst and jump to conclusions." "Look for the positive." "For now, give this person the benefit of the doubt." "Don't get defensive." "Try a cooperative approach." "Maybe we're both right."* If the other person is obviously pugnacious or obnoxious, you could say to yourself: *"Don't take it personally." "I wonder what's eating him." "It's really terrible how he's* acting." "He'll probably be sorry later." "For a person to be that irritable, he must be awfully unhappy."

When you think about it, angry explosions aren't all that sudden. There are many cues and hints that we ordinarily ignore, avoid, or rationalize away. But next time you feel annoyed or irritated in a conflicted situation, try to notice the anger immediately—before it takes over. By becoming aware of anger in its earliest stages, we can work to reduce the physical manifestations that tend to perpetuate it, like tensed muscles and hyperventilation. We should also notice our thoughts: are we beginning to fixate, react, sulk, resent? At times like this, we need to assess what is annoying us and deal with it *immediately*, before it builds into a reaction that will be unmanageable and regrettable as well.

You can design specific strategies for anticipating and averting anger-provoking situations and people. Though I think it's impossible to *choose* not to get angry (you'll only suppress your negative feelings and in the long run cause more trouble that way), I do think it's quite possible to choose to modify or even avoid situations that have consistently provoked your anger in the past. Look for alternative solutions so that you can either escape a situation or a person likely to irritate or even infuriate you, or consciously limit your exposure and provide yourself with an escape hatch. But it's also possible that by directly confronting people or situations that have annoyed you in the past and handling them *assertively*—instead of angrily or aggressively—you'll be able to change your pattern of relating. This might be effective, for instance, in dealing with close relatives with whom you have had difficulties.

There isn't equal potential for getting angry with *every* person in your life. So which people bother you the most? What types of interactions or issues are most likely to trigger your anger? If you *do* find yourself getting angry with a certain person, take some time after the confrontation to sit down and write in detail all the thoughts and feelings you had prior to, during, and after the explosion. Ask yourself this: before the blow-up, what were the *cues* and *signals* that could have warned me of these impending outbursts of anger? For example, if your mother criticizes your hair style, you may sense very strongly that the conversation is moving into "dangerous" areas. If you have had fruitless, unpleasant round-robin arguments about this subject in the past, you might want to simply change the subject and modify the situation as quickly as possible. Also, what were the *choice points* that you let go by—until you ran out of options and your emotions took over? For instance, if you already know that whenever Mom offers to help you clean your house it ends up in a fight over how the furniture should be arranged, decline her offers to help you in this way. Or, possibly, when you're on friendly terms with someone, you can productively discuss negative interactions you've had in the past. If this kind of discussion seems too threatening to you, consider writing down your thoughts instead, including your genuine desire to improve things to prevent future problems. Then consider giving those written thoughts to the other person. If that doesn't seem appropriate, you can describe the interaction to uninvolved friends and get some ideas about how to change things. You can even role-play to facilitate your responses and help you gain skill in interacting with a troublesome person and/or within a troublesome situation in the future.

In general, it is usually valuable to reduce the other person's defensiveness. The person's overreaction can feed into the already "primed" system and result in flared tempers that escalate together. *No one* feels good about momentarily losing control by exploding or engaging in a shouting match—in cases like this, we're unlikely to feel good even if we *do* win. The victory is mixed with guilt, anxiety, and perhaps embarrassment as well. And, sometimes, loss of self-esteem accompanies a loss of temper, even when that loss of temper is justified. Conversely, we often feel renewed self-confidence when the adversary fails to "get at" us.

But remember this—if you *do* get angry and "let 'er rip" on occasion: so long as you don't become completely irrational, it *is* healthy to let someone else know that there are definite limits to your tolerance for whatever he or she tries to dump on you because you've been mislabeled a victim.

References

1. Meichenbaum, Donald, and D. Turk. The cognitive-behavioral management of anxiety, anger and pain. In P.O. Davidson (ed.), *The Behavioral Management of Anxiety, Depression and Pain.* New York: Brunner/Mazel, 1976.

27.

Solicit Partner Cooperation

*". . . a relationship is a system; if half of it changes,
the other half cannot remain exactly the same."*

Any truly intimate relationship can serve as a solid base of support for
depressed people when they feel helpless, frightened, or despairing.
These relationships, when they are working well, provide a sanctuary
from the pain of isolation and alienation; they provide a hopeful
reality to counterbalance distorted perceptions and pessimistic
conclusions.

However, within the core of most intimate relationships lies a
vulnerability that can serve to catalyze earlier unresolved
developmental issues: sexual identity conflicts, intimacy and
autonomy problems, freedom or security needs. Many of us carry
around outdated models of marriage and intimate relationships along
with unfulfilled infantile needs, fantasies, and expectations. Often a
person's romantic but unrealistic hope that he or she will meet
someone who will completely make up for a deprived past or parental
rejection is quickly dashed by a lover's betrayal or marital
disillusionment. In these cases, the "loved one" is likely to have
served as a projected reflection of intense emotional needs that the
deprived self has not learned to satisfy or resolve. The depression-
prone person is customarily subject to severe depressions after his or
her fondest dreams are rudely shattered.

The open door of vulnerability in relationships lets in both deep
satisfaction and hurt, the powers of healing as well as the potential for
sabotage and self-destruction. When we allow ourselves to care about
another person and entrust our feelings to him or her, we drop our
guards and essentially become unprotected. Given these facts, it's no
wonder that an intimate relationship can correct misperceptions,
mistrusts, and old fears . . . *or* it can reinforce, catalyze, and confirm
them. If you can at least *postpone* blaming your partner or yourself for

your developmental vulnerabilities, conditioned personality characteristics, or style of relating to others, you might be able to correct negative patterns of communication and interaction. Too frequently, however, stresses and pressures in a relationship create defensiveness and self-protectiveness, characteristics which tend to further polarize two individuals. Instead of *appreciating* personality differences and expanding underdeveloped parts of yourself, you may become rigid and put your energy into blaming or changing your partner in order to accommodate your own neurotic needs.

You can help make your relationship and your life more peaceful if you recognize that trying to get your partner to change is more often than not a losing battle. The more you blame, attack, or demand during a conflict, the more rigid, defensive, and resistant your mate is likely to become. You don't have control over your partner's behavior, nor are you capable of reshaping his or her personality. What the two of you *can* do, however, is discuss incompatibilities during calm periods: make decisions, negotiate and bargain for changes, try to plug the "holes" in your relationship, develop and bolster its strengths. During the next crisis, however, old interactional patterns may automatically kick into play, so that agreements, negotiated rationally during a truce, may be momentarily suspended.

Sometimes, though, mutual agreements *do* hold up. But with respect to specific issues that are especially important to one partner, the other partner may have far less need and motivation to change. In other words, if something is particularly important to one partner, he or she can work to change his or her *own* feelings or reactions in this area of hoped-for change in the other. For example, instead of losing control and being reduced to ineffective rage, one partner can assertively and calmly hold the line; instead of withdrawing into cold aloofness, one partner can maintain contact and work through the issue; instead of withholding a response, one partner can share feelings; instead of angrily attacking, one partner can quietly confront; instead of passively withdrawing into helpless guilt, one partner can stand firm. These are all positive tactics a depression-prone person can utilize in a conflicted partnership that contains depression-causing ingredients.

One partner cannot remain the same if the other partner changes. For example, the guilt-inducer will eventually give up if the previously guilt-prone partner doesn't cooperate by becoming guilty; the passive-aggressive person will eventually stop sly attacks if the receiver ignores the insinuations; the provocateur will be more likely to change if the overreactor doesn't respond; the manipulator will become confused and abandon his or her efforts when the once-malleable partner maintains a stance. In other words, it "takes two to tango" in perpetuating a toxic interactional pattern in a committed relationship. If you don't automatically enter into the self-defeating fight rituals and/ or don't reward your sparring partner by getting angry, depressed, or otherwise upset, the interactional pattern will change. It will change because old behaviors are no longer being reinforced.

The partner motivated to change sometimes asks: *"But why do I have to do all the changing? Why can't he/she change too?"* That's a fair question. But if one partner is resistant to changing aspects of himself or herself and is stubborn about maintaining the marital status quo and the partner asking for change refuses to do "all the changing," you can guess what might happen: a couple could get stuck *for years* in a dismal holding pattern. But, surprisingly, when one partner stops trying to change the other and takes responsibility only for carrying out his or her own desired personal changes, the whole relationship is affected and sometimes even transformed. This happens because a relationship is a system; if half of it changes, the other half cannot remain exactly the same.

Sometimes depression-prone people are asked to change things they're doing as part of some "deal" struck between them and their partners in order to relieve tensions in the relationship. The following question is important for them to ask themselves in this case: *"Are the changes my partner would like to see in me compatible with my own goals for change?"* The test is whether the changes would make him or her healthier while improving the relationship as well.

If you deny or undermine your own potential when you try to change for the sake of a relationship, you may decide that you need to get out of the relationship rather than to stop growing. For instance, if you must stop expanding your interests and contacts, suppress legitimate needs, ignore healthy striving, and subordinate your whole being to a state of "togetherness" with your spouse, you are risking psychological death. Or if you have to give up meaningful friendships and remain dependent, weak, and compliant in order to keep your mate from feeling threatened, you need to take an objective look at what you're actually getting out of the relationship—in positive and negative terms. If by becoming positive, open, assertive, and focused on developing neglected potentials results in your partner becoming more rigid, demanding, undermining, or difficult in some other way (such as even adopting your depression- proneness), you need to ask yourself if personal growth is possible for you within the relationship.

On the other hand, those changes in you that are seemingly demanded by the needs of the relationship and are also productive and appropriate—changes that you should make whether or not you are involved with this particular partner—should be seen as positive changes beneficial to you and the relationship. A relationship that demands or stimulates healthy change in both partners can nurture the motivation for growth and provide ongoing support for that growth as well. Try to spot depression-causing elements in your partnership. When a partner who is depression-prone in the first place becomes significantly depressed during a conflict with an intimate, the depression itself may become the central issue in the relationship. Whether or not the depression was actually "caused" by unhealthy patterns in the relationship, it will eventually take its toll on that relationship. At that point, buried, unresolved conflicts brought into the marriage or relationship are likely to emerge.

Unfortunately, many people have "gaps" in their learning about relationships that correspond to the "gaps" in the relationship between their parents. For example, if parents don't know how to communicate, problem-solve, and fight in healthy ways, they might have demonstrated myriad ways to sabotage, criticize, and humiliate each other, thus perpetuating pathological interactions in their offspring. For instance, if, as a child, a person "practiced" short-circuiting—collapsing, exploding, or withdrawing—whenever he or she was being manipulated, controlled, criticized, or rejected, current susceptibilities may be nothing more than reflections of old vulnerabilities. But some of these patterns have been sufficiently reinforced so as to emerge automatically and full-blown during a conflict with an intimate. For example, if the depression-prone person had domineering, authoritarian, or controlling parents, he or she might passively give in to the partner and constantly be accommodating, compliant, and approval-seeking. Dependency, weakness, or passivity may cause a person to place his or her destiny in someone else's hands. If the depressed person depends upon the partner for his or her primary source of self-esteem and builds his or her identity or self-concept around the partner or the relationship, vulnerability to depression may increase.

Based upon *assumptions* and *expectations* consciously or subconsciously formulated during parental interactions, the depression-prone person may develop pessimistic expectations (*"No one will ever love me"*) or idealistically romantic hopes (*"Someday, someone will come along and make my life better"*). Unrealistic expectations growing out of childhood fears or dreams can pave the way for self-sabotage, disillusionment, and bitterness. Or *situational changes* may disrupt the balance of the marital or intimate relationship, and aggravate communication or interactional problems. For example, job changes, illnesses, or demands from children may increase pressure and reduce the availability of one or the other partner.

I have seen many cases in which one of the partners is more of a "giver" than the other. If the "giver" inherits excessive demands from other sources, the receiving partner—now "neglected"—may feel deprived and become confused, unhappy, resentful, or withdrawn. For example, a young married woman may be in a marriage in which both she and her husband expect *her* to be a good listener—sympathetic, and supportive. But if she has a demanding preschooler or two, acquires a full-time job outside the home, assumes increased family obligations because of an ailing relative or whatever, she may experience an emotional drain and consequently have less energy available for her husband. If he, in turn, becomes critical or demanding of her or—worse yet—pouts, withdraws from her, acts disappointed in her, or makes her feel guilty, she may find that she is getting depressed. Now, if her self-concept includes the view of herself as unselfish, loving, and always "there" for her husband, she may continue to neglect her own needs and try even harder, but still feel a reduction in self-esteem—and sink further into a depressed state.

Another source of depression may be unhealthy individual personality characteristics. One spouse may often act critical, withholding, demanding, negative, undermining, insensitive, or downright rejecting. If the other spouse is especially vulnerable to any of these personality patterns (and it would be hard not to be!) a depression may result. A far less obvious but parallel case might be the "perfect spouse." Beware of the "perfect person" who seems supremely well-adjusted, not at all needy, always in control—*but who may be undermining*. When the "well-adjusted" partner seems to have no emotional needs, is completely self-sufficient, is always giving yet seemingly not expecting to receive anything in return, a depression-prone mate may feel even more useless and burdensome. Many people actually begin to feel "sicker" when living with a "perfect" partner—for what do you give the person who already "has everything"?

Some people actually have a vested interest in maintaining depression in their partners. The non-depressed partner may be threatened by the depressed mate when he or she *isn't* depressed, so the non-depressive may say or do little things (especially subtle passive-aggressive things) to perpetuate or prolong a depression. Or the non-depressed partner may need to appear as the all-accepting "good guy" who gains praise from others for having to "put up with" his or her "bitchy" or irritable, unreasonable, oft-depressed mate. In order to look good, every "good guy" needs a "bad guy" around to ensure his or her positive image.

A rather dramatic and unfortunate example of a passive- aggressive "nice guy" contributing to a depression is reflected in a family problem I tried to deal with years ago, before I had sufficient experience in family dynamics. A 40-year-old woman named Hilda came to me for counseling, reporting periods of depression characterized by self-hate and angry outbursts aimed primarily at her three teenage children—all boys. Hilda acknowledged that her depression was the problem. Her husband Dave, she said, was a fine man—a good father and a patient husband. I believed her (to some extent) and invited her to bring her husband with her to the next session in order to help me understand her depression and the difficult situation that seemed to be developing in the family.

Hilda's husband Dave, a hard-working and successful lawyer, came with her to the session and immediately expressed his dismay about her depression. He felt that he was very successful financially and that they had a good family. Dave said he just didn't understand why Hilda was so depressed and angry and why she nagged the children so much. He remarked that he had no problem getting the boys to do whatever he asked of them. He said he sympathized with his children and felt that the reason they didn't mind their mother was because of her "bad attitude" and irrational, angry outbursts. Hilda admitted that everything Dave said was true.

As Dave spoke more about their family situation, I felt some vague annoyance that I couldn't quite put my finger on. Nevertheless, I encouraged him to talk further about his "concern." He then quickly described almost the prototype of a long-suffering nice-guy, ending with a story that proved to be devastating for Hilda. He said that Hilda's father, on his deathbed, told him that he expected Hilda to be as difficult for Dave to put up with as her mother had been for him! Even in my inexperience, I could detect a "curse of the cat people" script developing in this family situation. Despite Dave's obvious self-righteous stance, Hilda weakly admitted that he was relating the truth.

Containing my annoyance, I suggested that since Dave handled the children *so* well and had such good relationships with them, maybe he could completely take over the discipline for a period of two months, in order to show Hilda how it should be done. This would restore order (he said that they respected him) and it would remove Hilda from the disciplinary role long enough to re-establish positive relationships with the children. To my surprise, Dave agreed to this experiment. Hilda felt like a failure, but temporarily unburdened by the disciplinary role, she was able to concentrate on re-establishing positive, nurturing relationships with the children.

But as a result of this simple, temporary role reversal within the family, all hell broke loose! At first, the two teenagers were absolutely *delighted* that they had "bitchy" Mom off their backs and could take orders from their more reasonable father. But as I suspected, when the novelty wore off, the kids began to drag their feet and become as forgetful as they'd been with their mother. At first, Dave worked extra hard to make it appear that the system was working. Eventually, though, he became overburdened and displayed impatience. "Naturally" he yelled at Hilda because she was the one who had been responsible for establishing the pattern in the first place. Fortunately, Hilda deflected the blame, continued to leave the disciplining and chore-monitoring to him, and instead worked on improving her relationships with the children.

When I saw Dave and Hilda in a counseling session three weeks later, he blamed his lack of success on the long-term pattern his wife had been responsible for establishing. I didn't disagree with him, but simply suggested that if anyone could break the pattern, *he could*. Three weeks after that, Dave refused to return for counseling. Hilda reported that he was yelling at the children more and more; in response, the children were dragging their feet more and more. But, surprisingly, she was less depressed and her relationship with the children had improved. And, like Dave, she was angry with me for "screwing up the family." I apologized and expressed surprise that Dave was unable to manage the children as effectively as he thought he could; I also expressed some confusion that she felt so much better despite a growing family problem.

About two months later, Hilda returned for counseling. Her depression had dissipated; her improved relationship with the children had increased her effectiveness with them. As a result, she was now helping out with considerable effectiveness in monitoring their chores and behaviors. Overall, the family was functioning much better. But instead of being appreciative, Dave was moody and vaguely annoyed. I'm not sure if he was consciously aware of it or not, but he had been "found out." He had it made: a wife who blamed herself and through her angry outbursts and ineffectiveness made him look like the proverbial nice guy, and children who respected and adored him because, in contrast to their mother, he seemed perfect. Unfortunately, Dave's self-esteem (at least within the family) had been contingent upon an imbalanced and basically unhealthy family dynamic.

I didn't see Hilda and Dave again in counseling. But some months after my last session with them, I ran into Hilda in the grocery store. She looked energetic and alive. Though I don't know this to be true, I'm hoping that Dave was able to turn in his "nice guy" role with all its benefits for a more realistic role and a potentially more satisfying and balanced family environment.

Many of these apparent imbalances reflect behavioral patterns recognized by the skilled marital therapist as a typical "overadequate/underadequate" marital interaction style. In this type of arrangement, one partner is able to continually look good by inadvertently or consciously keeping the other partner "sick"—that is, off-balance, dependent, confused, or weak.

Relationship problems may emerge as a result of difficulties in the *interactional style* of the couple. If one partner becomes depressed, feels alone, and needs emotional closeness, he or she may experience the need for and become more demanding of the other partner for emotional expressiveness. If the partner is not a particularly warm or demonstrative person to begin with, he or she may become annoyed or alarmed, and withdraw. This partner may declare: *"No matter what I do, it isn't good enough"* or *"Your needs are insatiable. I can't fill you up."* Withholding from a depressed mate may be rationalized by, *"I don't want to give in to his unreasonable demands"* or *"I don't want to increase her dependency."* The depressed spouse may feel "sick" and overdependent, but because of this virtual rejection will experience increased helplessness, desperation, and alienation.

Such extreme cases in marital relationships are in the minority. I mention them here for emphasis, because many intimate relationships may contain faint echoes of any or all of these negative aspects. A relationship must be carefully scrutinized whenever there is a suspiciously negative interdependency or frequent conflict in an intimate association that is sustained by a chronic depressive or depression-prone person. These interactional elements and all others contributing to a crisis or stalemate in a troubled relationship are, of course, best sorted out by a competent, objective couple or family therapist, with both partners participating whenever possible.

When the Going Gets Tough

28.

Helping Your Depression-Prone Partner

Depressed people are often so preoccupied with problems related to their feelings that they fail to recognize or understand how their depression may be affecting family members, friends, and colleagues. If you are the partner of a depressed or depression-prone person, it is important for you to have an understanding of the emotional needs of the depressed person and the social consequences of the depression itself.

Depression and Relationships

A serious depression should not be allowed to continue unrelieved and untreated for a long period of time. Long-term and/or severe depression can create further and more serious problems because it has the effect of isolating the depressed person emotionally. Some of what I'm going to say in this chapter may sound like tough talk to a person who is experiencing depression, and/or to sympathetic family members and friends who are concerned about that person. My message here is intended as essential and practical advice; I share it directly and without frills, in an effort to alert you to some of the possible problems and complications of a continuing depression.

People who are depressed much of the time and tend always to lean on their friends may evidence little or no concern for the problems their friends are having; in fact, it may seem that the depressed person is actually *exploiting* his or her friends. And the help that most well-intentioned friends give a depressed person often serves only to keep that person from sinking into a deeper depression—in other words, this kind of help may allow the depressed person to remain in a "holding pattern"—rather than actively working his or her way out of the depression.

The Case for Professional Help

"The depressed person is afflicted, people around him or her subsequently become affected."

Some depressed people actually come to *expect* ongoing and supportive attention from concerned people in their lives. But when people are depressed so severely and/or frequently that their needs and demands begin to "drain" the energy of relatives and friends, it would seem that the depression is more than a passing thing and that professional help should be sought. A warning, though: depression-prone people often dismiss the idea of professional help by saying to themselves or others, "*I should be able to handle this myself!*" They also may castigate themselves for being so weak that they're unable to snap themselves out of their depression. But when they delay seeking professional assistance, severely depressed people run the risk of burdening others in their lives to the point where they ultimately *destroy* the very support systems they have created and learned to rely on. Severe and/or long-standing depression eventually proves to be costly in many ways—psychologically, socially, and financially.

The depressive's frequent glumness, unpredictability, negativism, and poor emotional control can bring on frustration, irritability, confrontativeness, disgust, and withdrawal in even the most compassionate and understanding friends and family members. To complicate matters, the fatigue and inertia that characterize a depression can result in work pile-ups at home, forcing extra duties on increasingly exhausted and resentful family members. Along with the sense of being "used" or overburdened by the depressed partner's emotional needs and functional inadequacies, a growing impatience with the depressed person may seriously undermine once satisfying relationships; indeed, the effects of a long-term depression may jeopardize the emotional and economic support systems of an entire family.

"*It's too expensive!*" That's another reason people frequently cite for not seeking professional treatment for depression. In my opinion, however, a seriously or frequently depressed person can't afford *not* to get help. When the depressed person works outside the home, it must be recognized that ongoing depression may, in time, affect that person's job performance and ultimately his or her job security. Job pressures in the form of seemingly overwhelming demands (which, prior to the depression, may have been rather routinely and easily handled), along with an almost inevitable drop in performance may ultimately cut the depressed person off from yet another source of personal satisfaction and self-esteem.

This, too, adds to the downward spiral of feelings. And it's no secret that not all employers are sympathetic and patient in dealing with employees who are struggling with personal problems. In fact, the slightest hint of emotional problems—whether directly observed by the employer or reported by other employees—makes some employers nervous and perhaps even intolerant. This is unfortunate and unfair, but it *is* true and it constitutes yet another reason to seek professional help for depression when it is severe, recurring, and/or long-standing.

If a person in a severely depressed condition does not seek professional help himself or herself, it is both appropriate and compassionate for someone else—spouse, relative, close friend, or associate—to actively seek out professional help for that person. Ideally, this help should commence as soon as it becomes evident that the depression is more than the blues and/or a passing mood and that the depressed person is not improving with self-help methods. The longer serious depression goes untreated, the more profoundly it will affect the depressed person's entire life—in ever-widening circles. The depressed person is *afflicted*, people around him or her subsequently become *affected*. Generally speaking, the more quickly the depressed person gets appropriate and effective help, the less lengthy and costly the course of treatment is likely to be. Postponing needed treatment until a person becomes so incapacitated that inpatient treatment is required will almost certainly have profound effects on the depressed person and many people in his or her life, as well.

Helping Your Partner/Helping Yourself

As the partner of a depression-prone person, there are things you can do—or consciously *avoid* doing—to help your partner, regardless of whether professional treatment is sought and carried out or not. Equally important, there are things you can do to help *yourself* by protecting your energy and looking after your own needs while you concentrate on providing effective support to your depression-prone partner.

Special Problems between Depressed People and Non-depressed People

"Take a good look at your partner's depression."

It does seem that depression-prone people are more likely to be attracted to people who are—or at least *appear* to be—relatively even-tempered and not depression-prone. It's almost as if a balance of temperaments has been sought in forging the relationship. Though it's probably fortunate when only one partner is depression-prone, that circumstance *does* make it difficult for the non-depressed partner to understand and empathize with what the depression-prone partner is going through. Some people have never struggled with an episode of depression in their lives; other people are not depression-prone; still other people have never *allowed* themselves to experience depression and have, in fact, succeeded in keeping the blues at bay by staying perpetually busy, with no time out for brooding. Each of these people may have difficulty understanding how it feels to be depressed.

When a partner's depression affects a person who is unfamiliar with the condition, he or she may be utterly mystified by it and fail to respond or relate to the depressed person's feelings in a non-judgmental way. Instead, this non-depressed person who does not know depression firsthand may see the depression as some sort of criticism, as if something he or she did or didn't do has *created* the depression in the other person. Some people may try to "handle" a partner's depression by behaving like military drillmasters, ordering the depressed person to shape up, then becoming *furious* when he or she is unable to do so on command. Not realizing that his or her depressed partner may feel unable to function at all, the non-depressed person may say, "Well, why don't you just *force* yourself to do something?"

A complicating factor in some relationships: when the non-depressed partner has strong susceptibilities to depression but has repressed these feelings and/or concealed them not only from others, but from himself or herself as well. For example, a frantic, achievement-oriented lifestyle may keep a person distracted or detached from feelings of depression. But when a depression-deflecting person is deeply involved with a depression-prone partner, he or she might be less successful in avoiding depression. A partner's depression may even trigger a panic reaction in a non-depressed person who was exposed at a very young age to a depression-prone parent. The fear of being dragged down into the pit of despair with the depressed partner may then be covered up with impatience, anger, or active avoidance. I saw this dynamic in a married couple I once counseled:

> When Marge had her first bout with depression, her husband
> Stan almost fled the relationship. Up to that point in their mar-
> riage, he had been quite supportive of her and she had been rela-
> tively independent. But when Marge discovered that her father
> had been having an extramarital affair, her whole world was
> shaken and she became very depressed. Stan was confused by
> her reaction and began staying away from home more and more.
> Through psychotherapy, we discovered together that Stan had
> grown up with a mother who was dependent and depressed.
> Throughout his childhood, he had guilt feelings related to his
> mother and felt burdened by her as well. Though as an adult,
> this man had all but "forgotten" about his childhood difficulties
> related to his mother, the onset of depression in his wife seemed
> to trigger his earlier conditioned response to his mother's chronic
> depression.

Take a good look at your partner's depression. Does it seem to be somewhat consistent with a long-established pattern in him or her— periodic blue moods that are more frequent and/or are now taking a more extreme form? Or is the depression an unusual new manifestation, not quite "in character" with the person you know so well? It could be that your partner is exhibiting more vulnerability and uncertainty than ever before because of ill health, the weakening of strong internal emotional controls, or because a general "busyness" that has deflected depression for him or her in the past has finally worn down. In other words: if you aren't familiar with depression yourself, try your best to understand your partner's situation and be sure to allow for your lack of comprehension of what he or she is suffering. Someday, you may have a bout with depression yourself. And then you'll begin to realize how helpless and hopeless and utterly depleted and disoriented a depressed person can feel. In the meantime, do the best you can to ease your partner through the difficult times.

Some of the special challenges inherent in relationships between depression-prone and non-depression-prone partners are illustrated in the experiences of Theresa and Frank, a married couple in their thirties:

Though Theresa's periodic depressions were not severe, they seemed to precipitate an inordinate amount of conflict in what was otherwise a good marriage. Theresa described her husband Frank as congenial, easy to get along with, and supportive. But it seemed to her that whenever she became depressed for a period of time, Frank would eventually lose patience with her and become agitated.

Theresa brought Frank with her for counseling; I liked him immediately. It seemed to me he had learned some good interpersonal skills from having both older and younger siblings. Frank had studied business administration and psychology in college and from his first job on, was considered an exceptional personnel director. Rational, clear-headed, and perceptive, Frank took pride in his ability to zero in on individuals and their problems and to help them find solutions, as well. Fortunately— or unfortunately, in this case—Frank had never been depressed in his life. The few times he'd experienced personal setbacks due to unforeseen circumstances, Frank said he was able to mobilize himself with this motto: "When the going gets tough, the tough get going." Sidestepping this cliche, I decided to try to help Frank understand Theresa's depression-proneness and along with that, explore his own reactions to this personality characteristic.

The causes of Frank's brief lapses from sensitivity soon became apparent: First, he loved Theresa deeply and couldn't stand seeing her so depressed. Unlike his appropriate and useful "detachment" from the people with whom he worked, Frank hurt as much in this situation as Theresa did! In fact, he would have done almost *anything* to soothe her pain. Second, Frank secretly felt responsible for Theresa's depression. At a deeper level, he naively believed that he wasn't everything she wanted or needed in a partner. Since he didn't understand her depression, he erroneously believed that if Theresa really loved him and was happy with him, she wouldn't get depressed *at all*. Thus, at the subconscious level, Frank felt that Theresa's depression was a negative reflection on him as a husband. Third, since Frank was justifiably proud of his professional ability to help other people solve their problems, he'd frequently ask himself this question: "What the hell kind of person am I when I can't even help my own wife?!" For Frank, Theresa's depression became an ongoing reminder of his failure in an important area of his life—and he certainly was not accustomed to failure.

As Theresa began to understand the sources of Frank's conflict, she took the first important steps toward resolving their trouble. "Look Frank," she said, "I had a lousy childhood. And I suffer from pre-menstrual syndrome as well as from some thyroid problems. Actually, I'm amazed that I don't get depressed more often than I do. You neither cause my depression nor are you responsible for curing it. I just want you to give up the savior role—and be supportive. Stop feeling so damn responsible and let me work out of my depressed feelings myself!" Frank followed Theresa's advice and the tension and conflicts between them over her depression began to lessen.

Avoid the Trap of Slipping into a Depression Yourself
" . . . there's a real 'demand quality' in depression . . ."

Whether or not the partner of a depressed person is depression-prone, he or she needs to be careful not to slip into the depression himself or herself. Understandably, this is a distinct possibility when partners are deeply devoted to each other and genuinely concerned about each other's well-being. This is another case for professional help: a more objective third party could be helpful because he or she would not have the illusion that devoted love alone can "cure" someone of depression.

Partners of depressed people can be most effective if they remind themselves that they're limited in what they can do. Unfortunately, there's a real "demand quality" in depression that makes it difficult for non-depressed people not to be dragged down when their partners are in so much pain. The more depressed their partners become, the more they feel compelled to help them. They might feel frantic and experience a tremendous desire to do almost *anything* to help their partners, at least in part to relieve their own feelings of helplessness. Sometimes, after trying very hard with little success to show for their efforts, these would-be rescuers become angry with their depressed mates for "making" them feel so ineffective in their efforts to help.

The following guidelines from *The Book of Hope* by Helen DeRosis and Victoria Pellegrino can be helpful for the partner of any depressed person, though they were specifically written for the partners of depressed women.

1. Depression is contagious, but try not to be overwhelmed yourself.
2. Don't put her worries down.
3. Show your kind concern, not your worried concern.
4. Remember that she'll get over her feelings.
5. Keep things light, playful if possible.
6. Distract as much as you can.
7. Remember, you may very well get the VIP treatment yourself when you need it one day.[1]

Alter Interactions

"*. . . no one can actually pull another person out of a depression . . .*"

To the foregoing list of guidelines, I'd like to add some other advice to partners of depressed people, advice that focuses specifically on altering interactions between the two of you:

1. When your partner is feeling depressed, don't spend time and effort trying to convince him or her that things aren't as bad as they seem to be. *The depressed person knows better—and knows that (in his or her perception at least) things are terrible!* It stands to reason that it will only aggravate matters if you point out how small his or her problems are or how distorted his or her perceptions or feelings are (to you, anyway). To the depressed person, this approach constitutes a put-down rather than reassurance. What he or she hears is this: "*You're ridiculous (or you have no reason) to feel that way.*" If you trivialize your

partner's feelings and concerns, you will succeed only in making him or her feel less important; if you make light of your partner's feelings, he or she will feel misunderstood and isolated. Depressed people often realize that they are, in fact, exaggerating reality; they don't need this pointed out to them. Partners of depressed people might consider this possibility: that the tendency of the depressive to exaggerate situations may be in response to the tendency of others to dismiss their feelings as unimportant.

2. Try to convey to your depressed partner your understanding that at times, situations can look very bleak and even relatively minor problems may seem absolutely overwhelming. If you evidence empathy for how your depressed partner feels, he or she will tend to feel less alone and less detached from reality. Sometimes, specific things *do* occur in one's life that contribute to depression. But in the midst of their perfectionism and self-criticalness, the depression-prone person may have overlooked certain situations as trivial when considering causes of depression. If you can somehow help your depressed partner see how the depression might have been triggered or just indicate that you understand why he or she might feel depressed, your partner may ease up on himself or herself and let go of the feeling that he or she is "crazy." Also, if you show empathy and understanding, the depressed person's need to exaggerate the condition in order to get attention will be lessened. If you can accept a depressed person's feelings as okay, he or she may be able to do the same. And, as a result, the intensity of the depression may lessen.

3. It isn't essential to know why a partner is depressed. In most cases, knowing the reason probably wouldn't help much anyway! If your first inquiry about the cause doesn't bring an answer, don't interrogate. (In their frustration to "get at" and "root out" the cause, I've heard some otherwise caring, concerned partners go so far as to say, "*Well, if you don't even know why you're depressed, how the hell can you feel so bad?*") But remember, people have a perfect right to feel a certain way without knowing exactly *why*. At any rate, immediate answers to "why" questions while one is in the midst of a depression could be

rationalizations, anyway. Paradoxically, when you stop asking "why" and instead make efforts to accept what your partner is feeling, he or she may no longer feel that it's necessary to justify his or her feelings to you. Consequently, the depressed person will be more relaxed, more reflective, and therefore more aware of some factors that may have contributed to his or her depression in the first place.

4. The best tone and approach to use in nurturing a depressed partner is one of concern, but not a hovering, fretful concern that may very well *add* to his or her anxiety. Strive to be available, but resist acting overly interested in pulling the person out of depression as quickly as possible. Over-involvement on your part may suggest to your depressed partner that it's not okay to be depressed; there may be an implicit demand that he or she should be able to conquer the depression immediately, if he or she would only *try* hard enough. The depressed partner may then feel the added burden of your displeasure and feel guilty for that. So, instead of conveying any sort of alarm or urgency to your depressed partner, just *listen*, be supportive, and reassure your partner that you will *be there* for him or her. Then, when you feel the time is right, you might gently point out that you believe the standards and expectations he or she is setting are too tough.

In implementing these suggestions, you can at times set up conditions that serve as *occasions* for your partner to work himself or herself out of a depression, and you can provide *opportunities* for him or her to take advantage of these things in overcoming depression. *But no one can actually pull another person out of a depression—that is clearly work for the individual affected, with or without professional help.* You are doomed to failure if you believe that you can bring your partner out of a depression *if only you try hard enough.* By taking responsibility for another person's depression, you are acting on an erroneous belief—that you are powerful enough to control the moods and feelings of another person. Quite frankly, this is a foolhardy and arrogant assumption that might even insult your depressed partner—particularly if he or she *already* feels dependent, helpless, or patronized. In this case, your efforts to take over *completely* may serve only to reinforce the depression. Your actions also subtly impose demands upon your depressed partner at a time when he or she is least able to handle demands. Of course, this over-involvement also makes you prone to taking things personally if your partner doesn't appreciate your efforts or fails to respond in a way you feel is appropriate.

Preventive Measures—Making a Difference

" . . . *ask your partner to tell you what is most helpful.*"

There are a number of preventive measures that will help diminish any depression-maintaining aspects of your relationship and also help your partner deal with his or her susceptibility to depression:

1. You can become *very explicit* in your communications with your depression-prone partner. In your efforts to keep peace or avoid conflict, do you sometimes find yourself "hemming and hawing" as a way of taking the edge off criticism or requests? Depression-prone people tend to be acutely sensitive to criticism and alert to negative reactions as well; this heightened awareness may lead them to read certain meanings into things that aren't intended or in any way based on reality. Your depressed partner needs to know *exactly* where he or she stands with you; he or she probably doesn't have the energy to detect subtle cues from you, anyway. Even with your criticisms and demands, you should be clear and straightforward, never covert. Be explicit, as well, in stating *your* annoyances and resentments. Above all, don't try to smooth things over by *denying* your anger. When you're angry but deny that fact, your depressed partner may sense your annoyance and imagine that there is even more anger present than what you are feeling. This kind of subtlety can trigger guilt and further undermine self-esteem in the depression-prone person.

2. When your depression-prone partner is not depressed, make a special effort to get in touch with your own needs and desires, and express them openly and honestly to him or her. Since your partner actively *experiences* more neediness, he or she is likely to be more overt with requests and demands than you are. Indeed, he or she may remark that you always seem satisfied and don't

appear to need help from others at all. You can help dispel this notion that you have no needs by determining what it is you want from your partner *and asking for it*—particularly when he or she is not in the midst of a depression. As I see it, there are at least three reasons for you, as the non-depressed partner, to be clear and explicit with your requests of a depression-prone partner: • your partner will feel needed • your partner can then take credit for accomplishing something you request when he or she is able to fulfill that request • your partner won't feel subtly manipulated. This clarity, in turn, will enable your depressed partner to refuse overt requests without feeling the intensity of guilt that he or she is likely to feel in refusing vague requests.

Concealing needs and refusing to formulate clear requests can actually be a subtle form of *withholding* on your part. The depression-prone person handles direct requests far better than diffuse general demands, backhand comments, or expectations subtly conveyed through fleeting looks of disappointment or disgust. Your depression-prone partner needs to feel needed and also needs to feel that he or she is an active partner in the relationship. That way, he or she won't feel so guilty when requesting something from you.

3. You must enlist some cooperation from your depressed partner. There are, however, two major stumbling blocks to this part of the helping process: • *the depressed person's vagueness and failure to provide feedback about helping behavior* • *the depressed person's anger.*

An important element in the depressed person's vagueness and failure to provide feedback about helping behavior is the fact that non-depressed partners are often truly in the dark about how they can be most helpful to their depressed partners. Thus, if you try several things in an attempt to make your depressed partner more comfortable, you can ask him or her to facilitate the process by indicating what is most helpful and by expressing genuine appreciation to further encourage you in your efforts. The depressed partner may not be clear about what he or she needs; but once you do a few things for him or her, you might ask for feedback regarding what was most helpful. In any case, *ask your partner to tell you what is most helpful.*

If your depressed partner does not make direct requests of you, his or her only recourse may be to drag around with a pained look, hoping against hope that you can read minds. But this technique is passively manipulative and while it may appear to work at first, ultimately it undermines the self-respect of the depressed partner. Furthermore, it could make you resentful of your partner when you fail to guess what he or she wants, then feel guilty about your inability to properly respond to unexpressed needs.

Don't allow your depressed partner to play the following game: "If I have to ask you for something, it's not worth it . . . it just doesn't count!" *When depressed people expect their partners to read their minds, they are operating within a very inefficient trial-and-error system.* Overall, it's much better for you to put your energies into *giving*, rather than guessing. *Anyone* would find it exhausting to be required to have antennae up all the time in order to pick up a partner's unspoken wants and needs. And when the "guessing game" goes on too long, you may become so resentful you won't want to give your partner *anything at all.* So get your feelings about this issue out in the open with your partner. By doing this, you will actively demonstrate that the best way for your partner to get what he or she needs or wants from you is to *ask* for it.

Of course, you might have to say "no" to some of your partner's requests, because you have needs and boundaries too. But, in the long run, your partner should realize that the more you are aware of his or her needs and wants, the more likely you are to be able to help in a timely way. And then, the more your depression-prone partner gets his or her needs met, the less resentful and deprived he or she will feel. That's one less complication for the depression.

But your depressed partner should not expect you to know intuitively what he or she wants (particularly if he or she is not clear on those issues). How can you possibly know what to do if he or she has only vague feelings of dissatisfaction and is unsure exactly what is needed? Take note that *no amount of love or concern on your part will help you read your partner's subconscious mind.* In a close and trusting relationship, you can *explore together* different kinds of attention-giving techniques.

Anger—another stumbling block in the helping process—is a rather complicated factor. At times, you may resent your depressed partner for "making" you expend so much effort to help or to just put up with the depression. Or you may feel sorry for yourself, convey your disapproval, or do something to make your depressed partner feel even *more* guilty than he or she *already* does. Eventually, your depression-prone partner may become angry when he or she realizes that your subtle disapproval and guilt-inducing maneuvers may have contributed to or aggravated the depression.

When you reach an impasse involving anger, take some immediate action: invite your depressed partner to go for a walk or to take a pleasant ride with you. Just getting out of the house and experiencing a change of scenery may provide a beneficial distraction for both of you. But if your partner is reluctant to go out, don't push or insist. Instead, you might make a few suggestions for pleasant, low-key diversions at home. You could suggest music, a back rub, reading, having a snack and watching television together. With some trial and error, you'll no doubt find a few activities and/or diversions that work better than others. But it's useful to remember that people don't tend to really get in touch with a need or a want until *after* it is met.

Another point about anger—it may be helpful for you to know that whether anger is subtly provoked or not, your depressed partner may feel less vulnerable when he or she is angry. But, in the final analysis, a temper-tantrum doesn't lead to feelings of competency or renewed self-esteem. It's particularly frustrating to a depressed person if another person simply withdraws before or during a confrontation of some kind. In fact, a frustrating and self-defeating *attack-withdrawal* pattern often develops between a depressed person and his or her partner: the more angry the depressed person becomes, the more passively withdrawn and detached the partner becomes while attempting to meet his or her needs and demands.

A *word about emotional withdrawal*—Some partners of depression-prone people become passive over time because they have "learned" that when they attempt to meet the expectations or demands of their partners, their efforts never seem to be fully appreciated *or even adequate*. But keep in mind that saying or thinking that your partner is never satisfied with your efforts may be a convenient excuse to do *nothing*. If you dislike this kind of no-win dynamic between the two of you—and I hope that you do—try to get your depression-prone partner to lower his or her perfectionistic standards so that you won't feel so frustrated when you *do* attempt to help out in some way. Try to help your depressed partner understand, too, that he or she should try to refrain from attacking you for not being sufficiently attentive or supportive. Let it be known that such attacks on your efforts drive you away and seem to make him or her feel guilty as well—in the end, no one's needs are met.

Depression-prone people who have unresponsive or emotionally withdrawn partners sometimes feel that they must *explode* in order to get their partners to respond to them at all. Any changes in a relationship that *do* take place as a result of these explosions are, more often than not, short-lived. Then, in no time, it's back to the depressed partner's script of "deprivation as usual." Or, both of you may decide to withdraw: you into passive resentment, your partner into helplessness and frustration. *But, is this any way to live together?* Couples' counseling is clearly indicated when negative interactive situations like this become a pattern in a relationship. As for the anger you feel as the partner of the depressed person, it may come simply from dealing with the demands of the depression. Accept the fact that you must get some rest, relief, and recreation that takes you away from the situation. These measures may include developing planned releases from the cumulative anger you might feel.

Maintaining Your Perspective

As a person who is willing to "hang in there" with the depressed partner, you may need to follow some specific suggestions in order to maintain a useful perspective and guard against becoming adversely affected by your partner's depression. Even a highly motivated, deeply loving, energetic helper may eventually suffer from a kind of "battle fatigue" as the added tasks and burdens and the inevitable energy-depleting activities and concerns take their toll. But nobody—not even you—can be perfectly patient, diplomatic, tactful, reassuring, and giving, particularly when—in return—you're encountering irritability, tears, apathy, complaints, or ongoing apologies. In time, you may find that you are neglecting your own personal needs, interests, and responsibilities while assuming more and more care of the depressed person.

Stay in Touch with Your Limitations

One of the characteristics of depression may be a lessening or lack of concern about personal care, nutrition, and maintenance of the environment. A caring partner will often see to it that the depressed person maintains his or her appearance, eats balanced meals, and has clean, orderly surroundings, so as to avoid a situation that might aggravate the depression. But taking on these kinds of responsibilities for another person's well-being is a *major commitment*. As a helper, you must stay in touch with the limits of your own time and energy. You need to recognize that overcoming depression may take *time*. For this reason, you would be wise to build in some personal survival tactics for yourself. Otherwise, your patience, sympathy, and giving will eventually lead to complete exhaustion. Even if you have willingly and lovingly volunteered to care for your depressed partner, the more worn-out you are, the more susceptible you are to negative feelings of frustration, helplessness, irritation, and eventually, anger and resentment. At times you may well feel unappreciated, used, "depleted," or neglected when you get little or nothing in return from your depressed partner. But remember that by acting angry or like a martyr, you'll only complicate the situation by adding to your depressed partner's feelings of guilt and self-criticalness.

Keep Your Own Needs in Mind

As the partner of a depressed person, you cannot continue to postpone your personal needs indefinitely, nor can you continue to suppress your anger. The first step is to recognize the anger you feel, rather than to suppress it and risk having it finally surface in vague and subtle ways or as a sudden (and seemingly inappropriate) explosion. (Either outcome would be damaging to both you and your partner.) The second step is to vent your anger on an ongoing basis. Do this when you're not around your partner, so that your anger won't reach volcanic proportions at times when you're together. This discharge may involve physical releases through jogging or pounding pillows, or it may take a verbal form through venting with other people you choose to share with and/or professional helpers.

It should be said that handling your frustrations may also include getting professional help yourself, particularly if you begin to see that certain elements in your relationship with your depressed partner may, in fact, be serving to aggravate or sustain the depression. If both your partner and his or her therapist are willing, you might also have joint sessions in which you receive professional assistance in order to help maintain and enhance your relationship.

Avoiding the Pitfalls and Problems

The suggestions that follow may help you avoid some of the pitfalls and problems so common to those who want to help a depressed partner:

• *Protect yourself.* Don't take the depressed person's irritability personally unless, of course, it's clear that you are somehow contributing to the depression.

• *Don't neglect your own needs.* You cannot postpone your own needs indefinitely. Since you can't depend on your depressed partner for help right now, find ways to nourish yourself emotionally, physically, and spiritually.

• *Limit your giving.* Don't keep giving until you are empty. Do what you can, but don't become "emotionally bankrupt." In fact, it's not at all productive to treat the depressed person as an invalid and allow him or her to remain totally immobilized.

• *Ask for assistance.* It's much better to work along with the depressed person than it is to do things always by yourself for him or her. Enlist help with tasks and chores. Depressed people sometimes are better able to mobilize themselves a bit when there is someone else to work with on a project or activity. Emphasize that this activity is no "big deal" for you, that the depression he or she is feeling is temporary, and that when it's over he or she can help you with some of *your* tasks.

• *Get away now and then.* Don't abandon your own interests, hobbies, or regular activities. Make arrangements to occasionally "escape" the burdens of your helper role so as to keep your spirits and your energy level up.

• *Don't cut yourself off from others.* If your depressed partner begins to feel uncomfortable socially or is too tired to socialize, go to the places you want to go alone. You must have an outlet for getting new energy, support, and encouragement from associating with other people. This will help you return to your partner in a better condition to resume the helper role.

• *Limit "depression talk."* Though it's helpful to listen sympathetically to the depressed person and to offer reassurance as well, constant analysis and review of old issues may encourage *indulgence* in the depression. Encouraging your depressed partner to ruminate over feelings of despair, failure, and incompetence may reinforce negative feelings rather than relieve them. Talk about other things, people, and events—positive things, that is—to help focus your partner away from himself or herself.

• *Try to stay "up."* Of course playing loud rock music, telling endless jokes, and acting like the court jester probably won't please or comfort the depressed person at all. (And, besides, you'd probably feel as if you were doing calisthenics in a morgue or stand-up comedy at a funeral.) But telling low-key, amusing stories, playing soothing music, sharing interests, and consciously keeping conversation light may temporarily distract both you and your partner from the pervasiveness of the depression.

In her book *Depression*, writer Wina Sturgeon says the following: *"Be mad at the illness, not at the person."* [2] When it seems to you that your partner is doing little to move out of a depression, remember that he or she is in pain and didn't *choose* to be depressed. *Who would?* Nevertheless, depression is a fact of your life together right now. Rather than indulging in blame, guilt, or games, your primary efforts on your partner's behalf (and your own as well) are best channeled into helping both of you get through the depression with hope and health intact.

References

1. DeRosis, Helen A., and Victoria Pellegrino. *The Book of Hope/How Women Can Overcome Depression.* New York: Bantam, 1977.

2. Sturgeon, Wina. *Depression.* Englewood Cliffs, N.J.: Prentice-Hall, 1979.

29.

Getting Professional Help

There are several questions that most people have as they consider seeking professional help for depression. Based on my experience and allowing for differences in service delivery throughout the country, I'll do my best to answer some of the most common questions here:

How do I know if I need professional help?

There's no absolute rule on this, but here's a rule of thumb: if your feelings and moods are disrupting your life frequently, severely, or on a more or less continuous basis, you would be wise to seek professional help.

It's important to remember, however, that when you're feeling down in the dumps or blue, you're not necessarily heading toward depression. Nowadays, people are inclined to label a dismal period in their lives or even recurring blue moods as "depression." There's a certain shorthand about that term that communicates a less-than-ebullient condition. But the fact is, most psychiatrists and psychologists use the word "depression" cautiously. What usually is meant by the word "depression" is a clinical syndrome, the salient symptoms of which are summarized in Chapter 1. In past years, this phenomenon was sometimes referred to as a "nervous breakdown." Before you describe a blue mood as "depression," give it some thought; it might be a bit like "crying wolf." Then, someday, if you *are* suffering from depression, other people may be less likely to take you seriously—even though you will realize the difference in your own feelings and responses.

There's another aspect to the misuse and/or overuse of the word "depression" in describing a feeling state: it can mask an inability or disinclination to *do* something—anything—to alter one's life circumstances, especially if this requires exertion and entails difficult disruptions. This kind of "depression" is really a hideout, a delaying of essential decision-making and the action that commonly follows.

But the stress of living and/or working in unhappy or painful circumstances *can* eventually lead to clinical depression, particularly in people who are predisposed to it. Therefore, if you're under increasing strain at home or on the job, can't seem to find the right approach to improving the situation, and are evidencing signs of severe or prolonged depression, *take action as soon as possible.* Likewise, when inertia and gloom persist, and/or if you experience anxiety attacks, phobias, or other disturbing and debilitating symptoms of serious depression, treat these symptoms as signs that point to the need for professional help.

How expensive is treatment for depression?

Although cost is a concern for almost everyone seeking specialized care, many health insurance plans now cover a significant portion of the cost of treatment by an accredited therapist, providing such treatment has been recommended or prescribed by a physician. But if you determine that your situation will result in your being responsible for all or most of the cost of treatment, you'll want to explore alternative ways to obtain psychotherapeutic help. Many people simply cannot afford the full cost of sessions with a psychiatrist (currently running over one hundred dollars per 50-minute hour). *Clinical psychologists* (Ph.D.'s) and *Psychiatric Social Workers* (M.S.W.'s) charge over seventy-five dollars per session—though reduced rates may sometimes be negotiated with these treatment professionals. Shopping around for therapeutic care—or having someone else shop around for you—can turn up some viable options for effective treatment at lower cost. *Community mental health clinics* usually provide sliding-fee schedules based on family earnings and expenses. Also, you may be able to reduce costs considerably by setting up a schedule of seeing the less expensive psychiatric social worker or experienced depression counselor for regular psychotherapy, and limiting visits to the more expensive psychiatrist or other qualified physician for medication and questions concerning your physical health.

Are there some guidelines I can follow that will lead me to a good psychotherapist?

If you decide to try psychotherapy but have no referrals to work from, you may discover that finding a suitable psychotherapist is no easy task. If you live in a small town or a rural community, you may find it necessary to look to the closest metropolitan area for the help you need. What are some guidelines? A first step might be simply to determine, generally, what kind of help is available locally. Start with the telephone directory. There should be listings under the *Mental Health* heading. Psychiatrists are frequently listed in the yellow pages under the general heading of *Physicians* or *Medical Doctors*. There also should be a heading for *Psychologists*. *Psychotherapists* may also be listed under one or the other of the following yellow-page classifications: *Pychiatric Social Workers, Social Workers, Social Services,* or *Marriage and Family Counselors*. Many of these listings include psychotherapists who are in private practice. Also, there are private group practices and nonprofit, volunteer-staffed and charitable organizations such as community family services and religious-affiliated agencies. (Note that in most cases, you need not belong to a particular church or religious denomination to seek help in one of these religious-affiliated agencies.) Often a local medical association (usually with the county's name) is prepared to provide referrals for mental health care. If cost is a major consideration, it may be possible to find a good therapist in the public sector, under such categories as *Human Services* or *Social Services*. All public, most nonprofit, and some private mental health agencies as well as counselors have sliding-fee schedules.

Don't overlook the possibility of seeking out a therapist who is still in training and is, therefore, closely supervised by an experienced professional. If there is a university or medical school near you, check to see if its department of psychology and/or department of psychiatry (or neuropsychiatry) conducts outpatient clinics. General hospitals and university hospitals (for medical training and research) usually maintain outpatient psychotherapy programs as well as inpatient psychiatric units. If you are a veteran, consider the V.A. hospital in your area a primary resource for treatment and referral.

Also, keep in mind that considerable success is often achieved with the kind of depression therapy that is carried out in small support groups and facilitated by a professional who is experienced in the treatment of depression. This kind of group therapy is often considerably less expensive than individual therapy; it might commence following a few initial visits to the therapist at the start of treatment. There are also supportive associations of people who may have been mentally ill, such as Recovery Incorporated, which are organized into local branches.

How does treatment for chemical abuse relate to treatment for depression?

If alcohol and/or chemical use are related to the depression—either as a primary causal factor or as a result of attempts to numb the effects of depression—chemical dependency treatment is almost certainly the most appropriate form of therapy needed on an immediate basis. The yellow pages of most telephone books include entries under *Alcohol and Drug Abuse* or *Chemical Dependency* that will lead you to sources of help. Dependency problems may call for an integrated program of inpatient or outpatient treatment, along with individual, marital, and/ or family counseling and attendance at Twelve-Step support meetings. In some cases, an inpatient treatment program may be advisable.

What if I sense that I need professional help, but just don't have the energy to seek it out?

If you're in a state of inertia and despondency and regard the prospects of seeking help as an oppressively overwhelming task, you might ask a trusted friend or relative for special assistance. *In any case, don't put off this quest if you recognize that you need—or want— professional help.* If all other channels seem closed and you reach the point of desperation, contact a mental health hot line for recommendations or referrals, or go in person to a hospital with a staff psychiatrist who is on emergency call.

Never hesitate to ask to see a therapist in a public or nonprofit facility. Don't spend time and energy ruminating because your funds are low or nonexistent. *Fight for your own survival.* Your life may be at stake, and if you permit yourself to sink deeper and deeper into a depression, you may reach a point where you are no longer aware of your need for help or are incapable of following up on good leads for help. If you fail to find the help you need in one place, try another— and keep trying until you succeed. *There is help for you.*

How do I know if a particular therapist is competent to deal with depression?

Whether or not you're in the position to choose your therapist, you should expect a prospective psychotherapist to have adequate training in the appropriate discipline. This is evidenced by a license issued by the state and/or a degree or certification conferred by an accredited university or professional organization. Mental health practitioners in both private and public sectors should be credentialed and accredited. A *psychiatrist* will not only have an M.D., he or she should also be board-eligible or board-certified in psychiatry and neurology. A *psychologist* should be licensed. A *psychiatric social worker* should have an M.S.W. degree and have certification (if the state he or she practices in has such a requirement) and/or be listed in the Registry of National Health Care Providers. A *counselor* or *therapist* must have an M.A. or M.S. degree and also have certification as a "Mental Health Counselor" or have an earned membership in the American Association of Marriage and Family Counselors.

Of course, education, experience, and the proper credentials certifications, licensure, and board or diplomate status do not guarantee that a therapist will be effective with a particular client. Therefore, if you are unable to "shop around," ask professionals (physicians, lawyers, and especially front-line helping professionals like nurses, vocational and school guidance counselors, and social workers) for recommendations. Nothing speaks better than experience—direct or secondhand through reputation—regarding therapeutic expertise. Also, consult with friends who have had firsthand experience with therapists.

What if you're so depressed that you feel you cannot take action of any kind?

If you feel too depressed to take any action whatsoever, or you lack the energy, assertiveness, or concentration to make inquiry calls, you could ask a friend or relative to do the initial calling and checking for you. Investigative questions should be straightforward: *Do you know this recommended therapist personally? What is his or her orientation in psychotherapy? Have depressed friends, relatives, or coworkers benefited from his or her treatment? What did they specifically say about the therapist?* If a particular therapist is recommended more than once, the chances are better that he or she is especially good than if only one person seems impressed. (It might also be wise to ask people for opinions of therapists to *avoid.*)

If possible, you or a friend who is helping you might even call therapists to discuss your situation personally—this personal contact can be helpful in determining whether a particular therapist would be suitable. If the therapist at least *sounds* both personable and knowledgeable, you'll probably feel reassured. If seeing a highly recommended therapist would, for example, involve driving an hour or two, the extra time and effort are likely to pay off.

Also, consider contacting a fairly large clinic or a group practice of psychologists or psychiatrists to inquire as to who in that clinic or group specializes in work with depressed people and, if marital issues are involved, the spouses of depressed people. If there is only one person, or just a few people on staff with this particular specialty and you're unable to get an immediate appointment with one of them, it might be worth the wait of a few days. (But try your best to get a definite appointment with this person within a week or two.) If, however, you sense that you need immediate help, you'd be better off consulting with someone who is not a depression specialist rather than no one at all.

If you feel uncomfortable about going to see a mental health specialist, you could ask your spouse, a friend, or relative to make the appointment for you, drive you there, and perhaps even accompany you to the first session. You may appreciate the involvement of a trusted third party because he or she might help facilitate the initial contact with a helping professional and "break the ice," making it easier for you to open up.

Are there any personal characteristics that I should look for in a therapist?

In my opinion, a person naturally works better with a psychotherapist with whom he or she feels comfortable. Of course it's normal to feel somewhat anxious before a session and to experience some pain during a session as well. Generally, though, an individual who is in therapy should have a good working rapport with the therapist and should also believe that this professional helper is clearly on his or her "side." Specific factors that create this kind of comfort are, of course, different for different people. For example, some therapists dress casually and ask clients to call them by their first names; this style makes some people feel quite comfortable. Understandably, though, some people feel more reassured by a therapist who has a more formal and "professional" demeanor.

But regardless of the specific preferences involved, you'll surely cooperate better and work harder with a therapist who you respect and trust and who you sense understands and approves of you. People usually don't get far in therapy with a therapist they don't like or a therapist they sense doesn't like them. It's sometimes true that in long-term treatment, working with a therapist who reminds you of a hated authority figure might catalyze vital material for working through deep-rooted problems and/or might stimulate projections and overreactions that could provide valuable insights. However, such lengthy, insight-oriented analysis usually involves investments of money, time, and energy that may not be the best solution for your *immediate* problems with depression.

What kind of therapist seems best suited to helping depressed people?

He or she must not come across as so aloof and detached that clients perceive him or her as being "above" human problems and, therefore, unable to understand their feelings. The therapist should be able to show interest and understanding, but should not be so empathically involved that he or she gets pulled into the depression. Over-involvement interferes with the therapist's objectivity at a time when he or she must remain clear-headed and focused. If the therapist has a personal investment in "saving" the client, he or she may over-identify with that client and lose objectivity and clarity pertaining to the therapy. An overly involved therapist may also give the client a sense that he or she disapproves of certain tactics or behavior changes. But the client simply doesn't need the added concern that he or she may be displeasing the therapist. The therapist should be able to strike a balance between being accepting and noncritical of the client and expressing disapproval of the client's self-defeating behaviors and erroneous beliefs.

When a therapist is too authoritarian, he or she may confront the depressed client in ways that cause unnecessary problems. A good therapist should be able to convey needed feedback, information, or interpretation in ways that minimize defensiveness and resistance. The therapist's primary roles are these: • to understand the client • to communicate that understanding • to simplify, clarify, organize, and advise. The therapist should be basically supportive—not in a hovering, dependency-producing way, but in a consistent, alert, and clear manner.

In short-term therapy, clients run the risk of wasting precious time and energy working and reworking their feelings about the therapist. These feelings may be based either on very real personality incompatibilities or on mannerisms, quirks, or superficial physical characteristics. For example, if a client feels that all Capricorns are too impersonal, that Catholics are too rigid, and that short men are insecure—*and simply can't get beyond these personal biases*—he or she may need to switch therapists if dealing with one answering to one or all of these categories. The immediate goal of therapy is to work through the depression and improve your life at home and at work; deep-seated prejudices against short, Catholic Capricorns should be worked out later. In other words, both personality incompatibilities and trivial personal biases may stand in the way of good therapeutic work and results. A depressed person doesn't have to *like* everyone. (Nor, for that matter, does a therapist.) If uneasy reactions that are not central issues in your problems with depression do, indeed, interfere with therapy, it might be wise to find a therapist with whom you feel more at ease.

What should a depressed person expect to accomplish through psychotherapy?

My own initial therapeutic goal with depressed people is to help bring about immediate relief of symptoms and help the client bring about small, specific behavior changes designed to lessen the depression and help him or her feel better. I focus on these immediate though relatively minor changes at first for a very specific reason: *the symptoms of a severe depression cloud the mind and immobilize the body, making it quite difficult at first to carry out a thorough and protracted exploration of causes.* I find that once patients experience symptom relief and get themselves mobilized, feeling better and "grounded," they're better able to look at causal factors and they have more energy to initiate therapeutic changes. At this point, then, they can begin to target specific attitudes and behaviors to be probed and altered, then work toward making some long-term and lasting changes. These somewhat later goals may involve working through and releasing negative or distorted feelings, modifying or abandoning obsolete or self-destructive beliefs, changing self-defeating behaviors, eliminating toxic relationships, and learning new coping skills for situations that must be accepted.

What ingredients make up the psychotherapeutic process?

Ideally, psychotherapy strikes a balance among these essential elements: 1. the *expression* of feelings and thoughts, 2. the *understanding* of experience and beliefs, and 3. *active work* in changing specific behaviors and attitudes.

The therapist should encourage enough expression of feelings to produce some immediate relief (and release) for the client through the processes of venting and unloading. Experiencing and verbalizing feelings and thoughts can help an individual gain new awareness of the depth and breadth of negative emotions while providing some hints and clues as to their causes. The processes of venting and unloading also help the therapist understand these emotions and the connection they have with depression so that he or she will be able, in turn, to convey that understanding to the client.

A brief history of family background and personal development, a chronology of "significant events," and an overview of pressure points in the individual's current life situation supply the therapist with clues as to what provoked the immediate depression and hints of what may have contributed to the underlying depression-prone personality in the first place. Usually the "logic" revealed in this progression helps a person reduce self-blame through the realization that no one is responsible for "choosing" parents unwisely, or for failing to circumnavigate earlier blocks to healthy psychic growth.

This objective understanding of developmental and situational factors contributing to the depression—gained through therapy—helps a person reorganize the elements of his or her life so as to bring about positive change through active work. As for the balance to be achieved between expression of feelings and work: a therapist should not be so preoccupied with feelings that he or she tends to encourage the client to overindulge in negative emotions and psychological pain. The therapist should not focus on feelings so long and so intently that the client feels *consumed* by them. On the other hand, the therapist should not dwell primarily with intellectual and analytical processes that either downplay the open expression of feelings or ultimately have the effect of *delaying* changes in behavior, attitude, and personality traits.

Even before they have experienced relief from the symptoms of depression, some people in therapy feel "short-changed" if the process somehow isn't "hurting enough." They insist that they must "dig deeper" (which usually means into their early development) or they feel that they must wallow around to find out what's really *wrong* with them—and locate their "missing" or perverse parts. They believe that only through a thorough analysis of the past and a complete probing of their psyches will they rid themselves of the "depression demon." In fact, in this post-Freudian era, I have had many clients who are so insistent about wanting a complete psychic dredging that I must assure them that we are only *postponing* a "deep" exploration into self and an examination of past painful experiences. This isn't a lie. If a depressed patient doesn't improve fairly rapidly with other techniques, we will retrace our steps and see whether a different, more analytical approach might be more helpful to them. Yet the feeling a person has that something is deeply wrong with him or her is, itself, a relatively common symptom of depression.

I have found that once depressed people begin to feel better about themselves, most of them no longer seem to feel the need to conduct excursions into inner space in search of invisible but suspected "black holes." When the depression begins to lift, the present begins to look far more inviting—and the past recedes into the background, where it belongs. Actually, there may be no valuable answers buried in the past or inhabiting the vast reaches of unexplored territory within the psyche. Usually a quick, systematic look at early patterns that shaped present feelings and behaviors is sufficient to change the current mechanisms perpetuating the depression. And, once symptoms are relieved and there is some understanding of the situational factors and personality characteristics contributing to depression-proneness, a person can undertake a program to reorganize or rehabilitate his or her life to help prevent future problems.

From my perspective, I believe that long-term psychotherapy or psychoanalysis may be a luxury for most people, other than the relatively small percentage of individuals who have the most debilitating and deeply entrenched conflicts and behaviors. Yet, long-term psychotherapy and psychoanalysis constitute excellent training ground for helping professionals; these processes may also serve to hone the sensitivities and enhance the insights of people who have experienced relief from the symptoms of depression, but who are still motivated to dig deeper and significantly expand their self-awareness. There is, however, a danger here: in long-term therapy, a client may develop unnecessary dependencies and nurture the conviction that he or she needs to *stay* in treatment just to function. Also, extensive therapy may reinforce the belief that one is "sick" and encourage the very same self-preoccupation and focus on pathology that the depression-prone person should be trying to work out of. In fact, there is little hard (or soft) evidence that long-term, more insight-oriented or psychoanalytic-type psychotherapy is more effective than short-term treatment in combating depression. On the contrary, psychotherapeutic research often seems to demonstrate the most positive results from the short-term, more cognitive and behavioral treatment. And, of course, short-term treatment is usually more affordable.

On the average, how long does treatment for depression last? How long before I can expect some positive results?

In most cases, there should be marked improvement in the major symptoms and accompanying psychological pain of depression in four or five sessions—most likely spread out over three or four weeks. It might take longer in the following cases: • if the person has been

depressed for several months before starting on a course of therapy
• if onset of the depression was sudden and severe • if factors
contributing to the depression—stressful job, troubled relationships,
poor health—have remained unchanged. In the absence of those
complicating factors, failure to get any relief from the first few weeks
of therapy may indicate that the depressed person needs medication
to take the edge off the depression and increase energy sufficiently to
implement needed changes. Sometimes, also, a patient-therapist
relationship gets in the way of progress. If a depression is not severe
and the individual being treated has made little or no progress within
the period of a month or two, a change of therapists may be in order.
Sometimes a friend, especially one who has benefited from counseling
or psychotherapy, may help evaluate therapeutic progress. If the
depressed person isn't getting better or has personal concerns about
the therapist ("I don't think she likes me" or "He seems disapproving,
and I feel worse after I see him"), the friend could encourage the
client to discuss these issues directly with the therapist. The
therapist's subsequent handling of the situation may indicate that the
client was incorrect in his or her impressions or was indeed picking
up subtle negative reactions from the therapist.

What if therapy doesn't help me?

In some cases, the situation becomes progressively worse and despite
therapy, depression intensifies. The depressed person may report that
the therapist is giving feedback or interpretations that relatives or
friends don't understand or agree with, if indeed the report is
accurate. Also, the depressed person seems to be getting more
depressed. In this situation, a concerned third party might request to
speak with the therapist directly, to determine whether or not the
depressed person is distorting the feedback. Then, if the therapist
acts rigid and defensive or holds a view of the depressed person that
the third party knows to be inaccurate, it is probably wise to consider
a change in therapists. One way to check out uncertainties or
misgivings about a particular therapist while sampling other options is
to visit another therapist.

There are, of course, people who change therapists everytime
the going gets tough—and eventually visit every available therapist in

town. *But dissatisfaction with a therapist should not be routinely dismissed as a defense mechanism.* Some clients just seem to get along better with a second therapist, then begin to make good progress. Assessing one's therapist requires honesty. Depressed people who are considering a change in therapists must ask themselves whether a new therapist is being considered because the present therapist isn't really helping them, or because the therapist is saying things they don't want to hear or suggesting changes they don't wish to make.

Actually, it's probably healthy for a depressed person to be a kind of "mental health consumer." If his or her condition is up to this investigative activity, it doesn't hurt to "shop around" before settling on a particular therapist. Or, if after several months there is only minimal progress—if any at all—going to a different therapist may well be a proper thing to do. However, if the therapy itself seems beneficially comfortable, medication may be considered. Both depressed people and their concerned associates must, of course, be realistic in gauging progress. Remember that while it can be very helpful, psychotherapy is never a "cure-all" or a quick panacea. When depression has been long-standing or severe, or its onset sudden and dramatic, it might well be that the best the client and treatments can do will be represented by slow yet perceptible progress—with some relapses now and then.

Except in severe cases, after a few months of weekly or biweekly therapy sessions, both therapist and client may begin to sense that they're at the point of diminishing returns. This is when the rate of increase of new insights or behavior changes isn't sufficient to justify ongoing therapy. At this point, something similar to the following might happen: in a needless dependency that is most likely false economy, the client may begin to "save up" decisions to be made or postpone independent action until he or she discusses it with his or her therapist. Reducing the frequency of therapeutic contacts at this time can accomplish three things: 1. cause more to happen between sessions, 2. give the client an opportunity to do more things on his or her own, and 3. allow time for the client to practice and consolidate new behaviors.

Also, with the reduction of psychological pain and an increase in symptom relief, it is often difficult for a person to maintain a high level of motivation to work on his or her personal issues. For various reasons, people may reach "plateaus" in therapy, times when they feel more centered and stable and things begin to settle down for them. At that point, decreasing the frequency of sessions to once a month or to an "as-needed" basis may be appropriate and even advisable. Clients who are functioning normally again and feeling good about themselves might be justified in questioning a psychotherapist's insistence that they continue coming in for help on a weekly or twice-weekly basis. (In some cases, the "need" may have become more the therapist's than the client's.)

Frequently, people continue to grow long after therapy has terminated. Therapy has served to provide direction and "get the ball rolling," so to speak. As the person confronts new situations, he or she should be able to apply learned skills and develop new skills as well. There are those clients who continue to work steadily and make progress for an extended period of time. The therapy hour always seems filled with active discussion: issues and feelings are revealed and dealt with, and behavior is changed. Therapy may then be continued as long as it appears to be useful and productive, so long as it doesn't create unnecessary dependency that turns the person into a "professional client."

One last general comment about psychotherapy: Whether long- or short-term, therapy may not help produce lasting results if the spouse, other family members, or deeply concerned companions are not involved in the treatment program somewhere along the line. For instance, it often develops that a person was depressed long before he or she got married. Through therapy, a significant relationship can serve as an important source of support as one works through old conflicts; a good, solid relationship can also be a "laboratory" for new behaviors and corrective experiences. Such deliberate therapeutic interventions in relationships may help strengthen the marital and family support systems so that the depressed person can gain the trust, warm assurance, and encouragement needed to effectively deal with and overcome depression.

About the Author

Dr. Jay Cleve is the Director of the Community Mental Health Clinic in Stevens Point, Wisconsin. He earned an M.A. in Clinical Psychology from the University of Arkansas in 1964 and a Ph.D. in Counseling Psychology from the University of Wisconsin-Madison in 1968. He completed post-master's internships at Manteno State Counseling Center in Madison and completed one year pre-doctoral and one year post-doctoral internships in Clinical/Counseling Psychology at Psychological Services, University of California-Riverside.

Dr. Cleve received training in Gestalt Therapy from the Gestalt Therapy Institute in Los Angeles and at Cambridge House Growth Center in Milwaukee, as well as six months training with couples at the Southern California Institute of Group Psychotherapy in Beverly Hills, California, and Encounter Group training at the Center for Studies of the Person in La Jolla, California, and Cambridge House in Milwaukee. He also attended biweekly family therapy seminars with Dr. Carl Whitaker for two years in Madison, Wisconsin, and received six months of training in clinical hypnosis at Cambridge House in Milwaukee. He has also received advanced training in projective drawing, the Rorschach Ink Blot Test, and art therapy.

While in California, Dr. Cleve worked in private practice at the Voorman Psychiatric Clinic at Upland, California, served as consultant to the Counseling Center at the University of California-Irvine, and conducted Sensitivity Training programs for non-commissioned officers in the Air Force at the Strategic Air Command Base in March, California.

Prior to serving in his present job, Dr. Cleve worked as a staff psychologist at the Psychological Services, University of California-Riverside and as Director of Staff Development and Resident Life Psychologist, Counseling Center Psychologist, and Assistant Professor of Psychology at the University of Wisconsin-Stevens Point (UWSP). While at UWSP, he also consulted at Norwood Mental

Hospital, Portage County Day Care Services, and has served as Acting Director of Human Services in Portage County on two occasions. Dr. Cleve conducts seminars and workshops on burn-out, stress management, depression management, relationships, and intimacy.